# Reformed

# With

# Power

Can a Calvinist believe the gifts are still used by God?

by

## Tom Pitman

# Table of Contents

# Preface

In the course of our lives as followers of Jesus Christ, we spend many hours poring over the Bible. It is an absolute joy, which permeates our hearts, our minds and our souls. I find that I am filled with joy as I encounter God in the Scriptures. Yet, a strange thing happens as I read and study the Bible. I come across verses that seem to have gone unnoticed. I read them and wonder how I ever missed them or missed their impact on my thoughts.

One such passage for me is 1 Corinthians 2:1-5.

"When I came to you, brothers, I did not come with eloquence or superior wisdom as I proclaimed to you the testimony about God. For I resolved to know nothing while I was with you except Jesus Christ and him crucified. I came to you in weakness and fear, and with much trembling. My message and my preaching were not with wise and persuasive words, but with a demonstration of the Spirit's power, so that your faith might not rest on men's wisdom, but on God's power."

This passage has changed much of the way I understand my faith. Having been raised in an evangelical church and from an ancestry of Reformed believers, my faith is based solely on the Word. But Paul also wanted the Corinthians' faith to be based on the power of God. Surely, Paul was talking about God's power for salvation and resurrection. Yet, how did they come to know the power of God for salvation? Paul gave them a demonstration of the Spirit's power. Whether this was by healing, casting out demons, prophecy or any other manifestation of the Spirit the passage is unclear. What is clear is that they were to rest their faith in this demonstration of the power of God.

It is my desire for the Church to return to a faith based on the Bible and on the power of God, demonstrated by manifestations of His Spirit. I believe that the power of God attests to the truth of the Scriptures and I believe that "The Bible, uniquely and fully inspired by the Holy Spirit, is the supreme and final authority on all matters on which it speaks." [1] In addition to my belief in the authority of the Bible I also want to acknowledge that "The Holy Spirit speaking in the Bible is the supreme judge of all religious controversies, all decisions of religious councils, all the opinions of ancient writers, all human teachings, and every private opinion. We are to be satisfied with the judgment of Him Who is and can be the only judge." [2] The Holy Spirit does not avoid His own writing and neither do I.

This work is nothing more than a pastoral letter. I am a pastor, not a theologian. I have served small churches around the U.S., which have grown in their knowledge of God's power. It is comforting to know that God even uses small, seemingly insignificant groups of believers to manifest some of His brilliant wonders.

When it comes to the power of God, I am just a learner who has enjoyed what I have seen God do in people's lives. Whether it is healing them, releasing them, speaking to them, or touching them in some new way, God is in the business of doing wonderful and compassionate ministry. I love God and I love His work.

I have two goals as I write. First, this is an apologetic for those who have questions about the gifts of the Spirit or are opposed to their use in the Church today. I will rely on the Bible, church history and current experience to make the case for their full inclusion in the Church.

My second goal is to give encouragement to those who want this aspect of the Holy Spirit in their lives. Sometimes it can seem as though something is missing. I read the New Testament and see the love and power by which ministry was done and I can't help noticing a glaring difference between the activity of the Holy Spirit then and now in many of our churches. People are still sick and demonized as they were then, but we have trouble believing that God wants to do anything about it. I believe He will continue to do powerful ministry through us.

I am writing from a Reformed perspective, because I am a Reformed pastor, but mainly because I believe that the Reformed Church is currently giving the greatest opposition to the operation of the gifts of the Holy Spirit in the life of the Church. It is my hope that the Reformed Church will one day be used by the Spirit in giving manifestations of power so that the world will come to know Jesus and its faith "might not rest on men's wisdom, but on God's power." [3]

# Introduction
## Definitions

It is always important to define the terms we use, especially in this topic, which touches the very core of our walk with God and His activity in our churches. Because of its significance, it is common to use words and labels without knowing or understanding the precise meaning behind them. As I have read through different publications I have noticed how some writers make broad presumptions which give a gross overstatement that result in making the statement a fallacy.

As a Reformed pastor I am going to look at the meanings of "Reformed Theology" and "Charismatic." I am not going to make the claim that the gifts are the sole possession of the Reformed faith. Rather, it is time for the churches of the Reformed faith to become receptive to the full work of the Holy Spirit.

### Defining the Reformed Faith

I have asked various pastors with a Reformed theological base to give me a definition of the Reformed faith in one paragraph. They haven't been able to do it without omitting too much. In order to give a concise explanation of Reformed theology I must list a group of ideas that outline this understanding of the faith. In writing this, I am sure that I will be leaving too much out. My apologies.

1) The Reformed faith holds to the absolute authority of the Bible. During the Reformation, one of the most important ideas was "Sola Scriptura." The "Scriptures Alone" have ultimate dominion over what we believe and what we do as followers of Jesus Christ.

The Reformation removed control from the hierarchy of the Church and returned that jurisdiction to the Bible. This was done by denying that the rulings and traditions of the Church are equal with the Bible. This also put the Bible into the hands of all believers by translating it into the languages of the people. Making it possible to know what God says in the Scriptures rather than depending on the Church to make official pronouncements.

2) The Reformed faith believes in the Kingdom of God. In holding to this biblical truth, we understand God's kingdom to be active here today on earth and also to be coming in full consummation in the future. Later in this work, I will give an explanation of the kingdom and explain its significance. The activity of God in His kingdom is viewed in different ways, depending upon whose work you read within the Reformed Tradition.

3) The Reformed faith believes in the sovereignty of God. This means that God has total dominion and authority over all that exists. The Triune God is separate from and above all that He has created, and He has the power to bring to fruition every plan He decrees.

4) The Reformed faith holds to God's act of predestination. As God has sovereignty over all creation, He also retains the right and power to determine who will live

with Him forever in Heaven. He elects those who He alone chooses to receive His mercy. Those whom He elects will at sometime in their life accept Christ Jesus as their savior and Lord.

5) The final distinguishing mark of the Reformed faith is "Sola Fide," meaning "faith alone." In opposition to the teaching of the Roman Catholic Church, the Reformers upheld the biblical truth that salvation is not achieved by good works mixed with faith, but only by faith in Jesus Christ, faith that Jesus was crucified for our sins and was resurrected from the dead.

This finds its summation in the Reformation statement, "Salvation by grace through faith." Any idea short of this is wrong, and leaves a person quite short of a true relationship with God.

With these as a basis, the Reformed faith then defines itself through many creeds such as the Westminster Confession of Faith, the Helvetic Confession, the Scot's Confession, etc. In these confessions you will find the above themes expressed in different ways.

Many people equate the Reformed Faith with Calvinism. Those who are Calvinists are definitely Reformed, but the Reformed body of churches and denominations did not start with John Calvin. Though he has been a great influence in forming the corpus of Reformed theology, you need not be a student of Calvinism to be Reformed, as long as you observe the basic ideas presented in Reformed theology.

There are some who believe that you are "truly" Reformed if you hold to the five points of Calvinism. [1] But these five points do not define the Reformed faith. As John R. de Witt writes, "It is also true that to be Reformed means different things to different people. Some tend to identify Reformed faith with the five points of Calvinism, forgetting that those five points only represent an expression of the faith." [2] De Witt continues by stating, "Beyond all dispute, however, the Reformed faith is much more comprehensive, much more all-embracing, than those five points."[3]

Believe me, I wanted to give you this definition in one simple paragraph. I have searched theological dictionaries and other works looking for a concise answer to what the Reformed faith is, but it doesn't exist. I am sure that I could write volumes (and it has been done!) if I were to expand on the points I have just given. The Reformed faith is best understood by the themes I have written.

Likewise, I cannot give you a one-paragraph description of the Charismatic Movement, without excluding too much pertinent information. I believe the following will be adequate to begin with.

## Defining Charismatic

The term "charismatic" is both a general label and a specific label. In general, it is used by many to identify any follower of Jesus who believes that the Holy Spirit still uses all of His gifts in the Church today. Not only does He use all of His gifts today, but He also has used them throughout Church history and will continue to use them until the end of the age. At that time Jesus will return to consummate history and His kingdom. When He returns there will then be no need of the gifts, since we will live in His direct presence for the rest of eternity.

When I state that Charismatics believe all of the gifts are being used by God in His Church, I am referring to the gifts listed in Romans 12:1-8, 1 Corinthians 12-14, Ephesians 4:1-16 and 1 Peter 4:7-11. We will examine what these gifts are and how the Holy Spirit uses them in a later chapter.

It was while I was attending seminary that I first became acquainted with the idea that "charismatic" was more than just a generic name for all "spirit-filled" Christians. C. Peter Wagner taught about the three waves of the Holy Spirit in the previous century.

The first wave was and is the Pentecostal Movement of churches and denominations. Starting in 1901 with a revival at Bethel Bible School and finding further definition in the Azuza Street Revival (1906-13), this movement has branched out into multiple denominations.[4] These denominations began as much from the power of the Spirit as from their rejection by the established ecclesiastical structure.

Though there are theological differences between Pentecostals and other believers who accept the gifts, the Pentecostals' main identifying feature is their contention that the sign of having been baptized by the Holy Spirit is speaking in tongues. The rest of the gifts tend to flow from the release of this gift within the believer.

The second wave of the Spirit came with a genre of individual charismatic churches. These churches are usually non-denominational in affiliation. Though they may have a wide range of theological backgrounds, a distinctive feature is their belief that the sign of having been baptized by the Holy Spirit is the use of any power gift in their lives. Whether it be healing, prophecy, tongues, miracles, etc., these gifts give witness to the presence of the Spirit in the individual believer's life.

The third group was called the Signs and Wonders Movement or the Third Wave. This was a move of the Holy Spirit to take His power and gifts back into the mainline churches. It did not matter if a believer was Presbyterian, Baptist, Congregational, Methodist or of any other denominational affiliation, the Holy Spirit was breathing powerful life back into His churches.

This movement had a different understanding of the sign of the baptism of the Holy Spirit. Activation of any of the gifts of the Spirit in a believer's life shows that a believer has been baptized by Him. The gift could be prophecy or serving; what truly matters to the believer is the reality of the Spirit's involvement and empowering of a believer and knowing that the gifts continue today as they did in the New Testament.

## Toward an Integration

Theologically speaking, there is nothing that prohibits the Reformed faith from receiving all that the Holy Spirit has for us. Reformed theology does not insist on the cessation of the gifts, rather I believe that the continuation of the ministry of the Holy Spirit is a valid and important part of the Reformed Church. Not one point of Reformed theology needs to be removed or changed in order to walk in the power of the Holy Spirit. However, there are some traditions and viewpoints that must change or be thrown out for the Spirit of God to move us freely in all that He would do.

# Chapter One
## Grounds of Disbelief

I get some of the strangest reactions from other believers when they find out that I am Reformed theologically and yet charismatic. It is almost as if I were holding two theological ideas that were mutually exclusive. Not only do some think they are opposites, but they are unable to find any form of reconciliation between the two.

When I was a candidate for the ministry and undergoing my trials for ordination in my Presbyterian denomination, I had preached a sermon against Dispensationalism. Part of my sermon touched on my belief that all of the gifts of the Spirit were still in operation in the Church of the first century.

During the time of questioning which followed the sermon, one of the pastors asked how I could be Reformed theologically and hold a charismatic view of the gifts. I was amazed at the question, as I believe they flow together.

This book is my endeavor to answer that question in a simple and coherent manner. I will show that there is harmony between Reformed theology and the continuation of all the gifts of the Spirit.

I suppose that I should not have been amazed that a Presbyterian pastor would ask that question. After all, I find that the Reformed tradition is one of the most resistant groups to the operation of the pneumatic or spiritual gifts in the Church today. Not only are the churches of the Reformed tradition resistant, they tend to lead in opposition to this work of the Holy Spirit.

Why is this so? Many of the Reformed churches' leading teachers and speakers have made statements, preached sermons and written books which vilify the charismatic movement through the centuries and today. Let me give you a few examples of statements given recently and in the past:

"We see the weakness of the miracles, even those performed by our Lord himself." [1] Michael Horton

"In spite of what is claimed, the working of miracles detracts from faith because it focuses attention, not on Christ, but on the miracle worker and because, in many cases, the miracle works independently of an individual's knowledge of the gospel, assent to it, or trust in its promises." [2] James Montgomery Boice

"Had any miracle perchance occurred beyond the Apostolic age they would be without significance; mere occurrences with no universal meaning." [3] B.B. Warfield

Each of these quotations demonstrates the basic attitudes that I have found within the Reformed tradition. They are also wrong, due to the fact that they are based on fallacies, not Scripture.

Even though this line of thinking demonstrated above seems to have captivated many in the Reformed tradition, there are many Reformed churches and teachers who would describe themselves as charismatic. The Holy Spirit is moving powerfully and sovereignly in many Presbyterian/Reformed churches.

The vast majority of denominations, churches and theologians of Reformed roots would say that the gifts of the Spirit have ceased. But where did this line of thinking come from? What is the basis for this opposition and refusal? It is to be found in the thinking and teaching of pastors and theologians throughout Reformed history. From the

Reformation until now, the vast majority of Reformed churches and theologians have not seen a need for the gifts of the Holy Spirit.

## John Calvin

The obvious starting place is to examine the views of Calvin. He was a strong proponent of the ministry of the Holy Spirit and the power of prayer. "Of all the great Reformers it was Calvin who undertook the most systematic exploration of the Spirit's work – notably in the third book of his *Institutes*, which reached final form in 1559." [4] Calvin did a great job of writing about the Holy Spirit's work in our lives, about giving us faith and sealing us in Christ, yet he did not believe in the continuation of the charismata of the Spirit into the 1500's.

I would say that the cessation of the gifts was not a fixation for Calvin. There were many other topics of concern to him that were essential to Reformed theology. That is why we associate subjects such as predestination, regeneration by the Spirit and others with Calvinism. Though we may differ on a number of topics, we find unity on many of these Reformed doctrines.

Calvin did write on the gifts of the Spirit in his *Institutes* and in his commentaries. From these writings we must conclude that Calvin thought that the gifts of power were no longer functioning. Calvin wrote,

"But those miraculous powers and manifest workings, which were dispensed by the laying on of hands, have ceased; and they have rightly lasted only for a time. For it was fitting that the new preaching of the gospel and the new Kingdom of Christ should be illumined and magnified by unheard-of and extraordinary miracles. When the Lord ceased from these, he did not utterly forsake his church, but declared that the magnificence of his Kingdom and the dignity of his word had been excellently enough disclosed." (5)

From this statement in the *Institutes*, John Calvin tells us he believes the gifts have stopped, his reason being that the revelation of the Kingdom and the Gospel had been unveiled. The idea that the power gifts were used by God primarily to attest to the truth of the revelation of the Gospel will become a major focus within the Reformed tradition and for other theological backgrounds as well.

In the "Prefatory Address To King Francis I of France" Calvin elaborates on his reason for miracles. He uses a few examples from scripture to show the view that miracles (and I believe Calvin would include the charismata in the word) were given by God to witness to the truth of the Gospel.

He wrote this in reaction to the Roman Catholic Church, which is "demanding miracles" of the Reformers. I agree with Calvin that there are no new Gospel revelations and therefore, there is no need for signs to substantiate a "new" gospel. Where I differ with him is that I believe that the Kingdom of God is still accompanied by healing and casting out of demons along with the rest of the gifts for other purposes. The Apostle Paul writes in 1 Corinthians 4:20, "For the kingdom of God is not a matter of talk but of power." It is very possible that Calvin overreacted to the demands of the Roman Catholic Church. This overreaction may have been the reason for his belief the gifts were no longer in use, allowing him to misinterpret scripture passages focusing on the charismata.

Calvin did believe in the continuation of miracles. He makes a statement at the beginning of his *Institutes of the*

*Christian Religion* that would lead me to this conclusion. In the "Prefatory Address" Calvin states, "Well, we are not entirely lacking in miracles, and these very certain and not subject to mockery." [(6)] I don't know to what kind of miracles Calvin refers. I wish Calvin had elaborated on the nature of these miracles.

Calvin also believed in the continuation of dreams from God. In his Institutes he wrote, "These are unfailing signs of divinity in man. Why is it that the soul not only vaguely roves about but conceives many useful things, ponders concerning many, even divines the future – all while man sleeps?" [(7)] and "Indeed, sleep itself, which benumbs man, seeming even to deprive him of life, is no obscure witness of immortality, since it suggests not only thoughts of things that have never happened, but also presentiments of the future. I have briefly touched upon these things which secular writers grandly extol and depict in more brilliant language; but among godly readers this simple reminder will be enough." [(8)]

John Calvin was only a partial cessationist since he believed that real miracles and dreams that revealed the future were happening in his day. Many in the Reformed tradition have used Calvin to reject the charismata. I am sorry he held the views he did on the gifts, whether they were because of an overreaction to Roman Catholicism or just the result of reading the Bible in light of his experience. Yet, Calvin is not the source who most Reformed Christians quote when saying that the charismata are no longer in the Church.

## B.B. Warfield

In many of the books and articles I have read that were against the gifts of the Spirit, I have frequently found references or quotes from Benjamin B. Warfield. He was a professor at Princeton Theological Seminary from 1887 into the 1900's and has become famous for a series of lectures that were published under the title of *Counterfeit Miracles*.

Like the vast majority of Reformed thinkers, Warfield used his reasoning capabilities rather than clear scriptural evidence to explain the cessation of the gifts. His thought on the subject centers on this quote:

"This, then, is the theory: that miracles having been given for the purpose of founding the church, they continued so long as they were needed for that purpose; growing gradually fewer as they were less needed, and ceasing altogether when the church having, so to speak, been firmly put upon its feet, was able to stand on its own legs." [9]

Warfield's feelings on the issue are essentially the same as Calvin's. The dividing line between him and Calvin is shown in the way his book was greatly negative in attitude. Warfield did a vicious job of criticizing other Christians. It seemed as if he put his theology above loving fellow believers. Calvin's treatment of the gifts was more a matter of the issue, rather than an attempt to discredit others in the body of Christ.

In *Counterfeit Miracles*, the main reason presented for the existence of the charismata, was "to authenticate the Apostles as the authoritative founders of the church." [10] This is surely one of the explanations for why the Spirit has given His gifts to the church. I will show later that there are a number of reasons the Spirit has given the charismata to us in the Church, yet Warfield limits it to this one. He is adamant to the point of saying that the Spirit could only be conveyed to others in the Church by the laying on of hands by the Apostles alone. [11] Any value these gifts would be to the Church was indirectly involved with authenticating the ministry of the Apostles. [12]

This prepares us for his belief that the charismata ended in the first century with the death of the Apostles. His contention is that, since the charismata were given for the sole purpose of lending credence to the message spoken by the Apostles, once that message was delivered, they ceased to be needed. Warfield believed that the gifts were not the possession of the Church, but were the sole property of the Apostles. [13] This view is the common rationale of many Reformed thinkers.

The Apostles were surely instrumental in the beginning of the Church, teaching the Church how to function with all of the love, grace and mercy of the Spirit. But I do not see any scriptures that clearly say that the gifts were the sole possession of the Apostles and lent out to any believers who came in contact with them.

To study B.B. Warfield is to realize that he was more complex on this subject than to simply deny the current power of the Spirit by leaving it with the Apostles. There was a philosophical grounding that would aid Warfield in feeling comfortable in his viewpoint called Scottish Common Sense.

## Princeton and Scottish Common Sense

When John Witherspoon came to be president of Princeton Seminary in 1768, he brought Scottish Common Sense Philosophy with him. As a line of thought, it was taught to and held by the prevailing Presbyterian theologians and scholars throughout early Princeton history. The list includes Archibald Alexander, Charles Hodge, A.A. Hodge, B.B. Warfield, and J. Gresham Machen (who would leave Princeton Seminary in 1929 to begin Westminster Theological

Seminary).  Scottish Common Sense would not only influence Northern Reformed circles, but Southern U.S. Presbyterianism as well.  As Luger G. Whitlock, Jr. wrote,

"Scottish Common Sense Philosophy dominated Princetonian thought from Witherspoon on and Old School Presbyterianism throughout the first half of the nineteenth century.  Princeton was by far the most influential of the northern colleges on southern education.  Therefore, it is relatively easy to see how Common Sense Philosophy would have become pervasive in the South.  Southern colleges offered courses in moral philosophy, required of all students, introducing Scottish Common Sense Philosophy to them in this manner." [14]

Thus, you can see how prevalent this philosophy was in the Presbyterian Church.  Since this "Common Sense" was held by Warfield and influenced a great many others, we will look at what it is and what it did.

Scottish Common Sense Philosophy (SCSP) was the brainchild of Thomas Reid (1710-1796), who was part of the Presbyterian clergy in Scotland.  He and others "attempted to overcome the epistemological, metaphysical, and moral skepticism of the Enlightenment philosophy of David Hume (1711-76) with a philosophy of common sense and natural realism." [15]  SCSP declares that humans have a "rational freedom" and can operate with "moral intuition" rather than being mere beings who react to "pain and pleasure." [16]  Basically, this philosophy tells us to make decisions on belief based on your rational intellect.

This "Common Sense" was a form of Enlightenment thought.  As Ahlstrom points out about SCSP, "(it) was a characteristic flowering of the Enlightenment and of Scottish renaissance of the eighteenth century." [17] Mark A. Noll agreed when he wrote, "These philosophers (Reid and Francis Hutcheson) were attempting to rescue the English "moderate" Enlightenment of Isaac Newton and John Locke from the skepticism of David Hume and the idealism of George Berkeley." [18]

The Enlightenment of the 18th Century had a great impact on Western Society as a whole. As much as we Christians like to think that our faith is void of cultural and philosophical influence, the truth is we are constantly being bombarded and these explosive fragments do affect our ways of thinking. Now, I am not totally against the Enlightenment, Scottish Common Sense or using our rational mind and engaging God intellectually. But, as Dr. Charles Kraft writes, "Our Enlightenment heritage has left us with a rationalistic, mind-oriented approach to everything. Even the Scriptures have come to be approached in a purely rational way."[19] We face the danger of God saying, "For my thoughts are not your thoughts, neither are your ways my ways." (Isaiah 55:8) Yet, our goal is to think like God and make His ways our ways.

That the Reformed tradition is married to the Enlightenment should be no surprise to anyone. We are an intellectually and rationally driven movement. The heroes of our faith are those who have written great volumes on theology or demonstrated prowess as instructors at a seminary level of education. This is probably why we love the Epistles and tend to place less emphasis on the Book of Acts. After all, there are some uncomfortable and even doctrinally messy situations in that book. It is Acts 10:44-48 that Peter, while beginning to preach a good sermon, is interrupted by the Holy Spirit releasing tongues upon Cornelius and his family. The worst part is Peter's willingness to baptize them immediately, because of their ecstatic experience. The sermon was cut off;

there was no confessional instruction to prepare them for baptism; and Peter considered them true believers. This is not a rational event.

This rationalism is a dangerous infection in the Body of Christ. About the effects of this danger Dr. Kraft writes,

"In the present day, however, Evangelicals tend to believe that God has stopped talking and doing the incredible things we read about in Scripture. Now we see God limiting himself to working through the Bible (the inspired record of what he used to do), plus an occasional contemporary "interference" in the natural course of events. What we usually call a miracle – the power of God used to manifest in healing – has been largely replaced by secular medicine. The speaking he used to do now comes indirectly through rationalistic reasoning in books, lectures, and sermons, similar to the process used by the secular sciences." [20]

The Enlightenment did not cause our teachers in the Reformed faith to become cessationist. It did aid and encourage them to maintain their cessationism. The activity of the Spirit does not always fit our conception of what is rational or intellectually acceptable. So Scottish Common Sense was a strong support in the wrong direction on this issue. I believe that the cessationist theory introduced into the Church by some during the Reformation left the Church wide-open for absorbing the intellectual, thought-only approach to seeing everything including a form of demythologizing day-to-day living for God.

## Abraham Kuyper

A professor of systematic theology at the University of Amsterdam, Dr. Kuyper held similar views to those of B.B. Warfield, who was a contemporary of his. Dr. Kuyper wrote a book entitled *The Work Of The Holy Spirit* in which he gave the Dutch Reformed churches an overview of the ministry of the Holy Spirit.

I have included Abraham Kuyper in this first chapter, because I believe that he had the same influence over the Dutch Reformed churches as Warfield had over the American scene. Kuyper has had some influence in the philosophy of Reformed thinkers in America too, even though he is rarely quoted when it comes to rejecting the charismata. His sphere of ideas tended to encompass the social and political needs of the Church in society.

Nevertheless, he did write a volume on the Spirit's work and his view of the charismata is summarily expressed in the following quote. "The charismata now existing in the Church are those pertaining to the ministry of the Word; the ordinary charismata of increased exercise of faith and love; those of wisdom, knowledge and discernment of spirits; that of self-restraint; and lastly, that of healing the sick suffering from nervous and psychological diseases. The others for the present are inactive." [21]

This is a common attitude towards the gifts of the Spirit, to say that the ordinary gifts are still active. Many Christians will say that the gifts of teaching, serving, and giving are still present. With that comes the perception that the extraordinary gifts such as healing, prophecy, tongues and the others were the ones that the Spirit brought to an end when the Apostles died, the idea being that the extraordinary gifts were needed to show the truth of the Gospel and establish it on earth.

One difference between Dr. Kuyper and the cessationists is the final sentence of the previous quote. Dr. Kuyper doesn't say the charismata ceased with the Apostles, he says they are inactive "for the present" leaving open the possibility of future use in his theology.

## Reformed Thinkers and the Cessationist Theory

There are certainly other Reformed theologians and pastors who have written on the gifts. I feel that these three men were probably the most influential and foundational in establishing the Reformed tradition's denial of the continuation of the gifts of the Spirit. I am sure that Charles Hodge or Cornelius Van Til wrote and spoke on the topic. I am convinced that they had great influence on the Reformed churches to this day, but not so notably on this subject.

As Calvin began the discussion within the Reformed camp, Warfield and Kuyper wrote directly on the subject of the work of the Holy Spirit. All three held to the same understanding, which is the cessationist theory. The basic idea of cessationism holds that the extraordinary gifts of the Spirit (healing, prophecy, miracles, tongues, interpretation of tongues, etc.) ceased to exist in the Church when the writing of the Bible was completed. These gifts were given only to validate the message of the Gospel as was given by the Apostles and the ministry of Jesus Himself. Once that was accomplished, there was no reason for the gifts to remain.

The problem with this theory is that it is not based on explicit passages from the Bible or even a clear theme of verses to be found anywhere in scripture. In other words, there are no verses in which God states that the gifts would stop once the Bible was written. So where does it come from?

Dr. Jack Deere, in his book, *Surprised by the Power of the Spirit*, makes a clear and reasoned argument that the cessationist theory is actually based on experience. As he writes, "No one ever just picked up the Bible, started reading, and then came to the conclusion that God was not doing signs and wonders anymore and that the gifts of the Holy Spirit had passed away. The doctrine of cessationism did not originate from a careful study of the Scriptures. The doctrine of cessationism originated in experience."[22] He is right. The believers I know who read all the verses having to do with the power of God and the gifts of the Spirit have all come to the same conclusion. They usually ask, "So, where does it say that the gifts have stopped? Everything says we are to seek them."

I am not going to make a complete argument against cessationist theory, as Dr. Deere has, since my focus is to give evidence of the continuation of the gifts. But I do want to focus our attention on Dr. Deere's answer of how the Reformers came to their conclusion about the cessation of the charismata. In reaction to the Roman Catholic Church and their use of miracles to support their tradition, the Reformers had to show that their theology was valid. Lacking experience in the miraculous, the Reformers decided to prove that the gifts had ceased. "Having been deprived of the most powerful weapon in their arsenal, specific statements of Scripture, the Reformers were forced to appeal to theological deductions. But how were they ever going to deduce that the miracles were intended to be temporary from a book that begins with miracles, persists in miracles, and ends with miracles?" [23]

According to Dr. Deere, the Reformers had experienced a lack of miraculous gifts, so they decided to theologize an excuse for this deficiency. Their answer was to say that the charismata were for the authentication of the Apostles, as was demonstrated in the view of Warfield. Warfield was not a Reformer, but a repository of this cessationist theory. As Dr. Deere writes in answer to this view, "When I looked up all of these references, I was astounded to discover that not one reference ever said that miracles bore witness to the apostles, confirmed apostles, or attested to the apostles. In short, miracles do not authenticate the apostles!" [24] He continues to point out that the purpose of the ministry of the Holy Spirit is the glorification of Jesus Christ.

There is one more theologian who must be mentioned in this chapter. The refusal to recognize the gifts and the power of the Holy Spirit in the life of the Church today also comes from the liberal viewpoint.

### Rudolf Bultmann

Rudolf Bultmann was a professor of New Testament studies at the University of Marburg, and a very influential scholar. Though Bultmann was Lutheran, his views have become a basis of the liberal side of reformed and Presbyterian theologians and church members.

He is known for the philosophy of demythologizing the Bible. That is the practice of boiling the Scriptures down to what he sees as the kernel of reality and removing every instance of myth from its pages. As you can imagine, he questions much of the New Testament as he wrote, "The world picture of the New Testament is a mythical world picture." [25]

Bultmann judged the Scriptures through the lens of reasoning based on known scientific discovery, which he felt had dismissed much of the truth revealed in the Bible. He demonstrated this by writing, "But it is impossible to repristinate a past world picture by sheer resolve, especially a mythical world picture, now that all of our thinking is irrevocably formed by science." [26]

As you will see in the following quotes, Bultmann includes demons, deliverance from demons, wonders and the Holy Spirit Himself as myth.

"Likewise, illnesses and their cures have natural causes and do not depend on the work of demons and on exorcising them. Thus, the wonders of the New Testament are also finished as wonders." [27]

"We cannot use electric lights and radios and, in the event of illness, avail ourselves of modern medical and clinical means and at the same time believe in the spirit and wonder world of the New Testament." [28]

"In both cases what the New Testament has to say about the "Spirit" (pneuma) and the sacraments is absolutely alien and unintelligible to us. Those of us who understand ourselves in purely biological terms do not understand how a supernatural something or other like the pneuma could intervene in the closed context of natural forces and be effective in us." [29]

We can see Bultmann came under the negative influence of Enlightenment thought as did those of cessationism. The difference being cessationism allows for the belief of miracles as revealed in the Bible, but not for today and demythologization rejects the power of the Holy Spirit in the Bible as well as today. Both views have roots in the Enlightenment and logical thinking as a basis of rejecting the power of the Spirit. Both use empirical means to back their erroneous theology. And both arrive at the same conclusion for the power of the Holy Spirit in the life of the Church.

## Results Within the Reformed Tradition

The consequences of cessationist ideas in present-day Reformed churches are consequences to beware of. The following are five residual problems that exist in the Reformed tradition. These problems are not simply limited to Reformed cessationists, but can be applied to any group or denomination from any theological background.

1.      One problem is how the Reformed churches and denominations have become dependent upon the *traditions of the elders* rather than the moving of the Holy Spirit. Alasdair Heron, Chair of Reformed Theology at the University of Erlangen, writes, "As the church consolidates into an ordered institution, there increases the danger of treating the Spirit as the possession of the church, which grows hardened and is no longer open to the Spirit's free energies. The resultant tensions between Spirit and structure have surfaced repeatedly through Christian history." [30]
Well, let's face it. Many of the congregations throughout the Reformed body do not want the open manifestations of the Holy Spirit. As much as we declare Him God, we become very uncomfortable when He moves upon people, whether He is demonstrating His gifts or causing people to physically manifest His presence. Why do you think Jonathan Edwards had to write a book defending the manifestations of the Spirit in the meetings he was conducting? The institutionalized churches were very upset and denounced the meetings.

2.    The Reformed tradition has become a community of disbelief when it comes to the power of God for the miraculous. Surely Reformed Christians believe in the miracles performed by Jesus and the Apostles and they even believe that God can do a miracle, once in a great while, in response to prayer. But, the majority of Reformed denominations do not believe God's miraculous power is normative to our Christian life. In other words, they do not believe that the Holy Spirit uses the present church in the same power as He did the Church in the New Testament.

How can I say this? Well, first I would like to be understood in what I mean by a community of disbelief. At the end of the thirteenth chapter of Matthew, we are told that Jesus spent some time in His hometown. The most remarkable part of this visit is stated in the last verse, which reads, "And he did not do many miracles there because of their lack of faith." The people didn't believe, so God didn't do much there. It was probably out of pure mercy that Jesus did any miracles at all amongst them. His hometown was a community of unbelief.

So, how do I apply this to the Reformed community? As I talk with different individuals from Reformed churches about the gifts, I usually find that they don't believe what I tell them I have seen God do with His power through His gifts. When I probe to find the underlying reason for their unbelief, I am told that they have never seen those gifts at work in their church. Yet, those very gifts would not be allowed to function in their churches. They don't believe all the gifts are active, so they won't allow them in their church. Yet, they don't see them, so they don't believe they are active. This is aided by some inferences from Scripture, which are viewed from and selected by their experience. This is an example of circular reasoning at it best.

Granted, we are not talking about unbelief in the deity of Jesus or of His incarnation. Even so, we are discussing an aspect of disbelief. Jesus clearly rebuked a lack of faith in any form. Whether the subject was Himself or the ministry, faith is requisite with Jesus.

3.    Another of the consequences is wrong generalizations about the charismatic movement. The most irrational generalization against the charismatic movement is to call it unbiblical. This allows Christians to easily disassociate with those who are seen this way. The reason being that anyone who is unbiblical is at best unsound and at worst heretical.

Certainly there are those within the Charismatic/Pentecostal movement who have stated or believe unbiblical doctrines. For that matter, we can find many people and movements within the history of Christianity who, though holding to the basic essentials of orthodox belief, allow for unbiblical ideas to flow through their theology. From my vantage point cessationism is unbiblical. The list can go on to Dispensationalism, Liberation Theology, Reconstructionism, etc. Obviously this is an abbreviated list, my intention is not to alienate my brothers and sisters in the Body of Christ.

Because some within the Charismatic movement have unbiblical ideas, it does not invalidate everyone who follows the Bible's teaching of the continuation of the gifts of the Spirit. We must study the Bible before we speak.

What makes a doctrine or practice unbiblical? Any time a person or group holds to a line of thinking that does not conform to the clear teachings of the Bible, it constitutes an unbiblical stance. My grandpa was an elder in his Presbyterian church and as such regularly taught adult classes on different books of the Bible. When students asked questions of an obscure nature, my grandpa would reply with

"The Bible plainly says…" followed by his answer. If something was taught over and over again through the Bible, then it met his criteria.

We can become sidetracked if we are not careful to be guided by the full counsel of the Bible. First, watch out when you hear that something is inferred in the Bible. I have seen Reformed publications that say the Bible infers that the gifts were to cease. An inference is not the same as a clear line of teaching from the Bible.

Second, some ideas are unbiblical because they twist the meaning of a verse. An example would be the use of Romans 8:29 to deny God's act of predestination according to His plan. Some use the verse to imply that God elected to salvation those who He saw would choose Him in the future. This makes God dependent upon us for His decisions. Though God clearly interacts with us in prayer and even allows for change of circumstances due to our petitions, Romans chapter 9 and Ephesians chapter 1 teach us that election is set by God's sacred choice alone.

Third, it is unbiblical to develop a theory and then try to find verses in Scripture to back it up. We call this nasty practice proof texting.

Finally, some people just ignore the Bible. They have decided that they are comfortable with the way their church does things and what they think they believe. After all, if it weren't right they wouldn't believe it or do it. Show these people the verses that instruct us to raise our hands to God's holy throne and they look at you as if you were from Mars. It doesn't matter that the Bible calls for this (Psalm 28:2; 63:4; 134:2; Lamentations 2:19; 3:41; 1 Timothy 2:8; and Hebrews 12:12), they don't want to do it.

4. The fourth problem that has crept into the Reformed Churches is the allowance for separatism from groups and

denominations in which the Spirit of God is using His gifts. Since charismatics are seen as unbiblical it is easy not to associate with them.

Not only does this take place on a denominational level, it also occurs between individual churches and fellow believers. At every level the cancer of disunity is allowed and the demonic forces make inroads as they attack the Church.

## How Does This Affect the Average Believer?

The average member of a church has no idea of what Calvin, Warfield or Kuyper taught in respect to the gifts. Likely they will go by what their pastor tells them on the topic. I have heard Christians say, "Well, my pastor studied the charismatic gifts and told me they don't happen anymore." What amazes me is the number of Christians who never read the verses in the Bible addressing this issue of the Faith. If the pastor says it, that's enough for them. Or perhaps they read their denomination's statements of belief and just go along with what it says. I was on the Internet one day looking at different Reformed sites and one link took me to the website of the Orthodox Presbyterian Church (www.opc.org).

Under the section called "What is the Reformed Faith?" is found "Part I: Reformed Principles." In this work on the sufficiency of the Bible the Orthodox Presbyterian Church states, "Continuing charismatic revelations, prophecies, or unknown tongues are no longer needed because God has spoken his final and all-sufficient word with the completion of the canon of Holy Scripture." Average members would assume this document to be right. And if they spent any time reading the works of the authors quoted above, they would assume this to be a Reformed doctrine.

With this as their basis, these members then avoid charismatic teaching with the thought that it must be from the devil, since God has stopped doing those things. They consider the manifestations that occur as a result of the power of God to be bizarre (though there are ample examples of these manifestations in the Bible), and they don't want these things in their church. It is more important to remain religiously respectable than to allow God Himself to do seemingly offensive manifestations in them or in their worship services.

They settle for a lack of the power and authority they read about in the New Testament, assuming it was just for the Christians of the 1st Century. Their spiritual life is void of powerful tools the Holy Spirit uses to advance His kingdom.

Yet, I believe that in their heart they want to know the power of God. There is a yearning to experience all that God has for us. There is a fascination and wonder that fills their minds and hearts when they see the power of the New Testament still functioning today by God's hand. I have seen too many Christians filled with joy and relief when they find out that God wants to use His gifts through them, that He speaks prophetically, heals and operates in His Church.

### Final Thought

Cessationism has been a factor in the Reformed tradition since John Calvin. Its consequences upon the Reformed churches as well as other Christian churches have been appalling. The greatest consequence of this line of thinking within the Church is the reality of being out of accord with the clear teachings of the Scriptures as to the gifts, so the Church has lacked power in its practice and spirituality. This does not mean that believers without the gifts are not Christians. But I want more for them and I believe God wants to give them more through the Spirit.  So, what does the Bible teach about the gifts of the Holy Spirit?

# Chapter Two
## Sola Scriptura

One of the key components of Reformed theology is the reality of "Sola Scriptura," which means "scripture alone." In the context of the Reformation in the 1500's it meant that as Christians, nothing was to be held as equal to the Bible. The Roman Catholic Church was guided more by the Pope and tradition than by the Bible. For them tradition was equal with Scripture.

But the Bible is the message of God, which governs what we think, do and believe. Traditions and church leaders can be good as guides for following God, as long as they don't contradict the Bible. The Reformers were raised up by God, because the Pope, the ecclesiastical institution and their traditions had both superseded the Bible and outright disregarded its teachings.

The idea of "Sola Scriptura" continues today with the Bible being our final rule for faith and life. We believe what the Bible says, thus what we believe must be brought into conformity with it. Our theology should not decide how we read the Scriptures, instead the verses of the Bible must inform our theology.

Rev. Jack Lash, a pastor in the Presbyterian Church of America, writes, "It is evident that no verse in the Bible explicitly states that these gifts have ceased. But, as all good Bible students know, that is never good enough. We must look deeper into Biblical theology in order to see what God is saying…" [1] He is telling us that he is going to allow his theology to inform him of how to read the Bible on this issue. He spends quite a bit of space in his newsletters showing how the gifts couldn't possibly function today the way they did in the first century, and upon this basis he has decided that the gifts of the Holy Spirit have ceased in operation.

I use this pastor as an example of why we must stick to "Sola Scriptura." We can theologize about many things in our faith and allow that mental exercise to take us out of accord with the clear teachings of the Bible. But it is the obligation of every follower of Jesus to believe and obey the Bible. Surely, there are verses in which God tells us what to do that make us uncomfortable, since they have never been a part of the way we live our faith. But that is what it means to grow spiritually, conforming our lives and faith to the Bible.

We cannot have a discussion of the continuation of the gifts of the Holy Spirit without starting with "Sola Scriptura." I believe the Bible has much to say on this issue, and states very clearly that the gifts are to continue until Jesus returns at the end of this age. Starting with "Sola Scriptura" we will pore over the verses that tell us that the gifts, and the use of the power of God, are to continue throughout the history of the Church.

### Jesus on Power Ministry

There are only a few places in the Gospels where Jesus specifically addresses the issue of our involvement in ministry with power. For me, power ministry and the use of the gifts are identical ways of speaking of the Holy Spirit's "charismatic" involvement in and through the Church. Though the references to the continuance of power ministry in the words of Jesus are not many, the ones He gave us are clear and concise.

## John 14:12

"I tell you the truth, anyone who has faith in me will do what I have been doing. He will do even greater things than these, because I am going to the Father."

While attending seminary, I took a class on healing and world evangelism under the instruction of Dr. C. Peter Wagner and Dr. Charles Kraft. One of the class sessions has stuck in my mind more than any other session of any other class I have ever taken. It wasn't actually the class period that was so remarkable, but just one question asked by one professor to another.

Dr. Lewis Smedes was a guest lecturer that day and during a forum discussion Dr. Kraft challenged him by asking what Jesus meant when He said, "anyone who has faith in me will do what I have been doing. He will do even greater things than these." Dr. Smedes replied that the Church has established hundreds of hospitals and schools around the world.

I can still feel in my heart as I did that day. I was amazed at Dr. Smedes answer. I was amazed that he could be so wrong. Atheists and Agnostics have also established schools and medical facilities. It didn't take the power of the Holy Spirit for them to do that.

The question still resonates in my heart and mind today. What did Jesus mean when He made that statement? First, Jesus says, "anyone who has faith in me..." This applies to people who believe in Him. The qualifier is faith in Jesus. He didn't put a time limit on this statement. He didn't put a number limit on it. He didn't say "anyone among you Apostles who has faith in me..." He said *anyone*. This can also be translated, "the one who believes in me." So, anyone who believes in Jesus from the moment He made that statement until now and beyond who has faith in Jesus will do the works Jesus did and even greater works than He did.

What kind of works did Jesus say we could do?  The works He did.  The word for works also translates to mean deeds.  In this case it translates specifically into the miraculous works of Jesus. [2] In other words, those who have faith in Him will do the ministry of power He did.

Consider what Jesus said to two of John the Baptist's disciples, when they were sent to ask if He was truly the Messiah in Luke 7:21-22, "At that very time Jesus cured many who had diseases, sicknesses and evil spirits, and gave sight to many who were blind.  So he replied to the messengers, 'Go back and report to John what you have seen and heard:  The blind receive sight, the lame walk, those who have leprosy are cured, the deaf hear, the dead are raised, and the good news is preached to the poor."

The works Jesus focused on to sum up His ministry were mainly of power.  Some could object to their being applied to us by noting that Jesus gave this as proof of His position as Messiah.  In that case, only the Messiah could preach the good news to the poor.

When Jesus said that we, who have faith in Him, "would do the works He did and greater works than these," He meant all of His works of power.  I also like to include His deeds of teaching and compassion, even though those are not the focus of the passage.  Let's also be clear that only Jesus could be crucified for the sins of the world.  This work belongs to Him alone.

### Matthew 28:18-20
"Therefore go and make disciples of all nations, baptizing them in the name of the Father and of

the Son and of the Holy Spirit, and teach them to obey everything I have commanded you."

Most evangelical Christians have memorized this passage or are at least very familiar with it. We know it as the Great Commission, the call of Jesus to spread the Gospel to all nations. Many have written concerning the first part of this passage. The importance of going and making disciples (evangelism) is definitely a central theme.

Actually, there are three parts to this commission: disciple making, baptism in the name of the Trinity, and teaching obedience. After evangelism and baptism, it is the job of the Church to teach new Christians to obey Jesus.

But what are they to obey? When I think of obeying Jesus the first thing that comes to mind is the greatest commandment of loving God with all my heart, mind, soul and strength in Mark 12:30. His ethical commands are also very important to me, such as the teachings found in the "Sermon on the Mount." These are surely the things Jesus wanted us to be taught to obey. But I believe there is more to this statement.

Jesus said to "teach them to obey everything I have commanded you." This included power ministry for the Kingdom of God. Let us look at an example, when Jesus told the Apostles to use power.

**Luke 9:1-2**
"When Jesus had called the Twelve together, he gave them power and authority to drive out all demons and to cure diseases, and he sent them out to preach the kingdom of God and to heal the sick."

Here Jesus sent the Twelve to preach the Kingdom and demonstrate its power. That demonstration was in the form of healing the sick and casting out demons. This was the paradigm of ministry the Twelve would use in the rest of their service to God. But how do I know this use of power wasn't just reserved for the Twelve? Go to the next chapter in Luke. In Luke 10:8,9 Jesus gave the following instructions to the 70 disciples.

### Luke 10:8-9

"When you enter a town and are welcomed, eat what is set before you. Heal the sick who are there and tell them, "The kingdom of God is near you.""

This is an identical command for ministry to the one Jesus gave to the Twelve in Luke 9:1,2. Therefore the use of kingdom power was not to be used only by the Apostles, but by the larger community of Jesus' disciples also. Proclaiming and demonstrating the kingdom of God has been passed on to us as well. It is the job of the Church to teach each generation of believers to keep all of Jesus' commands to the Apostles, with preaching the presence of the Kingdom, casting out demons and healing the sick included. As Dr. Don Williams writes, "And what is it that Jesus commands? In sum, in the context of Matthew, it is to preach the gospel of the kingdom, cast out demons, and heal the sick. To be a disciple of Jesus is to bear his message and continue his ministry. Nothing less will do." [3]

### Mark 16:9-20

"And these signs will accompany those who believe: In my name they will drive out demons;

they will speak in new tongues; they will pick up snakes with their hands; and when they drink deadly poison, it will not hurt them at all; they will place their hands on sick people and they will get well."

For many, this is a questionable passage from the Gospel of Mark. Many of our Bibles have a notation that says something to the effect that Mark 16:9-20 is not found in some of the early manuscripts. Does this mean that only the unreliable manuscripts have this passage? Not really. The real question we must ask ourselves is whether we believe Jesus said this or not.

I believe that Jesus made this statement. It is part of the canonized Scriptures. Some object to it because of the reference to snakes and poison. Yet, these verses were shown to be true in the ministry of Paul. In Acts 28:3-6 Paul had put a bunch of wood on a fire and a poisonous snake came out from the heat and fastened onto his hand. Those traveling with him saw the snake on his hand before Paul shook it off. They thought he would die, but he didn't. What Jesus said was true.

This passage does not instruct us to become poisonous snake handlers or drink poison as a show of faith. It is telling us that at times of great hazard, God will protect us. Some Christians will still make fun of this and claim that Jesus couldn't possibly have said such a thing. They sound like the "Jesus Seminar," [4] which tries to decide which parts of the Gospel Jesus really said and did and which parts he didn't. I choose to believe the entire Bible.

In his commentary on Mark 16:17, John Calvin shows the significance of Jesus' words when he wrote, "As the Lord, while he still lived with men in the world, had ratified the faith of his gospel by miracles, so now he extends the same power

39

to the future, least the disciples should imagine that it could not be separated from his bodily presence." [(5)] Calvin was right in thinking that Jesus was extending His power into the future for His followers. [(6)] That is the import of all these verses from the Gospels.

The indication of this passage is that there are certain signs that should accompany followers of Jesus. These signs are in keeping with the proclamation and demonstration of the Kingdom. Believers are to cast out demons, heal the sick and even speak in new tongues. Jesus used the term "believers" indefinitely, [(7)] because this was to apply to the Church until the end of the age. These are some of the signs of the true Church.

### Acts on the Gifts and Power Ministry

**Acts 1:8,9**
"'But you will receive power when the Holy Spirit comes on you; and you will be my witnesses in Jerusalem, and in all Judea and Samaria, and to the ends of the earth.' After he said this, he was taken up before their very eyes, and a cloud hid him from their sight."

These are the last words Jesus spoke to the Church before He physically left the earth. With this in mind, there gathers a weightiness to what was said. I am not trying to imply that the Gospels are somehow less important in comparison. By no means!

I see this statement to be in keeping with all that Jesus taught, but the weight of the statement is in the sense of focus it gives us. In this admonition, Jesus summarizes what He had prepared the Church for and what He calls us to receive and do.

One of the things Jesus prepared the Church for was the reception of the Holy Spirit. In the Gospel of John, chapter 14-16, Jesus told them the Holy Spirit was coming. He came to breathe life into the Church and empower it. Think about John 20:22, "And with that he (Jesus) breathed on them and said, 'Receive the Holy Spirit.'" This took place just after Christ's resurrection. As an event, it was to prepare them for what we are looking at right now.

I spent August of 1988 living with the leader of the underground Reformed Church in Hungary. His name was Istvan Bojtor and his ministry extended into Rumania and Czechoslovakia. There was a woman named Esther who helped his ministry. She was a strong Reformed believer and an obstetrician by profession. She told me of a wonderful thing that happened in the delivery room one day. She was delivering the baby of a family from her town. But the baby was stillborn. She said that she tested the baby for any signs of life, but there were none. It upset her greatly, yet she didn't lose her head or her faith. She took the baby in her arms and began to pray over him asking God to give the infant life. After about ten or fifteen minutes of praying, she said that warmth entered the little body, the eyes opened and the baby began to cry. Through her prayers, that baby was raised from the dead.

Jesus told the Apostles they would receive power and then He continued by telling them to be His witnesses starting in Jerusalem. The task would be finished when they took the Gospel to the ends of the earth. Jesus knew they would need the power of the Holy Spirit to be His witnesses to the ends of the earth. But the Apostles didn't take the Gospels to the ends of the earth. That job is still going on today. Dr. C. Peter Wagner, a professor of missiology, wrote,

"As this is being written, missiologists are suggesting for the first time in Christian history that there appears to be light at the end of the Great Commission tunnel! For the first time, there seems to be good reason to believe that the Body of Christ now has the human resources, the material resources and the spiritual resources to complete the task." [8]

I do not believe that Jesus was telling the Apostles that the job of the Church, taking the Gospel to the ends of the earth, would be completed by them. His words were a projection for the rest of Church history. We have His Word, but we also need His power until the task is complete.

**Acts 2:14-21**
"Then Peter stood up with the Eleven, raised his voice and addressed the crowd: 'Fellow Jews and all of you who are in Jerusalem, let me explain this to you; listen carefully to what I say. These men are not drunk, as you suppose. It's only nine in the morning! No, this is what was spoken by the prophet Joel: "In the last days," God says, "I will pour out my Spirit on all people. Your sons and daughters will prophesy, your young men will see visions, your old men will dream dreams. Even on my servants, both men and women, I will pour out my Spirit in those days, and they will prophesy...""

This piece of scripture is key in our understanding of three important biblical concepts. First, Peter tells us that we are in the last days. Ever since Jesus we have been in the last days. We have been in the last days for the last 2,000 years.

Second, Peter tells us how the Spirit will move in the last days. Throughout the last days God has been pouring out His Spirit, and it is important to understand from these verses the mode by which we can recognize His activity. As the Spirit moves in the Church He imparts the gift of prophecy. The Spirit of God speaks to His Church. We know that the Holy Spirit speaks to us through the Bible, but He also speaks to us in other ways. We will look at the nature of prophecy later.

Finally, the use of the gifts was prophesied in the Old Testament. God used the prophet Joel to speak of the use of prophecy in the last days (or in our time). Peter rightly applied this prophecy to the time of the Church. We are taught by these verses that prophecy was not just for the Apostles or those closely associated with the Apostles. The gift of prophecy would be used by the Spirit in the sons and daughters and beyond, to the generations of the Church until Christ returns and the moon turns to blood.

God says in Acts 2:18, "I will pour out my Spirit in those days, and they will prophesy." We are still in "those days" and the Holy Spirit is still fulfilling Joel's prophecy. According to this verse, the gift of prophecy has ceased if the last days have already come to an end. Otherwise, the Holy Spirit will use prophecy and other manifestations as a normal operation in the Church until the end of the age.

## The Apostle Paul on the Gifts

**1 Corinthians 1:7**
"Therefore you do not lack any spiritual gift as
you eagerly wait for our Lord Jesus Christ to be
revealed."

This is a verse that took me by surprise the first time I
realized what was being said. It tells us that the Church will
have all of the gifts of the Holy Spirit in operation until Jesus
returns in His second coming.

Some of you may have Bibles that translate this verse a
little differently. For example, the Contemporary English
Version (CEV) reads, "You are not missing out on any
blessings, as you wait for him to return." Because of different
readings of this verse I think it is important to establish a
common rendition.

*"do not lack"* In the BAGD lexicon the definition for
*ustereisthai* is "lack, be lacking, go without, come short of w.
gen. of the thing." [9] God would not have the Church "go
without" any of the gifts. In other words, we are to have the
full measure of the gifts of the Spirit.

*"any spiritual gift"* or *"any charisma" Charisma* means
"gift." This word seems ambiguous. It could mean salvation
or sanctification, but it doesn't. It is directly speaking of the
spiritual gifts. As Gordon Fee comments on the definition of
this word, "They have been enriched in every way, so that
none of the gracious endowments of the Spirit is lacking in
their midst. This also means that the word (charisma), which
could be seen to refer more broadly to the gracious gift of
redemption… is to be understood as in v.5 to refer more
specifically to those special endowments of the Holy Spirit in
chs. 12-14 (cf.12:6)." [10] These "special endowments" in
chapters 12-14 are the gifts of the Holy Spirit.

As in other letters, Paul gives thanks to God for the Christians in Corinth. He also gives thanks for what God has been doing in them as believers. Fee writes, "As with 1 Thessalonians, the first mention of Spirit activity in 1 Corinthians is found in the thanksgiving period; similarly it specifically reflects the issues that will be raised in the letter. What is most remarkable about this thanksgiving is the apostle's ability to thank God for the very things in the church that, because of abuse, are also causing him grief." [11]

What was the church abusing and what was causing Paul grief? The church was abusing the use of the spiritual gifts. The question for us is whether we can be like Paul and give thanks that God has given us all the gifts, even if their misuse causes problems. I am thankful that the Holy Spirit will use all of His gifts in us until Jesus returns. None of the gifts will cease until the end of the age.

**1 Corinthians 13:8-10**
"Love never fails. But where there are prophecies, they will cease; where there are tongues, they will be stilled; where there is knowledge, it will pass away. For we know in part and we prophesy in part, but when perfection comes, the imperfect disappears."

Many use this verse by itself to point out that the charismatic gifts have ceased. Their justification for such interpretation is that when the Bible (being perfect) was finished being written, the charismatic gifts (being imperfect) passed away.

The fallacy with this thinking is found in interpretation. The perfection to come was not the Bible. The perfection to come is Jesus Himself. F.F. Bruce writes, "**but when the perfect** comes at the parousia of Christ and the consummation is realized for which the sons of God at present long eagerly (Rom. 8:23), **the imperfect will pass away.**" [12] As in 1 Corinthians 1:7, we are waiting for the second coming of Jesus, His parousia, His revealing.

This passage and 1 Corinthians 1:7 complement each other. They teach the same thing. All of the gifts are active until Jesus comes back.

### 1 Corinthians 12:4-7
"There are different kinds of gifts, but the same Spirit. There are different kinds of service, but the same Lord. There are different kinds of working, but the same God working, but the same God works all of them in all men. Now to each one the manifestation of the Spirit is given for the common good."

This is a picture of the normal operation of the local church, in reference to the spiritual gifts. As we live out our lives as disciples of Jesus Christ, the use of the gifts is to be normative to our experience in fellowship and ministry to one another and to those outside of the Church.

Surely, there will be problems and conflicts that will arise in our churches over the gifts and their operation. The larger context of chapters 12-14 instruct the local church on the operation of the gifts and deals with problems which came along with the gifts. But Paul didn't say, "Avoid the use of the gifts, they are causing problems and will be done away with in a short time anyway." No, he wrote of how they can be used in worship and in ministry in a decent and orderly manner.

I believe these verses also teach us that the gifts were meant for the Church. I write this comment in opposition to the point brought up of B. B. Warfield's belief that the gifts were only for the Apostles. Paul wrote, "Now to each one the manifestation of the Spirit is given for the common good." Each believer is given manifestations of the Spirit. We know from the following verses that the word "manifestation" refers to the charismatic gifts. These charismatic manifestations were not just for the Apostles, or the 70 disciples, but also for each believer.

### 1 Corinthians 14:1
"Follow the way of love and eagerly desire
spiritual gifts, especially the gift of prophecy."

Many Christians believe something like this, "We don't need the gifts anymore, because we have the fruit of the Spirit, especially love." Since when does love displace the manifestations of the Spirit of God? Rather, this verse teaches us that the fruit of the Spirit, especially love, and the gifts of the Spirit go together. While walking the way of love we are to desire the gifts *in* the Church.

Paul tells the Corinthians to "eagerly" desire spiritual gifts. They are to exert themselves in striving for the Holy Spirit to manifest His gifts in their church. Why? 1 Corinthians 14:1 shows no sign of the gifts ceasing. I would say it demonstrates the complete opposite. If Paul foresaw that the gifts would cease in the near future, I don't think he would have instructed the church in Corinth to desire that the gifts, especially prophecy, be used in their midst.

The Bible is telling us that the gifts are going to continue throughout Church history and we should desire that the Spirit use His power in every local church. We must desire for the Holy Spirit to direct us through prophecy. I wish this were the attitude that I would find in the churches and Christians I know. Instead, I talk to too many Christians who didn't really want the gifts, and especially prophecy, to be used by the Holy Spirit in their church.

I was talking with one of my wife's uncles during a recent visit. He is a member in good standing in his church and teaches a Sunday morning adult class. We spent a long time debating the continuation of the charismatic gifts, and as we were discussing this verse I asked him if he even desires for the Holy Spirit to use His powerful gifts in his church. He said that he doesn't desire the charismatic gifts to be used in his church, because there are too many charlatans who are faking the gifts. I said that I agree there are charlatans, since the Bible promises that there will be false prophets and false teachers.

Even with this admonition from Scripture, he said that he would not desire the gifts. I told him that he was in disobedience to God. God has told us to "eagerly desire" the gifts. Ask yourself the same question. Do you eagerly desire for the Holy Spirit to use His gifts in your church or do you reject the exhortation of this verse?

**Galatians 3:1-5**
"You foolish Galatians! Who has bewitched you? Before your very eyes Jesus Christ was clearly portrayed as crucified. I would like to learn just one thing from you: Did you receive the Spirit by observing the law, or by believing what you heard? Are you so foolish? After beginning with the Spirit, are you now trying to attain your goal by human effort? Have you suffered so much for nothing – if it really was for nothing? Does God give you his Spirit and work miracles among you because you observe the law, or because you believe what you heard?"

The church in Galatia began with the power of the Spirit. This probably means Paul came to them, preached the Gospel and they started to believe in Jesus as they witnessed and were ministered to by the manifestations of the Spirit. It was the same for Thessalonica (1 Thessalonians 1:4,5) and Corinth (1 Corinthians 2:1-5), where Paul preached and demonstrated the power of the kingdom, so that their faith would be rooted in the power of God.

This was Paul's basic way of starting a new church. We can see that it was not enough for Paul that the church would experience a few miracles, come to faith and then allow the miraculous to cease so that they would build the church by their own effort. To "attain your goal" by human effort means to simply obey the law of God, be good people and try your hardest. This was being done by the Galatians to the exclusion of the Spirit and his manifestations.

I don't think Paul's understanding of the plan of God for the Church allowed for the cessation of the gifts. The power of the Spirit wasn't just meant to get the Church started. This passage shows that Paul expected the church in Galatia to continue in the power of the Spirit without end.

It is a matter of faith versus works and the power of the Spirit versus human effort all wrapped up into one argument. Paul expresses this argument for living by faith using inseparable terms. To live by faith includes living by the power and miracles of the Holy Spirit. These manifestations in the Church are a demonstration by God that mirrors our life in Christ, which is established by faith, not by works.

I think that the Apostle Paul would ask the Reformed Church the same question. "After beginning with the Spirit, are you now trying to attain your goal by human effort?"

## Final Thoughts on Sola Scriptura

I hope you will pore over these passages of Scripture. I hope you will do more than pore over them. Let these verses be the basis of your understanding on this issue. Again, being Reformed Christians we hold a value for "Sola Scriptura." The Bible must be the rule by which we decide what will take place in our churches and what we will believe theologically. As Luder G. Whitlock, Jr. writes, "(the) desire to understand the Scriptures and to seek obedient conformity to them in church and society is the essence of what it means to be Reformed." [13] Though I would presume Luder Whitlock is not charismatic, I find his statement quite applicable. I believe that if we are going to walk as the Reformed churches God planned for us to be, we will "seek obedient conformity" to these passages along with the rest of Scripture.

These verses are not inferences from the Bible. They clearly show that the power of God and the gifts of the Spirit are to continue to the end of the age. These are the teachings of Jesus and the Apostle Paul, and we see applications of these teachings in the Book of Acts. As these teachings are gathered together, they leave no doubt in my mind that the Spirit of God is still active in using His power to add to the kingdom and cultivate those within.

Now that we have a biblical basis for believing in the continuation of the charismatic gifts, do we have church history that concurs with these verses? That is the subject of the next chapter.

# Chapter Three
## The Power of God in Early Church and Reformed History

### Introduction to the Chapter

What place does experience have in our lives and faith? It should never be the sole determining factor in matters of faith. It must always be subjected to the Scriptures. That is why that last chapter was devoted to establishing a biblical basis for the gifts. Experience is still important, because it validates many of our beliefs and ideas. The Spirit of God shows us that His Word is true, by witnessing to our hearts and implementing it in our lives.

Many Christians believe the charismatic gifts have ceased being used as we discussed in chapter one. And many of those individuals base this belief on their experience. They have never seen the gifts in use. Furthermore, their pastors and other teachers tell them the gifts have not been used in Church history. Any examples given of power are usually spurious and used to convince the average believer that the gifts have stopped and any use of power in the Church is from the devil.

In 1989, my wife, Diana, and I studied Spanish in Costa Rica for 10 months. During our time there we made friends with another student and his wife. A graduate of Dallas Theological Seminary, he was an ardent cessationist.

One day while we were talking about the subject, he told me about a person who had been healed. After being healed the individual met with their pastor and elders, who said that God doesn't do that anymore and were concerned that the healing may have been from Satan. So the person rebuked the healing by saying, "If this healing is from the devil, then I reject it." The healed part of the person's body went back to the way it was. Having finished his story, the missionary looked at me and said something to the effect that this was an example of how the devil fools us into thinking God still does those things today.

The missionary used this story as the basis for his disbelief in God's use of power in the Church. This, of course, was a poor argument from experience. The problem we face in this situation is a belief based on a single story that lacks a biblical foundation.

We have displayed a biblical infrastructure for the use of the charismatic gifts in the Church, but that isn't enough for most Christians. They want to know if there is corroborative evidence to support this position. I believe there is ample documentation from Church history, and specifically Reformed church history, to show that the biblical basis is sound for the continuation of the charismatic gifts.

Witnessing the Holy Spirit's use of power and manifestations is an important and valid part of establishing the reality of His work among us. The Spirit maintains an accord between what He has revealed to us in the Bible and what He continues to do today. You will see this harmony in the following examples from our history.

## Charismatic Belief in the Early Church

In studying the charismatic gifts, it has been gratifying to read quotations from the Early Church Fathers. I have come across three great sources for this information.

Dr. James Bradley, a professor of Church History at Fuller Theological Seminary, wrote one of the most remarkable papers I have ever read on the subject of the power of God in Church history. It is titled "Some Theological and Ethical Aspects of Miracles in the Early Church" and it shows that the "second and third century Christians expected miracles to continue after the first century." This paper opened my eyes to the writings of Early Church Fathers and what they believed on the subject of miracles and the gifts in the Church.

Another source is Appendix A of John Wimber's book *Power Evangelism*. The appendix is titled "Signs and Wonders in Church History" and lists proponents of the gifts of the Spirit from Justin Martyr to John Wesley.

The third is a book written by Ronald A. N. Kydd titled *Charismatic Gifts in the Early Church*. This is the most extensive resource of these three authors. Kydd makes an extremely strong case for the existence of the charismatic gifts in the first three centuries of the Church. He also shows that the gifts were being used by the Church throughout the Roman Empire rather than being limited to one geographic area.

The following are quotes of Early Christian leaders, which are found in the works just listed. Listen to what the Early Church Fathers believed:

**Ignatius of Antioch** was a bishop who wrote seven letters from 98 A.D. to 117 A.D., which show him to be a prophet. [1] In a letter to the Philadelphians Ignatius wrote,

"While I was among you, I cried out, I was speaking with a loud voice,  God's voice, 'Pay attention to the bishop, to the presbytery and deacons.' And some were suspecting that I said these things as one who had had prior    information about a division which certain people had caused, but he for whom I am in bonds is my witness that I did not get this information from any man. But the Spirit proclaimed aloud, saying 'Do nothing without the bishop; keep your flesh as the temple of God; love unity; flee divisions; be imitators of Jesus Christ as he is of his Father.'" [2]

In another letter to Polycarp, bishop of Smyrna, Ignatius wrote, "ask for invisible things so that they may be made manifest to you in order that you may lack nothing and abound with all spiritual gifts." [3]

**Justin Martyr** (c.100-165 A.D.) wrote, "For the prophetical gifts remain with us even to the present time." [4] And "Now, it is possible to see amongst us women and men who possess gifts of the Spirit of God." [5] In light of these quotes and others made by Justin Martyr, Kydd comments,

"On several occasions in the record of this conversation with Trypho, he refers to the gifts of the Spirit as though they were a part of the Church of his day. The one gives concrete evidence for things which happened in the atmosphere that we sense in the other. The Church of the mid-second century was charismatic." [6]

**Irenaeus** (c.130-c.200 A.D.), Bishop of Lyon, wrote in his work *Against Heresies*,

"And some have foreknowledge of things to be, and visions and prophetic speech, and others cure the sick by the laying on of hands and make them whole, and even as we have said, the dead have been raised and remained with us for many years." [7]

In another passage from *Against Heresies* Irenaeus wrote,

"Just as we hear many brethren in the church who have gifts of prophecy, and who speak through the Spirit with all manner of tongues, and who bring the hidden things of men into the clearness for the common good and expound the mysteries of God." [8]

**Tertullian** (c.160-220 A.D.) is quoted by Bradley as writing, "Now all these signs (of spiritual gifts) are forthcoming from my side without difficulty, and they agree, too, with the rules, and the dispensations, and the instructions of the Creator; therefore without doubt the Christ, and the Spirit, and the apostle, belong severally to my God. Here then is my frank avowal for anyone who cares to require it."

**Cyprian** (c.200-258 A.D.) Cyprian, the Bishop of Carthage, was known by some to be prophetic. Some persecuted Christians once wrote the following in a letter to him,

"For by your words you have both provided those things about which we have been taught the least and strengthened us to bear up under the sufferings which we are experiencing, being certain of the heavenly reward,   the martyrs' crown, and the kingdom of God as a result of the prophecy which you, being full of the Holy Spirit pledged to us in your letter." [9]

Of his own experiences, Cyprian wrote,

"In fact I remember what has already been shown to me, indeed what has been taught to an obedient and fearing servant by the Lord God, who thought it worthwhile to show and reveal these things among other things and who adds this, 'Therefore he who does not believe Christ who makes the priest, shall later begin to believe him who avenges the priest.' And yet, I know that to some men dreams are seen to be ridiculous and visions silly, but certainly more so to those who choose to think badly of the priests than to those who are favorable to them." [10]

And, "Because of this the divine judgment does not stop restraining us night and day. In addition to visions in the night, during the day also among us the innocent age of childhood is filled with the Holy Spirit. It sees with its eyes in ecstasy, it hears, and it speaks those things of which the Lord thinks it is worthwhile to warn and to instruct us." [11]

As a comment on this last passage, Kydd wrote, "Here Cyprian refers to prophetic messages which he was hearing while in hiding and which were relevant to the subject he was discussing. The agents of these messages appear to have been children." [12] In an overall statement Kydd also wrote, "From all of these passages, we conclude that North Africa was not foreign to the gifts of the Spirit around the mid-point of the third century." [13]

**Origen** (c.185-c.254 A.D.), a leader and teacher in the Church, had the following to say about the gifts in a work called *Against Celsus*.

"Traces of that Holy Spirit who appeared in the form of a dove are still preserved among Christians. They charm demons away and perform many cures and perceive certain things about the future according to the will of the Logos." [14]

"They no longer have any prophets or wonders, though traces of these are to be found to a considerable extent among Christians. Indeed, some works are even greater; and if our word may be trusted, we also have seen them." [15]

**Dionysius**, Bishop of Alexandria (serving from 247 to 264 A.D.), wrote about an experience he had. It reads, "But a vision sent by God came and strengthened me, and a word of command was given me, saying expressly: 'Read all things that may come to thy hand. For thou art able to sift and prove each matter; which thing was originally the cause of thy faith.' I accepted the vision." [16]

Besides the examples given here, there are others throughout Church history (including Clement, Bishop of Rome and Eusebius) who have believed the gifts were in use or were said to have experienced them. In addition to these individuals, Early Church writings such as the *Didache* and *The Shepherd of Hermas* give instruction for the use of prophecy in the Church.

Now that we have established that the gifts of the Spirit were seen to be active in the first three centuries of the Church, I would like to turn towards the Reformed tradition for the rest of our examples of God's power continuing to be used in the Church.

## Augustine of Hippo (354-430 A.D.)

Augustine is recognized as probably the most formative theologian in Reformed doctrine before John Calvin. Calvin himself refers to and quotes him some 100 times in his *Institutes of the Christian Religion*. Augustine is well known for his propounding on predestination and total depravity. He wrote on these Reformed doctrines in his many volumes of theological writing.  Though we appreciate his applications to our theology, very few people know of his experiences with the power of the Holy Spirit.

Augustine's mother, Monica, spent much of the first part of Augustine's life praying for him.  He was a man who was given to enjoying his sinful nature.  In his Confessions, Augustine tells us of how his mother wept in prayer for him, knowing that her son lived a life leading to death.  God heard Monica's prayers for her son and answered her by giving her a vision.

Augustine writes, "She dreamed that she was standing on a wooden rule, and coming towards her in a halo of splendor she saw a young man who smiled at her in joy, although she herself was sad and quite consumed with grief. He asked her the reason for her sorrow and her daily tears, not because he did not know, but because he had something to tell her, for this is what happens in visions.  When she replied that her tears were for the soul I had lost, he told her to take heart for, if she looked carefully, she would see that where she was, there also was I.  And when she looked, she saw me standing beside her on the same rule." [17]

God proved the vision to be true as He saved Augustine and gave spiritual life to him.  But Augustine was not saved in an ordinary manner.  Likewise, God called him in a supernatural manner.  Augustine was sitting alone under a fig tree in deep despair and weeping when he heard the voice of a child singing a chant from a nearby house.  The words he heard repeated in the song were "Take it and read; Take it and read."

Augustine could not remember a children's song with these words.  He wrote, "I stemmed my flood of tears and stood up, telling myself that this could only be a divine command to open my book of Scripture and read the first passage on which my eyes should fall." [18] So he returned to where he had left his Bible. He then writes, "I seized it and opened it, and in silence I read the first passage on which my eyes fell: 'Not in reveling and drunkenness, not in lust and wantonness, not in quarrels and rivalries. Rather, arm yourselves with the Lord Jesus Christ; spend no more thought on nature and nature's appetites.' I had no wish to read more and no need to do so. For in an instant, as I came to the end of the sentence, it was as though the light of confidence flooded into my heart and all darkness of doubt was dispelled." [19]

His conversion is marked by a prophetic vision given to his mother, and audible voice commanding him to read the Bible and the Holy Spirit using Romans 13:13, 14 to bring Augustine into complete faith in Jesus Christ. As if these weren't enough, he would experience more of the Holy Spirit later in his life.

In Chapter 22 of *The City of God*, Augustine writes, "To what do these miracles witness, but to this faith which preaches Christ risen in the flesh, and ascended with the same into heaven?"[20] For him, the central reason God gives miracles is to glorify Jesus. He used this chapter to write of a number of miracles, some of which he saw.

Innocentius was an ex-advocate of the deputy prefecture, who was sick and had a fistula. Though the doctors tried to fix the condition with medications, they were ready to perform an operation. The day before surgery, Augustine was present with a few others, including a bishop named Aurelius, to pray for Innocentius. After a time of emotional prayer, they agreed to return the next day to be there for the sick individual while the doctors worked on him. On the next day when they removed the bandages to begin the operation, they found Innocentius to be completely healed. As

Augustine wrote, "a cure wrought at Carthage, in my presence, and under my own eyes." [21]

Innocentia was a woman suffering from breast cancer, which she had been told was incurable. Her only hope was found in prayer. Augustine tells us how God answered her petitions. "On the approach of Easter, she was instructed in a dream to wait for the first woman that came out from the baptistery after being baptized, and ask her to make the sign of Christ upon her sore. She did so, and was immediately cured." [22]

Augustine continues to write of a doctor and an aging comedian both of whom were cured of gout by being baptized. In both cases the individuals were found to be free from their afflictions as they rose from the act of being baptized. [23]

There are more healings related to us, even a person who was raised from the dead. I think it is important to write on them, since the way in which the healing was brought about is controversial. Two men were healed in relation to dirt from Jerusalem and others were healed by the use of the bones of Stephen, the deacon and martyr. I do not adhere to the use of relics when it comes to praying for someone who is sick. I believe we are instructed by the Bible to pray for the sick and use oil to anoint them for healing. Sometimes the simplest prayer to God will move Him to use His power for healing. But that does not mean that God cannot use such items as listed above to free someone from sickness.

In 2 Kings 13:21 we are told, "Elisha died and was buried. Now Moabite raiders used to enter the country every spring. Once while some Israelites were burying a man, suddenly they saw a band of raiders; so they threw the man's body into Elisha's tomb. When the body touched Elisha's bones, the man came to life and stood up on his feet." This event in Israel's history is not meant as a justification for the use of relics in healing. Yet, we must stand back and let God be God. No one prayed for the man, he was simply dropped on Elisha's bones. This was a sovereign act of God.

This is not the only place in Scripture where God is known to allow for power ministry that is distributed through objects. We are told of a particularly strange happening in Acts 19:11, 12. It reads, "God did extraordinary miracles through Paul. Handkerchiefs and aprons that had touched him were taken to the sick, and their illnesses were cured and the evil spirits left them." When I say that this is strange, I don't mean that it is weird. Rather, this is not common to our experience. The thought of touching something to someone who is greatly anointed by the Spirit and using it to heal someone who is sick or to cast out a demon just doesn't fit in 20th or 21st Century Christianity.

God used both Elisha's bones and pieces of cloth, which had touched Paul, to heal, cast out demons and raise the dead. With this in mind, I don't want to dismiss Augustine's accounts of individuals being healed, even by Steven's bones. Augustine is a pillar of Reformed theology and is given respect for his theological mind. We must also respect his experiences of the power of God.

As much as I enjoy what Augustine has to say to us in his witness of God's power in healing, it is time for us to turn our attention to the accounts from the Reformation. I believe the strongest historical evidence for the continuation of the charismatic gifts comes from the Scottish Reformation. In essence I am saying that the Presbyterian Church was birthed by the very power of God its larger body tries to ignore and deny. Return with me to Scotland in the mid 1500's.

# George Wishart (1513-1546 A.D.)

This man was the lightning rod of the Reformation in Scotland. He was known for having started the Reformation in Scotland. In this cause of God he was martyred for the sake of Jesus Christ. Wishart was a man of great learning and moved powerfully in the Spirit of God. He was also a mentor to John Knox. Knox wrote, "Also he was so clearly illuminated with the Spirit of Prophecy, that he saw not only things pertaining to himself, but also such things as some towns and the whole Realm afterwards felt, which he forespake, not in secret, but in the audience of many." [24]

John Knox is a firsthand witness to his mentor being filled with the gift of prophecy. Knox is not writing about the ability to preach, but the power of God to "forespake" or prophesy a future event. These events were "afterwards felt" or experienced later by Knox and others as they had been spoken.

Once, while George Wishart was preaching in a town called Dundee, he was ordered to stop by the authorities. He prophesied that they would be stricken with the plague because they rejected the Word of God. A couple of weeks later while ministering in another town quite a distance away he was informed that the people of Dundee were dying from a plague. He immediately rode his horse back to Dundee and began to care for the people of that town.

John Knox goes on to give two examples of prophetic words given by George Wishart. The first was spoken against the town of Haddington. Wishart was supposed to preach a sermon on the Second Table of the Law. But he didn't give it much time. Instead he spoke this word to the few who attended the service.

"O Lord, how long shall it be that Thy Holy Word shall be despised, and men shall not regard their own salvation? I have heard of thee, Haddington, that in thee would have been at a vain Clerk (or Miracle) Play two or three thousand people; and now, to hear the Messenger of the Eternal God, of all the town or parish cannot be numbered a hundred persons! Sore and fearful shall the plagues be that shall endue upon this thy contempt! With fire and sword shalt thou be plagued! Yea, thou Haddington, strangers shall possess thee, and you, the present inhabitants, shall either in bondage serve your enemies, or else ye shall be chased from your habitations; and that because ye have not known, nor will not know, the time of God's merciful visitation." [25]

After quoting this prophetic word given to the people of Haddington, Knox makes this statement, "In such vehemency and threatening continued that servant of God near an hour and a half, in which he declared all the plagues that ensued, as plainly as after our eyes saw them performed." [26] So John Knox said that the very plagues prophesied against Haddington came to that town. The prophecy was fulfilled.

George Wishart also predicted his own capture that would lead to his death. After he was finished speaking against Haddington and was preparing for the night, Knox wanted to stay with him and probably protect him. But Wishart said to Knox, "Nay, return to your bairns (pupils), and God bless you. One is sufficient for one sacrifice." [27] With that he had Knox give up the two-handed sword he was carrying and go with Hugh Douglas. Knox writes that he obeyed Wishart and went.

That night Wishart reflected on the "comfortable purpose of the death of God's chosen children, and merrily said, 'Methinks that I desire earnestly to sleep.'" [28] I believe he was referring to sleeping in Jesus or, in other words, his death. During the night the place where he was staying was completely surrounded. Without a fight the Scottish reformer said, "Open the gates. The Blessed Will of my God be done!" [(29)] With that he was taken into custody.

George Wishart's final prophecy was spoken while he was being burned at the stake. It was a gruesome end to a great reformer. The fire had been lit and bags of powder tied to his body had exploded. The executioner realized that Wishart was still alive and spoke words of courage to him. I can only imagine what went through his mind when Wishart replied, "This flame hath scorched my body, yet it hath not daunted my spirit; but he who from yonder place, beholdeth us with such pride, shall within a few days lie in the same, as ignominiously as he is now seen proudly to rest himself." [(30)]

This prophetic word was given against Cardinal Beaton, who as the Pope's agent had tried to kill the Reformation in Scotland by hunting down Wishart. The prophecy came true less than three months later when men broke into those same chambers and stabbed the Cardinal to death.

John Howie gives a great summary to the power of God in Wishart's ministry when he wrote, "Through the whole of his sufferings, his meekness and patience were very remarkable, as was that uncommon measure of the spirit of prophecy which he possessed. Witness the circumstances relative to Dundee, Haddington, the reformation from Popery, and the Cardinal's death – all of which were foretold by him, and soon after accomplished."[(31)]

We can only conclude as John Knox and John Howie have that God used the gift of prophecy in the ministry of George Wishart. But Wishart wasn't the only reformer in whom God used this gift. Let's examine the use of this gift in the ministry of John Knox.

# John Knox (1515-1572 A.D.)

He was called the "prophet and apostle of our nation" by James Melville [32] and the "great apostle of the Scots" by Beza. [33] Every Presbyterian knows that God used Knox to begin the Presbyterian Church in Scotland, but we don't know him by such strong appellations as used by these two men who were his contemporaries.

John Knox walked powerfully in the Spirit, especially in the gift of prophecy. Jasper Ridley writes, "The stories about Knox's prophetic powers, showing how his prophecies came true, were also circulated within a very few years of his death by Smeton, and were later repeated and elaborated by James Melville and many other Scottish Protestant writers."[34] The following are three examples of prophecies given by John Knox.

While Knox was in Central Europe under the guidance of John Calvin, he was called to pastor an English-speaking church in Frankfurt, Germany. The congregation was an assemblage of English Protestants living in exile. "At first he hesitated to accept, but Calvin persuaded him to do so and he went. He had hesitated because of a premonition that trouble over doctrine would arise, and sure enough – he had been there only a short time when exactly such trouble arose." [35] The word "premonition" is a weak way of saying that he prophetically knew what would take place should he go to Frankfurt. I would venture to say that the Holy Spirit had warned him not to waste his time serving that congregation.

John Knox gave a prophecy to a man by the name of the Earl of Morton. Morton was about receive the position of Regency when Knox recounted how God had blessed him with many good friends and good things. He also charged Morton to use his position for the advancement of the Gospel through the Church. Knox concluded by saying, "If you act thus, God will be with you; if otherwise, he shall deprive you of all these benefits, and your end shall be shameful and ignominious." [36] John Howie, in his book *The Scots Worthies*, tells us the outcome of this prophetic word by writing, "This threatening, as Morton to his melancholy experience confessed, was literally accomplished. At his execution, in June 1581, he called to mind John Knox's words, and acknowledged, that in what he had said to him he had been a true prophet." [37]

While Knox was on his deathbed, William Kircaldy (the Laird of Grange) was making ready in the Castle of Edinburgh to defend against the King. John Knox loved Kircaldy very much as a friend and fellow reformer. And as David Lindsay was visiting Knox, the dying leader said, "Well, brother, I thank God I have desired all this day to have had you, that I might send you to that man in the Castle, the Laird of Grange, whom you know I have loved dearly. Go, I pray you, and tell him from me, in the name of God, that unless he leave that evil course wherein he has entered, neither shall that rock (meaning the Castle of Edinburgh, which he then kept out against the King) afford him any help, nor the carnal wisdom of that man, whom he counteth half a god (meaning Maitland of Lethington); but he shall be pulled out of that nest, and brought down over the wall with shame, and his carcase shall be hung before the sun; so God hath assured me." [38]

When the battle was over and it was time for Kircaldy to surrender, he could not leave the castle through the gates due to the damage from English bombardment. Instead, they tied a rope around him and lowered him from the wall. Later, they took him to the market cross to hang him until dead. As his hanging began, he was facing the east, but swung around to the west, towards the sun, as he died. [39] Thus, John Knox's prophecy came true in how Kircaldy was removed from the castle and the manner in which he would die. It cannot be doubted that Knox walked in the Spirit with the gift of prophecy.

## Samuel Rutherford (1600-1661 A.D.)

Scottish covenanter, theologian, minister and author, Samuel Rutherford is best remembered as one of the Scottish Commissioners to the Westminster Assembly in 1643-1649. In helping to write the Westminster Confession of Faith, he has demonstrated his credentials as a Reformed theologian.

While serving as Professor of Divinity at the University of St. Andrews in Scotland, Rutherford wrote a book called *A Survey Of The Spiritual Antichrist* in which he addresses four kinds of prophecy. In the following quote he writes about third prophecy or prophetic words given to people since the Bible was completed. It is clear Samuel Rutherford believed the gift of prophecy was still active in the Church.

"There is a 3 revelation of some particular men, who have foretold things to come even since the ceasing of the Canon of the word, as John Husse, Wickeliefe, Luther, have foretold things to come, and they certainly fell out, and in our nation of Scotland, M. George Wishart foretold that Cardinall Beaton should not come out alive at the Gates of the Castle of St. Andrews, but that he should dye a shameful death, and he was hanged over the window that he did look out at, when he saw the man of God burnt, M. Knox prophecied of the hanging of the Lord of Grange, M. Joh Davidson uttered prophecies, knowne to many of the kingdome, diverse holy and mortified preachers in England have done the like" [40]

## John Scrimgeour

A minister at Kinghorn, who later spent time as chaplain to King James VI, John Scrimgeour, "… was also an eminent wrestler with God, and had more than ordinary power and familiarity with Him." [41] There are only two instances of the power of God in his ministry as recorded by John Howie.

The first is the healing of a woman with "a very lingering disease" and possible mental illness. After a time of sweet and encouraging ministry to her, Scrimgeour prayed, "in the name of Jesus Christ, who obeyed the Father, and came to save us; and in the name of the Holy and blessed Spirit, our Quickener and Sanctifier, I, the elder, command thee, a daughter of Abraham, to be loosed from these bonds." She was instantly healed. In the other case, his daughter was sick. John prayed and she was healed.

## John Welch (1568-1622 A.D.)

According to John Howie, writer of *The Scots Worthies*, John Welch was a great and dedicated servant of Jesus Christ. His life was devoted to prayer as Howie writes, "from the beginning of his ministry to his death, he reckoned the day ill-spent if he stayed not seven or eight hours in prayer." [42] This aspect of Welch's spiritual life has challenged me in ways I could not have imagined. His prayer time of seven or eight hours leads me to want to spend more time with God during my day. As you will soon read, John Welch was well acquainted with our Lord.

Besides being a prayer warrior, he was quite possibly a central figure in the continuation of the Reformation in Scotland. John Welch was John Knox's son-in-law. He married Knox's daughter Elizabeth and together they had three sons. Yet, his position in the history of the Reformation is not due to his marriage, or some doctrinal thesis. John Welch was used by God with prayer and power. Like Knox, Welch would ask God, "Lord, wilt Thou not grant me, Scotland?" [43] In answer to this question, Welch prophesied, "a sad time was at hand, but the Lord would be gracious to a remnant." [44] But this wasn't the only prophecy God would give John Welch.

While being the pastor at Kirkcudbright, Welch met a man named Robert Glendinning. The man was definitely worldly, but Welch told him to begin studying the Scriptures. Welch prophesied that Glendinning would take his place as minister at Kirkcudbright. Robert Glendinning later became the minister at Kirkcudbright. [45]

John Welch foresaw judgments coming against Scotland [46] and he spoke prophecies against a few individuals. There was a man who "greatly profaned" the Lord's Day. God finally had Welch warn the man to respect God on Sundays or God would cause him to lose his house. When the man did lose his house, "he told his wife and children that he had found Welch a true prophet."[47]

As for the Archbishop of Glasgow, John Spottiswoode, Welch prophesied, "He shall be cast away as a stone out of a sling, his name shall rot, and a malediction shall fall upon his posterity, after he is gone." [48] Spottiswoode soon died in a foreign land and his son, Robert, was later beheaded by order of the Scottish Parliament.

While visiting in the home of Lord Ochiltree, Welch was talking with all present about things concerning God. There was a young Catholic man who made fun of Welch by laughing, mocking and making faces. "Thereupon Mr. Welch brake out into a sad abrupt charge upon all the company to be silent, and observe the work of the Lord upon that mocker, which they should presently behold; upon which the profane wretch sunk down and died beneath the table, to the great astonishment of all the company." [49]

Once when his wife was about to travel, he told her to bypass the town of Ayr, "for before you come thither, you shall find the plague broken out in Ayr." [50] As he had prophesied, the plague did break out in Ayr. The people of that town asked him for help and he said that Hugh Kennedy was to pray for them. They took his advice. Mr. Kennedy gathered a few others of the town and they prayed. Soon after the prayer, the plague began to decline.

At another time while John Welch was living and ministering in Ayr, the plague was spreading through many other towns. The town officials had posted guards at the entrances. One day two merchants came asking to enter and sell their goods. The guards sent for the magistrates who sent for Mr. Welch (the leaders of the town would not do anything without consulting him) who came and spent a moment looking up to God in personal prayer. He then told them to send the merchants on to the next town, because their goods were infested with the plague. The merchants went on to the town of Cumnock and that town received the plague from their goods as Welch had said. An interesting thing is that the merchants had just come from a town that was free of the plague and the merchants held passes from that town saying they should be accepted. [51]

Finally, Lord Ochiltree's son was staying in Mr. Welch's home. The young man had become sick and died. Mr. Welch liked the young man very much and was grieved by this death. Mr. Welch asked that he be alone with the body and began to pray. After three hours they came for the body, but Welch asked for another 24 hours. At the conclusion of this time, there was a desire to prepare the body for a coffin, since the weather was very hot. Yet, Welch asked for more time. After 48 hours had passed, Welch's friends decided to prove to Mr. Welch that the young man was dead and not just asleep. Physicians came and "twisted a bow-string around his head with great force" [52] and pinched the young man with pinchers. The doctors said that the young man was dead. John Welch then asked for a couple of more hours and they agreed.

John Howie writes at this point, "Then Mr. Welch fell down before the pallet, and cried to the Lord with all his might, and sometimes looked upon the dead body, continuing to wrestle with the Lord, till at length the dead youth opened his eyes, and cried out to Mr. Welch, whom he distinctly knew, 'O sir, I am all whole, but my head and legs' and these were the places they had surely hurt with their pinching. When Mr. Welch perceived this, he called upon his friends; and showed them the dead young man restored to life again, "to their great astonishment." [53]

## Robert Bruce (c.1554-1631 A.D.)

As a minister in Edinburgh, Robert Bruce was held in high regard. That doesn't mean he escaped persecution for the cause of Christ. Through the trials of the Reformation many recognized the authority and power of God resting on this man. He was known for speaking prophecy and having those prophecies come true. God also healed many through Bruce's ministry, including epileptics. [54]

In the matter of God's use of the prophetic in Bruce, John Howie relates the following, "About this time he related a strange dream, how he had seen a long broad book, with black boards, flying in the air, with many black fowls like crows flying about it; and as it touched any of them, they fell down dead. Upon this he heard an audible voice speak to him, saying, *Haec est ira Dei contra pastores ecclesiae Scoticanae*, (this is the anger of God against the pastors of the Scottish church); upon which he fell a-weeping, and prayed that he might be kept faithful; and not be one of those who were thus struck down by a touch of His wrath, through deserting the truth. He said, when he awakened, he found his pillow all wet and drenched with tears. The accomplishment of this dream I need not describe." [55]

Like John Welch, Robert Bruce was known as a prayer warrior. Once while praying through a matter with other ministers, it is said that he prayed down the Holy Spirit. The evidence of the Spirit's presence was an "extraordinary motion on all present." [56] I can only assume that this motion was probably something like shaking, since it was out of the ordinary. The account also says that the ministers present "could hardly contain themselves." [57] I imagine that Jonathan Edwards would have felt at home in this prayer meeting. Edwards was accustomed to such manifestations of the Spirit in his meetings.

### Alexander Peden (c.1626-1680's)

One of the most fascinating figures in Presbyterian history was a man known as Prophet Peden. Peden was a graduate of the University of Glasgow and could have done as he pleased. Instead, he followed God. His life was marked by godly poverty as he lived in caves while ministering God's grace.

As a picture of his relationship and intimacy with God, Smellie writes, "the heaven from which issue answers to human prayer, and divine interpositions, and great and precious promises, and disclosures of things unseen, was nearer to him than it is to many; by continual trust and daily speech with the King, he accustomed himself to 'climb higher than the sphery chime.'" [58] From this relationship with our Lord, Peden walked in the gift of prophecy.

After performing the wedding of Isabel Weir to John Brown, Peden told the bride, "Isabel, you have got a good man; but you will not enjoy him long. Prize his company, and keep linen by you to be his winding-sheet; for you will need it when ye are not looking for it, and it will be a bloody one." [59] Three years later in 1685, a Capt. Claverhouse and some troops captured Brown who was out working with a shovel in his fields. They took him back to his house and told him to prepare to die by saying, "Go to your prayers, for you shall immediately die." Brown knelt and prayed for the people of Scotland and that God would save a remnant. Following prayer Claverhouse told Brown, "Take good-night of your wife and children."

Brown said goodbye to his wife and children, who were present. Claverhouse ordered his execution and the troops shot Brown to death. After Claverhouse left, Isabel gathered his body together, covered him and wept next to his body.

That same morning, Peden was about ten miles away. Entering the house of a friend approximately an hour after the shooting had occurred he said, "Lord, when wilt Thou avenge Brown's blood? O, let Brown's blood be precious in Thy sight!" This is a prophetic word given by Peden to those in that house, since he wasn't present at Brown's execution.

The owner of the home, John Muirhead, asked Peden what he was talking about. Peden answered, "What do I mean? Claverhouse has been at Priesthill this morning, and has murdered John Brown. His corpse is lying at the end of his house, and his poor wife sitting weeping by his corpse, and not a soul to speak comfortably to her." [60] He went on, "This morning, after the sun-rising, I saw a strange apparition in the firmament, the appearance of a very bright, clear, shining star fall from heaven to the earth. And indeed there is a clear, shining light fallen this day, the greatest Christian that ever I conversed with." [61]

Prophet Peden had not only prophesied the death of John Brown to his bride, but spiritually saw the fulfillment of that word as it was completed. This is an example of one of Peden's prophecies. But Peden was also known for miraculous escapes from those who would arrest him for being a part of the Reformed Church.

Once while being chased by troops, Peden escaped by crossing a river. It was spring and the river was at a flood stage with strong currents. Peden rode his horse into the river and it seemed that he crossed easily, but the troops did not enter, knowing the currents would sweep them away and probably kill them. "Then turning in his saddle, he saluted his baffled antagonists. 'Lads,' he cried, with the gleam of fun in his looks, 'ye want my boat for crossing waters, and will certainly drown."[62] So, he warned them not to try the crossing. He knew that God had supernaturally given him passage through danger.

At other times, while being chased on horseback, he would pray to the Lord, "Cast the lap of thy cloak, Lord, over puir auld Sandy." [63] A mist would then cover him and hide him from his pursuer's eyes.

Probably the most fitting statement about Alexander Peden came from Smellie when he wrote, "Peden was the friend of God, and therefore the thin veil which hides the future became sometimes more transparent and diaphanous." [64] He was a man who preached the Gospel as if he heard every line from the Holy Spirit and was loved and respected by all who heard him. [65]

# The Huguenots (1560-1600's)

Back on the European Continent were the French Calvinists known as Huguenots. They were primarily located in the Southeastern quarter of France and were ruthlessly persecuted by the Catholic Church under the support of the King, especially Louis XIV. Their persecution was in the form of governmental restrictions and military attacks against their lives. Some Huguenots immigrated to England as a result of this oppression.

Though I had heard of this Calvinistic movement in France, I did not know until recently of their use of spiritual gifts. It makes me wonder what other groups of Christians in Church history were used by the Spirit with the gifts, and we remain somewhat unaware of it.

Of all the charismatic gifts, there was a fluent use of prophecy amongst the Huguenots. Interestingly they would prophesy while they were asleep or in a sleep state. It began in 1688 with a young sixteen year old named Isabeau Vincent. "Asleep in the home of an uncle with whom she lived, she suddenly cried out and began to sing the Ten Commandments. Each night thereafter when Huguenots sat in the room, she sang, preached and prayed while asleep." [66] Besides speaking the Ten Commandments it is recorded that, "In her nights of prophecy, Isabeau exhort[ed] all to repent, for suffering was the result of disrespect for God's Word." [67]

She was not the only one gifted with prophecy. Imprisoned in June of 1688 as a threat to the Catholic-run government, she prophesied "others younger than herself would take her place." [68] Within a year many other young people would begin to prophesy, both male and female. They were given the name *Inspires*.

It was also common for the Inspires to have physical manifestations such as shaking and falling to the ground as they entered the sleep state to prophesy. Schwartz writes, "Like Isabeau Vincent, they would be passive but agitated, asleep but awake, unconscious but perceptive, exhausted but refreshed. Their sermons and predictions betrayed a similar strain, a tension between mercy and judgment." [69] From the reading, it seems that most of their prophecies of judgment were spoken against Roman Catholics and those who were swayed to return to mass.

I was amazed to read of accounts in Hillel Schwartz of infants who spoke up under the Spirit to refuse baptism in the Catholic Church. Or in the appendix of John Wimber's book *Power Evangelism* where he quotes Henry Baird saying that the illiterate peasant children would prophesy in good French. [70]

There were also examples of healings amongst the Huguenots. Due to prayer and reading of the Bible, Mary Milliard was healed of lameness. [71] In all of this, it seems that prophecy and healing were a normal part of the Huguenots' life in Christ. They expected to hear from God on a regular basis.

### Hector McPhail (1700's)

Rex Gardiner, in his book, *Healing Miracles*, informs us about Mr. McPhail. Gardner writes, "In Presbyterian Scotland we find continuing evidence of the miraculous gifts of the Spirit. For the eighteenth century we can turn to the *Synod of Ross* volume in the authoritative series, *Fasti Ecclesiae Scoticanae*." [72] Where it normally records lists of names the volume tells us of how McPhail prayed for a woman who was "violently insane." He prayed, "O Thou who are three times holy, I implore Thee not to allow me to rise from my knees should they rot to earth, until Thou makest it visibly known here that there is a God in Israel." [73] The woman immediately got up and praised God.

In the other account, McPhail was eating at a friend's home when he suddenly got up, left the house and entered the forest in close proximity. He continued until he found a woman about to kill herself by drowning in a small lake. After a little while she gave herself to God and turned from her self-destruction. [74] This is what most charismatics call the "gift of word of knowledge." He couldn't possibly have known that the woman was about to drown herself. I can only imagine how God told him to go and where to find her. The great part of this testimony was McPhail's obedience to the Spirit of God in both of these situations.

## A.B. Simpson (1843-1919 A.D.)

Most Christian scholars of Church history know A.B. Simpson as the man who began the Christian and Missionary Alliance (C&MA) denomination. What few realize was his earlier involvement in the Presbyterian Church. Albert Benjamin Simpson was born into a Scottish Presbyterian family and described his father as "a good Presbyterian of the old school." [75]

Simpson was ordained as a Presbyterian minister in 1865 and became the pastor of Knox Presbyterian Church of Hamilton, Ontario. From there he would serve as pastor of Chestnut Presbyterian Church in Louisville, Kentucky and finally at Thirteenth Street Presbyterian Church in New York City.

It was during his third pastorate that a great event took place in his life. Simpson was "'miraculously' healed of a chronic heart disorder during a vacation at Old Orchard Beach, Maine." [76] Due to this experience and other criteria, Simpson decided to leave the Presbyterian Church for an independent ministry. But I must wonder if he knew he would not be accepted by the very theological home in which he was raised. I wish he had stayed; the Presbyterian Church would be stronger if he had given us what he knew and experienced.

Simpson would strongly teach against the cessation of the gifts. He could find no evidence of cessation in the Bible. His experience of the charismatic gifts was based on Joel 2 and 1 Corinthians 12. From these texts he came to the understanding that the gifts were to continue until the 2nd Advent of Christ. [77]

## Final Thoughts

Why don't we know about the use of the gifts in Reformation History? Why? Because you can't teach what you don't believe. Reformed pastors, teachers, and theologians have been under the presumption that the gifts ceased with the Apostles, therefore they have taught this fallacy to the Church.

The purpose of this chapter has been to provide historical evidence that the charismatic gifts of the Spirit have not ceased, but have been active throughout Church history. Yet, more specifically, the charismatic gifts have been operating in Reformed Church history.

It may be asked why I have not included examples from other theological traditions and movements. There is certainly ample historical documentation from other denominations, but many people do not know of the rich heritage of power given by the Spirit in the Reformed tradition. Since this work is from a Reformed perspective, it is fitting that I restrict the case histories to what the Holy Spirit has done in this tradition.

The examples given in this chapter of John Knox, Augustine, George Wishart, John Welch and the others are just those that were actually recorded. I know that more happened, since some of the biographies mentioned other healings and prophecies without expounding on them. I have to wonder what was taking place amongst the members of their churches. We know that prophecy was widespread within the Huguenots and testimony was given that prophecies were issued during Knox's sermons. Take the example of Grange's hanging mentioned above. Ridley wrote, "Melville states that Knox, in his sermons, had been prophesying that Grange would be hanged in the face of the sun." [78] So prophecy was somewhat common in the church with Knox, but I hope evidence will be found to show that Knox allowed for others under his ministry to prophesy in the church.

As the evidence shows us, the Presbyterian Church was born out of the Reformation in the gift of prophecy and other manifestations of the Spirit's power. This is part of our heritage that must be reckoned with. We must also realize that it is fully consistent with Reformation history to encourage the gifts in the Church. I also believe that Reformed theology and the charismatic understanding of orthodox pneumatology naturally work together under God's plan for the Church.

# Chapter Four
## Reformed Faith and the Charismata

### Defining the Charismatic Movement Theologically

Some within the "Reformed" camp have said that the Charismatic Movement is Arminian. Some claim it to be a resurgence of Roman Catholic mysticism. Some see any use of the power gifts as being a Pentecostal thing. If you identify the use of God's power with any of these groups as a way of discrediting this aspect of ministry, you are wrong.

The use of the Spirit's gifts is not something to be identified with any one group within Christianity. The gifts are to be identified with the Holy Spirit alone. As 1 Corinthians 12:11 says, "All these (the gifts) are the work of one and the same Spirit, and he gives them to each one, just as he determines." The Pentecostal churches have been very receptive to this work of the Spirit, so He has determined to use His power in them. Many within Arminian theological circles (including Pentecostals) have been open to the gifts and the Holy Spirit has used His gifts in them for ministry.

But, if someone experiences the gifts of the Spirit, it would be a fallacy to conclude that they are Arminian or Roman Catholic theologically. If this were true, we would have to conclude that John Knox was either Arminian or Roman Catholic. Yet, we all know that Knox was clearly Reformed in his theology.

The Holy Spirit has used His gifts within all major theological groups. In the last decade I have heard of the use of the gifts by Baptists, Pentecostals, Episcopalians, Methodists, Charismatics, Nazarenes, and even Presbyterians.

The Spirit does not seem to be a respecter of theology. He tends to use those who will be used by Him, except cults and those walking in heresy.

## Is There Supposed to be a "Charismatic" Theology?

There have been comments made that the Charismatic Movement is theologically weak. The idea being presented is that there has been very little scholarship to develop a theological grid for supporting this movement of the Spirit. But the use of the gifts in the Church is not to have its own theology.

I don't believe the Holy Spirit ever intended for power ministry to be a separate theological movement. But then again, I don't think He ever wanted there to be separate theological movements anyway. Consider what Paul wrote in Ephesians 4:4-6, "There is one body and one Spirit – just as you were called to one hope when you were called – one Lord, one faith, one baptism; one God and Father of all, who is over all and through all and in all."

I use the gifts within a Reformed theological belief system. I do not need to have two different theologies for what the Holy Spirit does in me and through me. I do not hold to Reformed Theology on one hand and some Charismatic Theology on the other hand. That is not the way the Holy Spirit has moved with me.

Personally speaking, I believe that Reformed Theology is a great foundation for the use of the gifts in the Church. This is not meant as a statement of pride over other theological backgrounds. What I am saying is that I have never found it necessary to give up Reformed Theology in order for the Holy Spirit to use His gifts through me. To go further, Reformed

Theology has broadened my understanding of how the Spirit uses the gifts.

## Does Power Ministry Really Fit With Reformed Theology?

I obviously believe that all of the gifts fit with Reformed Theology. Now I want to show you how they mix. It is one thing to say that Jesus and the Apostles taught the doctrines which led to Reformed Theology and were ministering in power. To stop there would quit short of building the bridge between Presbyterian and Reformed churches and the power God has given us.

John Knox and others in the Scottish Reformation were clearly Reformed and operated in the gifts as they served Jesus. Loraine Boettner quoted Philip Schaff on Knox when he wrote, "The hero of the Scottish Reformation, though four years older than Calvin, sat humbly at his feet and became more Calvinistic than Calvin." [1] No one will argue that Knox wasn't a Calvinist and from the evidence presented in the last chapter no one should argue that Knox didn't walk in power ministry.

So how do we present a theological framework for us to be Calvinistic like our spiritual leader Knox and be used by the Spirit with power in ministry? We will look at four central items of Reformed Theology: the kingdom of God, the sovereignty of God, grace and faith. The undergirding of our framework begins with the kingdom of God.

## The Kingdom of God

God's kingdom is the central teaching of the New Testament, and as well as the whole Bible. All other parts of our faith must be understood from the foundation of this kingdom.

The kingdom is defined as the reign or rule of God. [2] It is not to be equated with a geographical location, a political ideology or only with the Church itself. The Church is a product of God's kingdom rule.

With this definition stated, how should a Reformed believer view the significance of God's kingdom? First, we must recognize its importance to Jesus. In Luke 4:43 Jesus said, "I must preach the good news of the kingdom of God to the other towns also, because that is why I was sent." The Father sent Jesus to present the reality of the kingdom. This is why Jesus is constantly speaking of the kingdom and telling parables about it.

For most of my life I couldn't tell you what the kingdom was or why it was significant. Yet, this is the most important concept of the Gospels. Conveying this message was central to Jesus' mission. The reason my knowledge of this was insufficient lies with the teaching I received from the Church. It was unimportant for many of those who discipled me to focus on God's kingdom.

In their minds, the Kingdom was something for the end times. In fact, the kingdom was a footnote to Jesus' return at the end of this age. Unless a believer sees that everything we have in relation to God comes from the kingdom, it will remain an insignificant footnote to them.

To see the establishment of God's kingdom as purely a future event is a grave mistake. Jesus taught of the kingdom as being present in His ministry, but not brought to completion until the end of this age. George Eldon Ladd's teaching and writing has led many to realize the nature of the kingdom as being "already but not yet." Let me show this to you from the Gospels.

In Matthew 12:28 Jesus said, "But if I drive out demons by the Spirit of God, then the kingdom of God has come upon you." When Jesus began His ministry He initiated the direct application of the Kingdom into our lives on earth. The Holy Spirit is the active ingredient that propels the Kingdom's power and influence in the world in order to bring about God's plan of salvation.

As the Holy Spirit ministered through Jesus, our Lord was able to say that the kingdom was present, or as in the quote above, "the kingdom of God has come upon you." This is the good news that the kingdom is present and we can enter it for eternity.

While the kingdom is present, it is not in its completion here on earth. We are waiting for Jesus to return and consummate His kingdom. What is given and promised now will be brought to fruition. God has given me eternal life, but I do not live in an eternal state yet with a glorified body.

The reality of the Kingdom being here already, but not yet consummated is recognized in Reformed Theology. John Calvin, writing on the interaction of God's spiritual government with civil government, states, "For spiritual government, indeed, is already initiating in us upon earth certain beginnings of the Heavenly Kingdom." [3] He went on to show that the Kingdom of God "is now among us." He understood that the kingdom had arrived in part, but not in whole.

Charles Hodge expounded on this view of the kingdom when he wrote, "the New Testament announces the establishment of a new kingdom as consequent on his advent." [4] He is saying that when Jesus came He brought the present form of the kingdom with Him.

Louis Berkhof gave the most abridged and best Reformed affirmation of this view of the kingdom in his

84

*Systematic Theology* writing, "It is a kingdom that is both present and future. It is on the one hand a present, ever developing, spiritual reality in the hearts and lives of men, and as such exercises influence in a constantly widening sphere. Jesus and the apostles clearly refer to the kingdom as already present in their time..." [5] Berkhof, Hodge and Calvin all recognized the "already, but not yet" kingdom of God. God reintroduced His kingdom on earth in the ministry of Christ Jesus.

One of my favorite statements on the kingdom comes from Don Williams. He wrote, "We can sum up the thought in this way: the kingdom is really here but it is not fully here. Believers, then, live in a kingdom come and coming." [6]

How do we know that the kingdom is really present? We know the kingdom is present because the Bible teaches us this truth. We also know it is a present reality when we see the power of God's kingdom. Spiritual power is an integrated part of God's work in His kingdom. Paul wrote 1 Corinthians 4:20, "For the kingdom of God is not a matter of talk but of power."

When Jesus brought His kingdom, He did so with demonstrations of power. As we quoted a little earlier from Matthew 12:28 Jesus said, "But if I drive out demons by the Spirit of God, then the kingdom of God has come upon you." When Jesus ministered in power, it was to demonstrate the kingdom. When Jesus healed the sick it was to demonstrate the kingdom. C. Peter Wagner quotes the Dutch theologian Herman Ridderbos as writing, "This factual relation between the coming of the kingdom and Jesus' miracles is also brought out not only by the casting out of devils but also by Jesus' other miracles, for they all prove that Satan's power has been broken and that, therefore, the kingdom has come." [7]

Likewise, when Jesus sent out His disciples it was for the purpose of proclaiming and demonstrating the kingdom. Look at what Jesus said to the Twelve when He sent them out in Luke 9:1,2, "When Jesus had called the Twelve together, he gave them power and authority to drive out all demons and to cure diseases, and he sent them out to preach the kingdom of God and to heal the sick." Jesus gave the same orders to the 70 disciples in Luke 10:9, "Heal the sick who are there and tell them, "The kingdom of God is near you."

The proclamation of the kingdom is the good news of eternal life through the blood of Jesus on the cross. We can enter the kingdom and live with God forever! The demonstration of the kingdom is God's power and authority given to the Church to cast out all demons and to heal the sick. God's kingdom beats the kingdom of Satan.

Some people object to this by asking why healers don't enter hospitals and heal everyone who is sick. This is actually based on a pretty good question. Why aren't all the sick healed when we pray for them? The answer is that the kingdom is not consummated yet. Remember, the kingdom is "come and coming." The presence of the kingdom now is only a part of the kingdom that will come with Jesus at the end of this age when He returns.

The book of Revelation tells us what life will be like when we live in the fullness of the kingdom. "He will wipe every tear from their eyes. There will be no more death or mourning or crying or pain, for the old order of things has passed away." (Revelation 21:4) The previous question accidentally presupposes that we are living in the consummated kingdom after God has destroyed the "old order of things." Instead, we live in a time when the benefits of the kingdom can be had now, but not completely. So we will see many who are healed and freed from demons, yet tears, death, mourning, crying and pain will continue to be a part of our lives. Some will be healed and some won't when we pray for them. For the kingdom is not completely here.

That is not to say that God won't do amazing shows of power. There have been times when God has healed groups of people at a single meeting. There have been believers with gifts of healing who have seen many healed by the Spirit through their ministry. God certainly has the choice to empty hospitals and I hope this is something we will see in the future. Until such a time, I am just excited with the power God is giving to the Church as is.

Many people do not understand the powerful nature of the kingdom of God, especially cult members. I was speaking with a couple of Jehovah's Witnesses at my front door one summer day. I am always trying to find new ways to make them think about the Gospel and possibly respond. While conversing with them I asked if they believed in the kingdom of God. (Their belief is wrong, of course)

After they answered affirmatively, I had them turn to Luke 9:1, 2 and 10:9. I pointed out the relation of the proclamation of the kingdom and the demonstration of the kingdom. I then asked them if they had seen anyone healed in their group or if any demons had been cast out. They began to tell me that those things don't happen anymore. Other than that they had no response to the power of God. I informed them of the healings we had seen in our church and of the demons that had been cast out. I told them that if they did not have those demonstrations of the kingdom's power in their group then I didn't want to hear about their organization, since it wasn't the kingdom Jesus was proclaiming. (There was more to our conversation. I just wanted to relate to you the part about the kingdom.)

Our understanding of God's kingdom is incomplete if we do not incorporate all that Jesus showed us and taught us about it. Jesus taught us and commanded us to minister with God's power for His kingdom as well as to live kingdom lives.

## God's Sovereignty and Power Ministry

The power of the kingdom leads us to the sovereignty of God. When we speak of God's sovereignty we have in mind His dominion and control. As God rules and reigns over His kingdom, He exercises His control over what He has made.

We believe in God's sovereign decrees, by which He has decided the course of history and the timing of events. So, if God has set human history, does our use of God's power fit with His sovereignty? For many God's sovereignty and our use of His power are inconsistent. There is an attitude which believes that everything is set in cement and unchangeable. The thought is, "What will happen, will happen." A sort of fatalism sets in. If someone is sick, they will get well if it is meant to be or they will remain sick.

While many events are unchangeable, God seems to allow for change in other events. Some events and occurrences are conditional upon our petition before Him.

Under God's sovereignty He has given us the use of His power and authority. God has decreed that some things will not happen if we don't pray for them. Some sicknesses will continue if we let them. God has commanded His Church to use the authority and power He has given us. One passage which brings God's sovereign control and our use of His power together is Acts 4:23-31.

"On their release, Peter and John went back to their own people and reported all that the chief priests and elders had said to them. When they heard this, they raised their voices together in prayer to God. 'Sovereign Lord,' they said, 'you made the heaven and the earth and the sea, and everything in them. You spoke by the Holy Spirit through the mouth of your servant, our father David: "Why do the nations rage and the peoples plot in vain? The kings of the earth take their stand and the rulers gather together against the Lord and against his Anointed One." Indeed Herod and Pontius Pilate met    together with the Gentiles and the people of Israel in this city to conspire against your holy servant Jesus, whom you anointed. They did what your power and will had decided beforehand should happen. Now, Lord, consider their threats and enable your servants to speak your word with great boldness. Stretch out your hand to heal and perform miraculous signs and wonders through the name of your holy servant Jesus.' After they prayed, the place where they were meeting was shaken. And they were all filled with the Holy Spirit and spoke the word of God boldly."

In this prayer the Apostles acknowledge a key idea in Reformed theology, the sovereignty of God. They prayed, "Sovereign Lord" and go on to praise God for what He has made and said. To say that God is sovereign is to realize His control of all that exists. As an earthly king is "sovereign" over his domain, so God is King over all that He has created.

But what is the nature of that control? The Apostles went on to pray, "They did what your power and will had decided beforehand should happen." We, in the Reformed Tradition, believe that God's control over creation is not just in His right of ownership and the right to establish His law over that possession. We believe that God has predestined the outcome of each life on this earth and those of the spiritual realm as well. The Apostles showed us that the actions of

Herod, Pontius Pilate, the Gentiles and the Jews were predestined. They had no choice but to act in accordance with the will and power of God.

Predestination is a hard reality for many Christians to accept; yet it is clearly taught throughout the Bible. You can read of it in Romans 9, Ephesians 1 and many other passages of Scripture. It is not a matter of deciding if God predestines people; it is accepting that he does.

Predestination is based on the decrees of God. As the Westminster Confession of Faith states, "From all eternity and by the completely wise and holy purpose of His own will, God has freely and unchangeably ordained whatever happens. This ordination does not mean, however, that God is the author of sin (He is not), that He represses the will of His created beings, or that He takes away the freedom or contingency of secondary causes. Rather, the will of created beings and the freedom and contingency of secondary causes are established by Him." [8]

God has decreed everything from the creation of the world to the day when Jesus will return in His second coming. You may be wondering if we still have a will of our own. The Westminster also states, "God has given man a will, which by nature is free, i.e., it is not forced or necessarily inclined toward good or evil." [9] Yes, we make decisions and act by the volition of our own will. We are called to interact with God and to use our will to glorify Him.

To overly focus on God's eternal decrees can make us fatalistic in our thinking. We can start to act as if our participation in the plan of God is unnecessary, since God has already decreed everything that is going to happen. I don't need to share my faith, since God will save the elect. I don't need to pray, because my prayers will not have any real effect on the outcome of anything. These types of attitudes deny the commands of God in the Bible. God commands us to preach the Gospel and to pray.

Fatalism can lead to the thought that we can't really use God's power to heal someone. People will get well or remain sick, because that was the way things are meant to be. The Apostles did not have this fatalism in their minds as they continued to pray in Acts 4. They prayed, "Now, Lord, consider their threats and enable your servants to speak your word with great boldness. Stretch out your hand to heal and perform miraculous signs and wonders through the name of your holy servant Jesus." They prayed for the boldness to proclaim the Gospel and for the power to heal and minister with signs and wonders.

They knew that God is in sovereign control, through His eternal decrees, of all that exists. In light of this they ask for power ministry in Jesus' name. In response to their prayer, God shook the building and filled them with the Holy Spirit. He gave them what they asked for. Surely, God willed for them to minister in power. Would the young man have been raised from the dead if Rev. John Welsh had not remained in prayer for some 48 hours? I don't think he would have returned to this earth.

Here is a question for the fatalists who will read this. If they had decided to skip that time of prayer, would God have shaken the house and filled them with the Spirit for power ministry anyway? I believe the answer is no. We must desire to proclaim the Gospel with boldness and to minister with power.

### Grace and the Gifts

In God's sovereign control, He gives grace to those He has predestined to receive it. Grace is an important topic in

Reformed thought. As stated earlier, the climactic statement of the Reformation was "Salvation by grace through faith." It is grace that empowers us to believe and be saved. It is also by God's grace that we live and have our being.

In order to talk about grace, we need to define what it is. A most commonly stated definition of grace is God's unmerited favor. We surely receive grace due to God's favor, but I would not limit His grace to this definition. God's mercy is His unmerited favor.

Probably the most accurate definition of grace is God's riches at Christ's expense. Through the crucifixion and resurrection of Jesus, the Father has been pleased to pour out His riches for salvation, spiritual growth, daily living and power ministry. Grace is the empowering of God for us to receive and live with all of these wonderful things.

Consider 1 Corinthians 1:4-9 as Paul wrote, "I always thank God for you because of his grace given you in Christ Jesus. For in him you have been enriched in every way – in all your speaking and in all your knowledge – because our testimony about Christ was confirmed in you. Therefore you do not lack any spiritual gift as you eagerly wait for our Lord Jesus Christ to be revealed. He will keep you strong to the end, so that you will be blameless on that day of our Lord Jesus Christ. God, who has called you into fellowship with his Son Jesus Christ our Lord, is faithful."

According to this passage, what does God give us by the free gift of grace? First, the "testimony about Christ was confirmed in you." That confirmation of the testimony is salvation. The believers in Corinth were saved when they confirmed the testimony of the Gospel.

Another benefit of grace is that "He will keep you strong to the end." In classic Calvinistic language we call this the perseverance of the saints. By His power and plan, God keeps elect believers from falling away from the faith. I know that God has saved me and I will never lose my faith, because of Him.

The passage continues to say "that you will be blameless on that day of our Lord Jesus Christ." God sanctifies us by His grace. As the kingdom is already and not yet, so is our sanctification. When I was saved by Jesus, I was sanctified. I was made holy by God through the blood of Jesus. If I die I will go to heaven. Yet, I am also in the process of sanctification. I am growing more holy in God's likeness every day. Why do I need to grow in sanctification? Because I still have moments when I sin.

So this passage gives me hope. It tells me that by God's sanctification of me by His grace, I "will be blameless on that day of our Lord Jesus Christ." This is just another example of God's riches at Christ's expense. God's grace is great!

Finally, I need to back up in this passage to where it says, "Therefore you do not lack any spiritual gift." The Holy Spirit, by His grace, empowers us with all of His gifts. You see, all of the gifts are a by-product of grace. How can this be?

If you look at the word for gift in the Greek (*charisma*) you will notice that it comes from its root word for grace (*charis*). So from grace (*charis*) we get "gracious gift" [10] (*charisma*) and "gifts of the Spirit" [11] (*charismata*). [12] Gordon Fee explains our understanding of the word in the sense of being a gift from the Holy Spirit when he wrote, "the word frequently relates to special manifestations or activities of the Spirit, indicating 'gracious gifts' of the Spirit, which is why it has come to be thought of as a Spirit activity as such." [13]

It should be no surprise to us that the Holy Spirit empowers us with His gifts by grace. As Paul writes in

Romans 12:6, "We have different gifts, according to the grace given us." The Apostle is saying that everything from prophecy and tongues to gifts of healing come by the empowering of the Holy Spirit by grace. This is why I believe a great definition for grace is the empowering presence of God.

We will find references of power in conjunction with grace in the New Testament such as the following:

Acts 4:33, "With great power the apostles continued to testify to the resurrection of the Lord Jesus, and much grace was upon them all."

Acts 6:8, "Now Stephen, a man full of God's grace and power, did great wonders and miraculous signs among the people."

Acts 14:3, "So Paul and Barnabus spent considerable time there, speaking boldly for the Lord, who confirmed the message of his grace by enabling them to do miraculous signs and wonders."

These verses confirm for us the "graceful" nature of God's power and gifts. Whether it is the Apostles, the deacon Stephen, Paul or Barnabas, God gave them the use of His power through His grace.

Since grace is freely given and not based upon works, this tells us something about how the gifts are given to us. You cannot earn the gifts of the Spirit. Rather, the Spirit "gives them to each one, just as he determines." (1 Corinthians 12:11) Because they are a gift, no believer can claim that God owes them the use of the charismata due to their morality or good deeds, just as they cannot claim salvation on the same basis. Any principle that applies to the doctrine of grace is applicable to the gifts of the Spirit, since the gifts come by grace.

I have never heard anyone preach or teach that God has ceased giving some area of grace to us. Or that certain grace was given only to the Apostles but not to the rest of the Church. I would not see this as a biblical teaching. Yet, there is one condition put on grace. In 1 Peter 5:5, the Apostle tells us "God opposes the proud but gives grace to the humble." [14]

As we walk humbly with God, He does great things for us through grace. In Acts 4:33 it says, "With great power the apostles continued to testify to the resurrection of the Lord Jesus, and much grace was upon them all." The King James says that "great grace" was on them. This seems to be a reference to a quantitative amount of grace. Could it be that they were walking humbly before God and He was pouring out more grace than usual? This would lead us to ask if the times when the Church has not seen much in the way of kingdom power if the Church has not been walking as humbly with God as it should.

The New Testament commands us to desire the gifts and even more so to prophesy (1 Corinthians 14:1 and 14:39). Yet, there are believers who will tell you not to desire these things in our walk with God. For whatever reason they justify this line of thinking, it is rebellious to not desire all of the gifts of the Spirit to be active in the Church. So, humble yourself to what the Bible teaches and ask God to release more grace in your life and the life of your church.

At a General Assembly of the Evangelical Presbyterian Church, we were told that the Church is in decline in the United States. The growth of the Church is not keeping up with the birth rate. Since we are not seeing evangelism or power ministry flourish in our churches, I must assume that we are seeing a lack of God's grace. But can you really see grace or its effects?

In Acts 11:19-24 we are told that "the Lord's hand was with" the believers in Antioch and many were coming into the faith. So much so that Barnabas was sent from Jerusalem to see what was going on. Acts 11:23 says, "When he arrived and saw the evidence of the grace of God..." The New American Standard Bible translates this verse as, "Then when he had come and witnessed the grace of God..." The literal translation of this is that Barnabas went to Antioch and saw the grace of God. It is something that can be witnessed and experienced.

I don't think that we are witnessing the grace of God in the United States that we should be. We don't see the evangelism we should see. We don't witness the power of God as much as we should.

We want grace. We want "much" grace and "great" grace. We must ask for great grace in the Church, but it takes faith to ask for such grace. If you think about it, grace and faith are totally intertwined ideas in the Bible. As Paul wrote, "For by grace you have been saved through faith." (Ephesians 2:8). God enabled you by His grace to have the faith to be saved.

As God builds faith in our lives by His grace, what should that faith look like? Are there levels of faith? Does God's power move by faith?

### Having Faith

Faith is a key ingredient as the Spirit uses His power and gifts in us. We must believe that God will use His power through us and receive what He is doing. But before we examine the use of faith in conjunction with the charismata, let's get back to the basics. What is faith?

Louis Berkhof gave a great definition of faith when he wrote that it is, "a confiding trust or confidence in God..." [15] This is what it means to say that you have faith in God. You trust Him. In order to be saved, you must have faith that God will save you by grace. You believe that eternal life is a free gift paid for by Jesus' death on the cross for your sins. Furthermore, you believe that He is resurrected from the dead to give you life.

Faith is a gift from God. It is something He gives to us by the power of the Holy Spirit. As He implants it in our hearts and minds, we are to walk by this faith and grow in it.

What does this have to do with faith in the miraculous? Faith is more than a gift from God unto salvation, though this is the central function of our faith. God has expectations of what we should be doing with the faith He has given us.

It is not enough to just believe in God. In our covenantal relationship with Him, God desires for us to have strong and effective faith. This is the kind of faith that expects power ministry to take place and for God to work marvelous things through the prayers of the Church.

Jesus rebuked His followers for not having great faith. The New International Version of the Bible quotes Jesus as calling His followers, "you of little faith" (Matthew 6:30). But wait a minute. Many people think that faith is just something God puts in you and you either have it or you don't.

Not so, according to Jesus. In fact, Jesus points out the "little faith" of His followers a couple of other times. In Matthew 14:31, Peter is told he has little faith after sinking into the sea, because he doubted while walking on the water to Jesus. In each of these situations, Jesus expected His followers to have more faith. But how much more is more?

In Matthew 17 the disciples attempted to cast out a demon, but failed.  They asked Jesus why they couldn't do it and He replied, "Because you have so little faith.  I tell you the truth, if you have the faith as small as a mustard seed, you can say to this mountain, 'Move from here to there' and it will move.  Nothing will be impossible for you" (Matthew 17:20). [16]  I believe that Jesus was speaking about faith great enough to move mountains.  We should be striving to see our faith grow.

As God has been giving miraculous answers to the prayers of the people in the church I pastored in Santa Maria, I saw their faith grow.  It has grown in what they were willing to ask God for and what they believed God would do, from healings to direct guidance.

Not only should Reformed Christians differentiate between little and big fish, but we know that there are different types or levels of faith also.  Dr. Berkhof in his *Systematic Theology* states that there are two types of faith for a true believer, habitus and actus faith.

Dr. Berkhof also stated that there is a miraculous faith. He wrote of this faith as a companion to saving faith and defines it as "a persuasion wrought in the mind of a person that a miracle will be performed by him or in his behalf." [17]  But he saw no need for miraculous faith today, even though he wrote, "the Word of God leads us to expect another cycle of miracles in the future." [18]

I think that Berkhof was on the right trail, but didn't go far enough.  C. Peter Wagner teaches that there are four levels of faith.  These four range from saving faith and sanctifying faith all the way to "a kind of faith which releases the power of God for supernatural signs and wonders." [19]  He explained what he means by this kind of supernatural faith when he wrote about "faith for healing."

He replied, "By 'faith' we mean a willingness to come before Jesus and expectantly ask for His healing touch while releasing ourselves into His loving care trusting Him to do what is best for us. We do not believe that faith is a tool for coercing God to heal. Nor is it a level of credulity heightened by excessive emotionalism which seeks to deny the reality of symptoms." [20]

He would apply the same understanding of this kind of faith to any other use of the supernatural gifts. In this level of faith God wants us to expect miracles to take place. We are to have a faith that expects the supernatural. Think of the conversation between Jesus and Martha in John 11:39, 40. "'Take way the stone,' he said, 'But, Lord,' said Martha, the sister of the dead man, 'by this time there is a bad odor, for he has been there four days.' Then Jesus said, 'Did I not tell you that if you believed, you would see the glory of God?'" Jesus wanted Martha to have a faith that would expect to see the glory of God in the act of raising the dead.

The gifts operate in relation to the amount of faith we have. Consider Romans 12:6 where Paul wrote, "We have different gifts, according to the grace given us. If a man's gift is prophesying, let him use it in proportion to his faith." The greater amount of faith the more one will prophesy, or if one has small faith in this area, there is a chance they won't prophesy at all. If you don't believe God still gives prophecy or that God wouldn't use you, then you probably won't be used for prophecy if that is your gift.

The idea of proportion of faith to the use of gift applies to the situation stated earlier when the disciples couldn't cast out the demon. Jesus told them they were of "little faith." They probably didn't believe the demon would come out even if they rebuked it. So, they didn't.

This takes us to the problem of churches that don't believe the gifts are still in operation. The gifts will operate in their church in proportion to the faith they have for God to work supernaturally among them. If they don't have faith, they won't see the gifts. Now God will move sovereignly among them with different manifestations, but they usually won't recognize the gift in action and it won't be common.

I think about the testimonies I have heard concerning the "Jesus" movie, where some who saw the movie came to faith in Jesus. They proceed to pray for the healing of others and they are healed. They were asked why they prayed for the healing of others and they said they saw Jesus doing it in the movie. [21] The answer to this is that hearing the Gospel of Luke gave them great faith to see God do that ministry among them.

Faith is a key ingredient when we pray. In the book of James, we are taught to pray with faith. James 5:15 says, "and the prayer offered in faith will make the sick person well; the Lord will raise him up." This is prayer that not only believes God can heal the sick, but that He will heal the sick. God wants our faith to grow to this level and beyond so that we will do the work that Jesus was doing and even greater works (John 14:12).

Coming into the orthodoxy and orthopraxy of the charismata has also helped me to understand and believe some of the tough statements of Jesus. Here are a couple examples of these tough statements. In Mark 11:24, Jesus said, "Therefore I tell you, whatever you ask for in prayer, believe that you have received it, and it will be yours." And in John 14:14 He said, "You may ask me for anything in my name, and I will do it."

I used to ignore verses like these because I didn't understand them and they made me uncomfortable. I was never taught to incorporate these teachings of Jesus into my prayer life. It was almost as if many Christians had wished Jesus had never made these statements. God now uses these verses to challenge me to grow spiritually.

## Final Thoughts

Is there anything in Reformed Theology that would exclude the gifts? There is nothing theologically in the Reformed Tradition that says that the gifts don't fit. In my opinion, true Reformed Theology would conclude that the gifts must be active today and work well within a Reformed framework. After all, if we believe that Jesus and the Apostles gave us a clear guideline for Reformed Theology in the New Testament, we must also believe that there was no contradiction between their theology and their practice of the power of God in the use of the charismata.

In fact, I think that much of what is taught within the Charismatic Movement is acceptable by the standards of Reformed Theology and will be found to be orthodox. As was demonstrated, the key Reformed doctrines of the kingdom of God, the sovereignty of God, grace and faith all uphold the use of the charismata from the beginning of the New Testament until Jesus returns at the end of the age.

# Chapter Five
## Charismatic Ministry of Jesus

"All these (charismata) are the work of one and the same Spirit, and he gives them to each one, just as he determines." This quote from 1 Corinthians 12:11 is the simplest understanding of how the gifts are used within the Church. The Holy Spirit uses His gifts as He wants in whom He desires. But some want an explanation with depth. At least I did, so the following is what I believe is a biblical philosophy of ministry for the use of the *charismata* in the Church.

In order to understand the use of the gifts in the Church, we must look at the ministry of Jesus. In the first chapter, I quoted James Montgomery Boice as saying that the problem with the working of miracles is that it takes away from our focus on Jesus and our knowledge of the Gospel. [1] My experience with the miraculous has been the exact opposite. I have had to focus even more on Jesus and the Gospel since our work in the miraculous is based directly on Jesus Himself, what He did, and what He commanded us to do.

### Focusing on Jesus

Everything in our faith is motivated by love for God. Loving God is, after all, the greatest commandment given in the Bible. As we grow deeper in our love for God, His love dwells more and more in us. When we were saved by God, the heart of our conversion experience was a love for Jesus and what He did for us in His crucifixion and resurrection. As we grow to know the Father better, His love for Jesus increases in us as in John 17:26. It is by the Holy Spirit that this love increases in our hearts.

I have found that every experience I have had with the power of God has greatly increased my awe and love for Jesus. At the same time, these experiences of God's power have made me want to see more of Jesus in the Scriptures. The Scriptures and these experiences have let me see the love and compassion of Jesus, both then and now. It is hard not to be infected with His love as the Holy Spirit teaches me and ministers through me.

As we focus on Jesus in the Gospels we realize that He not only did His ministry out of love and compassion, but also because He was on a mission. Jesus said in Luke 4:43, "I must preach the kingdom of God to the other cities also, for I was sent for this purpose." His mission was to proclaim the coming of the kingdom of God. As I showed you in the last chapter, the kingdom was brought with proclamation and demonstration.

Throughout Jesus' ministry, He continually preached the kingdom as well as demonstrated its presence by healing people and engaging in spiritual warfare. The use of power was a major component of His work on earth.

Consider the summary Jesus gives to the disciples of John the Baptist in Luke 7:21-23.

"At that very time Jesus cured many who had diseases, sicknesses and evil spirits, and gave sight to many who were blind. So he replied to the messengers, 'Go back and report to John what you have seen and heard: the blind receive sight, the lame walk, those who have leprosy are cured, the deaf hear, the dead are raised, and the good news is preached to the poor.

Blessed is the man who does not fall away on account of me.'"

Here Jesus stated to John's disciples that He has been busy demonstrating and proclaiming.  What Jesus said in Luke 7:21-23 should not be surprising at all in light of what happened in Luke 4:18, 19 when He read from the scroll of Isaiah.  For Jesus read the prophecy of His ministry that said, "The Spirit of the Lord is upon me, because he has anointed me to preach good news to the poor.  He has sent me to proclaim freedom for the prisoners and recovery of sight for the blind, to release the oppressed, to proclaim the year of the Lord's favor."  Jesus was telling John's disciples that He was fulfilling the prophecy of Isaiah.

## Jesus and the Holy Spirit

What did it mean when Jesus acknowledged that He was anointed with the Holy Spirit?  Why did Jesus have to be anointed with the Spirit?  What difference would it make?  These questions lead to understanding how Jesus did His ministry.  As the passage from Luke 4:18, 19 points out, Jesus did His entire ministry by the anointing and sending of the Holy Spirit.

When we say that Jesus was anointed by the Spirit, we mean that He was filled and empowered by the Spirit.  The Holy Spirit enabled Jesus to preach, proclaim, release and give recovery (healing).

Luke gave us great insight into the interaction of the Holy Spirit in the life and ministry of Jesus when he wrote, "Jesus, full of the Holy Spirit, returned from the Jordan and was led by the Spirit in the desert." (Luke 4:1) and "Jesus returned to Galilee in the power of the Spirit," (Luke 4:14a).  Luke wrote this leading up to when Jesus read from Isaiah, so I believe these two verses inform us of the meaning of this prophecy and its fulfillment.

The verses say that Jesus was "full of the Holy Spirit" and "in the power of the Spirit." From this we know that when the Spirit anointed Jesus He dwelt in Jesus and empowered Him.

In explanation of Luke 4:14, Dr. Gerald Hawthorne wrote,

"With this extraordinary prefatory remark Luke makes it clear that, as far as he understood things, Jesus did not begin to preach, teach, or to perform miracles, nor did he continue to do such things (cf. 4:14b, which presupposes an extended ministry) on his own initiative or by virtue of his own skills or because he possessed inherently some power for healing or exorcising. Quite the contrary, Luke precisely identifies Jesus' power as the power of the Holy Spirit, and thus attributes those things Jesus did, which caused people to spread his fame far and wide (4:14b), to the *dynamis*, "the power," of the Spirit." [2]

Luke gave us more understanding when he wrote, "You know what has happened throughout Judea, beginning in Galilee after the baptism that John preached – how God anointed Jesus of Nazareth with the Holy Spirit and power, and how he went around doing good and healing all who were under the power of the devil, because God was with him." This verse teaches us that when Jesus did good, healed and freed people from the devil, it was by His anointing by the "Holy Spirit and power."

Jesus even stated that the Holy Spirit did ministry through Him when He said, "But if I drive out demons by the Spirit of God, then the kingdom of God has come upon you." (Matthew 12:28) Here Jesus tells us that He cast out demons by the power of the Holy Spirit, for it is the Holy Spirit who brings the power of the kingdom.  So we can see that there is a clear teaching in Scripture that Jesus didn't do His ministry from His own power, but by the power of the Holy Spirit.

## The Deity and Humanity of Jesus

Why would Jesus need to be anointed by the Holy Spirit?  After all, we believe that Jesus was and is God.  As the Westminster Confession of Faith states, "The person Jesus is truly God and truly man, yet one Christ, the only mediator between God and man." [3]  As Colossians 2:9 states, "For in Christ all the fullness of the Deity lives in bodily form."

We know that Jesus Himself claimed to be God.  Jesus made a classic statement in John 8:58 when He said, "I tell you the truth... before Abraham was born, I am!"  When Jesus used the "I am" in addressing Himself, He was claiming to be Yahweh.  We know Yahweh more commonly as "I Am Who I Am" from Exodus 3:14.  Jesus claimed to be Yahweh in more than one passage of Scripture.  So we know that Jesus is one with the Father and the Holy Spirit.

As the Westminster Confession of Faith states, "The Son of God, the second person of the Trinity, is truly the eternal God, of one substance and equal with the Father." [4]  This is basic, true Christian belief.  To deny this essential truth about Jesus is to be a heretic and fall short of salvation.

The Confession goes on to say, "In the fullness of time He took on Himself the nature of man, with all the essential qualities and ordinary frailties of man – except that He was sinless." [5]  In the incarnation the divine was "inseparably joined together" [6] with the human.  Jesus took the form of a servant.  He lived a human life on our planet.

Philippians 2:6, 7 adds to our understanding of what took place in Jesus' incarnation.  It reads, "Who being in very nature God, did not consider equality with God something to be grasped, but made himself nothing, taking the very nature of a servant, being made in human likeness." The key point in this passage applicable to this discussion is the phrase "made himself nothing." [7] Other translations say, "emptied himself." [8] Berkhof told us what this meant when he wrote, "…He laid aside the divine majesty, the majesty of the sovereign Ruler of the universe, and assumed human nature in the form of a servant." [9]

Jesus was still fully God while He was on Earth. He still had all the immutable power of being God. He was omniscient and omnipotent, but He chose not to use these sovereign powers of being God. As Hawthorne wrote, "The particular view of the person of Christ which seems to me most able to do this and which seems most in harmony with the whole of the teaching of the New Testament is the view that, in becoming a human being, the Son of God willed to renounce the exercise of his divine powers, attributes, prerogatives, so that he might live fully within those limitations which inhere in being truly human." [10]

Any theology that takes away from the deity of Jesus as Yahweh is wrong and full of error. Likewise, any theology that takes away from Jesus' full humanity is wrong and full of error also. There are many heresies that have come about in Church history because people try to twist what happened in the incarnation. Take Monophysitism [11] for example. It is a heresy which teaches that Jesus was a divine being wrapped in a human body. That is false. Jesus was fully God and fully human, inseparably joined together.

Jesus chose to "make himself nothing" by taking the form of a human servant and not use His divine power. [12] That is why Jesus had to be anointed with the Holy Spirit and with power, and that is why God was with Him in His ministry. Jesus cast out demons by the power of the Holy Spirit so that the power of God the Spirit worked through God the Son as the decree of God the Father.

## Jesus and the Gifts

So we know that Jesus accomplished His ministry with the power of the Holy Spirit. In fact, we can see many of the gifts at use by Jesus. Though the Bible does not refer to Jesus with the terminology of "using the gifts" we can see many of the gifts at work by looking at Jesus' ministry in the Gospels. I am equating the ministry of Jesus with the gifts listed in Paul's writings, because both are manifestations of the Holy Spirit. I believe we can see the gifts of words of knowledge, healing, miraculous powers, prophecy, and distinguishing between spirits in Jesus' ministry as shown in the Gospels. I believe that Jesus used all of the gifts, but they weren't all demonstrated by Jesus in the Gospels.

Let me give you some examples of the gifts in His ministry. In Mark 2:6-8 we see what I think is the gift of a word of knowledge. It says, "Now some teachers of the law were sitting there, thinking to themselves, 'Why does this fellow talk like that? He's blaspheming! Who can forgive sins but God alone?' Immediately Jesus knew in his spirit that this was what they were thinking in their hearts, and he said to them, 'Why are you thinking these things?'" Jesus supernaturally knew what they were thinking. You can also see the same demonstration of this gift in Matthew 9:4, Matthew 12:25 and Luke 5:22.

There are many examples of Jesus healing people in the Gospels. Whether He was healing Peter's mother-in-law from a fever in Matthew 8:15 or healing everyone who touched Him in Luke 6:19, we know this was a major part of His ministry.

There is a verse in Luke 5 that gives us a clue that Jesus healed by gifting. Luke 5:17 says, "One day as he was teaching, Pharisees and teachers of the law, who had come from every village of Galilee and from Judea and Jerusalem, were sitting there. And the power of the Lord was present for him to heal the sick." This verse would imply that there were other times that the power of the Lord was not present for Jesus to heal the sick. I believe that Jesus could ask for the power at any time and it would have been given to Him. However the idea being presented is that when Jesus healed the sick it was a manifestation of the Holy Spirit. But then again, any gift of power is a manifestation of the Spirit.

All of the Gospels tell us that Jesus demonstrated the gift of miraculous powers. John begins with Jesus turning water into wine (John 2:1-11). Luke speaks of Jesus raising a man from the dead (Luke 7:11-17). Mark says that Jesus walked on water (Mark 6:45-52). And Matthew describes how Jesus miraculously fed 5,000 people at one time (Matthew 14:13-21) and 4,000 people at another time (Matthew 16:29-39). [13] These are just a taste of the miracles Jesus did, but they show the gift of miraculous powers at work as Jesus did His ministry.

As for the gift of prophecy, Jesus prophesied many things as an active prophet. He spoke of His second coming (Matthew 24:30; 26:24), the fall of Jerusalem in A.D. 70 (Luke 19:39), Peter's denial of Him (Matthew 26:34), and of His own crucifixion (John 3:14 and Matthew 12:39). Jesus gave many other prophecies, but these offer just a picture of the breadth and power of His prophetic gifting.

An interesting sign that Jesus ministered by prophetic gifting is that there was something that even Jesus didn't know. Jesus said, "No one knows about that day or hour, not even the angels in heaven, nor the Son, but only the Father."

(Matthew 24:36 and Mark 13:32) During His days on Earth, He didn't know the "day or hour: of His second coming. This is something the Father would have to reveal to Him.

Finally, we can see Jesus use the gift of discerning between spirits during His ministry. In the first chapter of Mark, Jesus is teaching in the synagogue when a man cries out, "What do you want with us, Jesus of Nazareth? Have you come to destroy us? I know who you are – the Holy One of God!" (Mark 1:24). Now the passage tells us that the man had a demon, but how did Jesus know? Had we been there, I am sure that we would not have known by outward appearances that the man had a demon. The average person in that synagogue probably would not have understood what the demon said through the man. Jesus knew who was really addressing Him supernaturally.

Another situation needing the gift of distinguishing between spirits occurs in Mark 9:14-29. Jesus casts a demon out of a boy after His disciples had already tried and failed. Later, they ask Jesus why they couldn't cast it out and Jesus replied, "This kind can only come out by prayer and fasting." How would anyone know what kind of demon He is casting out? The answer is found in the gift of distinguishing between spirits. Jesus knew what kind of demon it was supernaturally.

So we can see different manifestations of the Holy Spirit in the ministry of Jesus. But what does that have to do with us in the Church? Look at what Jesus said in John 14:12, "I tell you the truth, anyone who has faith in me will do what I have been doing. He will do even greater things than these, because I am going to the Father." As we established in the second chapter, these things that Jesus is referring to are His works of power. Anyone who believes in Jesus will do the power ministry He did.

But how is this possible?  Remember that one of the focuses of the 14$^{th}$ chapter of John is the promised coming of the Holy Spirit.  Jesus said that the Spirit would come and live in us.  So, if the Holy Spirit is the one who anointed and empowered Jesus, He can continue His ministry by anointing and empowering us also.

A serious question arises at this point.  Which parts of Jesus' ministry were unique to Him alone?  Having the Holy Spirit in our lives does not make us equal with Jesus.  Here is a short list of items that are unique to who Jesus is and what He did in ministry.

1) Jesus always has been, is and always will be God Almighty.  John 1:1 teaches us that Jesus is God.  Later in the same gospel, Thomas is given the invitation to touch the wounds in Jesus and he exclaims, "My Lord and my God!" (John 20:28)  Along with these two examples are numerous times when Jesus applied the title of "I am" to Himself.

There are also a number of times in the Gospels when Jesus was worshiped.  Both Matthew 14:33 and John 9:38 tell us of times when people recognized Jesus' divinity and began to worship Him.  This is significant because Jesus would not have allowed Himself to be worshiped if He was not Yahweh.

2) Only Jesus could initiate the kingdom of God on Earth, since He is the King.  The Church is the product of the activity of the kingdom, but Jesus is the King of kings who brought it and called us to enter into it.  As Revelation 17:14 states, "They will make war against the Lamb, but the Lamb will overcome them because he is Lord of lords and Kings of kings – and with him will be his called, chosen and faithful followers."  Jesus is the King, we are just followers, who proclaim and demonstrate His kingdom by His command.

3) Jesus is and was the only mediator between God and the human race.  As 1 Timothy 2:5 says, "For there is one God

and one mediator between God and men, the man Christ Jesus." There is no other way to be with the Father. Only Jesus can bring us into His presence. Jesus made such a statement during His ministry when He said, "I am the way and the truth and the life. No one comes to the Father except through me." None of us can make that statement, since the Church is not the mediator between God and people. That role belongs solely to the Lord of the Church, Jesus Christ.

4) Finally, Jesus is the only one who could be the sacrifice for our sins and be our atonement by what He did on the cross. 1 John 4:10 tells us, "This is love; not that we loved God, but that he loved us and sent his Son as an atoning sacrifice for our sins." The sacrifice for sins is done.

Though Jesus called us to proclaim and demonstrate the kingdom with power and to do the works He did by the power of the Spirit, these four items are what separate our ministry from His. I am sure that there may be other ways in which His ministry is different from ours, but what is important is that we do what Jesus has commanded us to do and emulate His ministry in every way we can. Ministry under the Holy Spirit with power is a great way to respond to the call to imitate Him.

# Chapter Six
## Person and Empowering Work of the Holy Spirit

### Knowing the Holy Spirit as God

As I thought about writing this chapter, I wanted to convey how truly exciting the Holy Spirit is. Every time the Bible speaks of Him and what He did and does, I find they are some of the most exhilarating things I have ever heard. From Genesis 1:2 where He is hovering over the waters and creating the planet to the New Testament, the Holy Spirit is awesome.

So many writings about Him are seemingly cold and overly systematic in describing Him. Yet, He is alive and constantly moving in ministry through the Church.

I once heard it said, "If you only know the Holy Spirit as It, you don't know Him." This is a truthful statement. Many Christians will acknowledge that the Trinity is the Father, the Son, and the Holy Spirit, but experientially, their Trinity is the Father, the Son, and the Holy Bible. They have relegated the job of the Holy Spirit to simply teaching us what the Bible says, since their seemingly exclusive interaction with Him is reading what He did in the Old and New Testaments. The Bible shows us so much more than that.

The Holy Spirit empowered Jesus' ministry and He is the one who empowers the Church for salvation, life and ministry. In order to understand how the Spirit uses us, we must look at what the Bible teaches us about Him. As we grow in knowing Him we will know better how to be used by Him.

He is God the Spirit. We theologically recognize Him as the third person of the Trinity, since the Holy Spirit is Yahweh. The Trinitarian formulas given in the New Testament teach us that the Spirit along with the Father and the Son together are Yahweh (i.e. Matthew 28:19 and 2 Corinthians 13:14). It is important for us to recognize the full deity of the Spirit.

2 Corinthians 3:17-18 says, "Now the Lord is the Spirit, and where the Spirit of the Lord is, there is freedom. And we with unveiled faces all reflect the Lord's glory, are being transformed into His likeness with ever-increasing glory, which comes from the Lord, who is the Spirit." This clearly teaches us that the Holy Spirit is God Almighty. As the Father and Jesus are Lord, so the Spirit is equally Lord.

As R.A. Torrey wrote, "If the Holy Spirit is a divine person, worthy to receive our adoration, our faith and our love, and we do not know and recognize Him as such, then we are robbing a divine Being of the adoration and love and confidence which are His due." [1] We must know the Holy Spirit as fully divine. We can call the Spirit by the name of Yahweh. To do any less is to see Him as less than God and that would make us heretics. We owe Him all of our love and we must glorify Him as God Almighty.

### The Holy Spirit is to be Worshipped

Not only is the Holy Spirit equally Lord as the Father and the Son, so He is equally worthy of worship as God. Some of the confessions recognized by Reformed churches confirm this truth. The Nicene Creed says, "And we believe in the Holy Spirit, the Lord and Giver of Life, who proceedeth from the Father and the Son, who with the Father and the Son together is worshipped and glorified, who spoke by the

114

prophets." [2] Or consider the Second Helvetic Confession as it states, "and the Holy Spirit truly proceeds from them both, and the same from eternity and is to be worshipped with both." [3] And finally the Westminster Confession of Faith instructs us that, "Religious worship is to be given to God, the Father, Son, and Holy Ghost." [4]

Growing up a Christian, I remember hearing Christian leaders warn me about churches that worship or focus on the Holy Spirit. It didn't take long for me to realize the error in this warning. It is the same as warning someone to stay away from any church that worshipped and focused on God the Father. The error is that some Christians think that by worshipping the Spirit, we are somehow doing less than truly worshipping God.

In being Trinitarian, we are to focus our worship on the Father, Son and the Holy Spirit. Each person of the Trinity is fully worthy of worship and obedience. In the course of the life of any Church there will be times of learning and focusing on each person in the Trinity.

I have found that when a church begins to focus on the Holy Spirit, He turns our attention on the Father and the Son. When we look to the Father, He pours out the Spirit on us and builds our love for the Son. And when we center our attention on the Son, He leads us to the Father and gives us more of the Holy Spirit. I believe this is characteristic of the Triune God.

There is no sin in loving the Trinity and going through times of focusing on any one person of the Trinity. There is sin in avoiding or devaluing any person of the Trinity. This can lead to a less than Trinitarian theology. Surely there are Christians who will give assent to belief in the Trinity for orthodoxy's sake, yet functionally and experientially deny the Trinity.

The United Pentecostals denomination holds to what is called Oneness Theology. This belief system claims there is only one person of God, saying that the other parts of the Trinity are merely names or manifestations of the one person. They only baptize their members in the name of Jesus, rather than the full Trinity (which is in disobedience to Jesus' great commission in Matthew 28:18-20). This group eventually broke from the Assemblies of God and was rightly designated as heretics by the Assemblies of God and other orthodox denominations. Any time we forget to follow the full Trinity, we are in danger of becoming like the United Pentecostals. We can give mental agreement to the doctrine of the Trinity and still become unorthodox in our experience of God, which leads to unorthopraxy in reality.

So, we not only believe in the existence of the Holy Spirit and His deity, we worship Him as God. One of the great things about the Holy Spirit is that we worship Him as a present reality in our lives. Jesus promised the coming of the Holy Spirit to us (John 7:39; 20:22; Acts 1:8). And His coming was wonderful because He came to dwell in us as true believers.

As Paul wrote in 1 Corinthians 3:16, "Do you not know that you are God's temple and that God's Spirit dwells in you?" The Spirit of God inhabits us and as He lives in us we live with Him and His empowering presence. Since the Spirit dwells in us, He calls us to an intimacy with Him.

### Fellowship with the Holy Spirit

This intimacy is built as He fellowships with us and we fellowship with Him. 2 Corinthians 13:14 says, "May the grace of the Lord Jesus Christ, and the love of God, and the fellowship of the Holy Spirit be with you all." God gives us the fellowship of the Holy Spirit.

When some Christians read this verse they look at the fellowship of the Holy Spirit as being the fellowship between believers when we worship or study the Bible together. This is a misunderstanding of the verse. In order to read this verse correctly we must decide what "of the Holy Spirit" really means. Dr. Gordon Fee writes,

"There has been some debate as to whether 'of the Spirit' is an objective or subjective genitive. That is, are we in fellowship with the Spirit, or does he create the fellowship of the saints, as it were? Since the two prior clauses reflect something both of God's character and of his activity on behalf of his people in light of that character, it seems most likely that something similar is presented here seems to capture the essence of the 'direction' of the Spirit's activity and of the meaning of the word itself." [5]

So, this verse shows the Spirit's activity toward us as drawing us into fellowship with Himself, rather than our fellowship with each other. It would be easy to interpret this verse as fellowship with one another if fellowshipping with the Holy Spirit was not part of a person's experience. If believers have never sought to fellowship with the Holy Spirit, then that type of intimate relationship with Him wouldn't mean anything to them. The Spirit remains a remote being in our conscious reality.

Surely the fellowship of the Church flows from our fellowship with the Holy Spirit. We love each other because we have learned how to love from the Spirit. We value each other and spend time together because we see the work and fruit of the Spirit in each other's lives. But the fellowship of

117

the Church is really a by-product of our relationship with the Spirit as He dwells in us.

Dr. Fee thus writes, based on what was just quoted from his book, "Through the gift of his Holy Spirit, the Spirit of the living God, God has now arrived in the new creation as an abiding, empowering presence – so that what most characterizes the Holy Spirit is *koinonia*, which primarily means "participation in," or "fellowship with." [6] He is present to fellowship with us.

So, how do we fellowship with the Spirit? First, you have to spend time with Him. Many of us have time that we set aside to pray for different needs. While that is good and biblical, I am suggesting that we have to spend time in the Spirit's presence. We must devote our quiet times to being with the Holy Spirit. As we spend time with Him we will learn how to listen to Him.

There is a great picture of this in Acts 13:1-3 which tells us,

"In the church at Antioch there were prophets and teachers: Barnabas, Simeon called Niger, Lucius of Cyrene, Manaen (who had been brought up with Herod the tetrarch) and Saul. While they were worshipping the Lord and fasting, the Holy Spirit said, 'Set apart for me Barnabas and Saul for the work to which I have called them.' So after they had fasted and prayed, they placed their hands on them and sent them off."

As the teachers and prophets had been spending time with the Spirit, He spoke to them. Due to the intimacy the Holy Spirit had developed in these people, they knew His voice and obeyed Him in preparing Barnabas and Saul for what He had called them to do.

Most of us Christians are not that sensitive to the Spirit, nor do we expect Him to speak that directly to us. I believe there are a number of reasons for this, but a primary reason is that we fail to have fellowship with the Spirit Himself. Let me ask you a question. Do you know the Holy Spirit? I am not asking if you know about Him or if you know what the Confessions teach about Him. I am asking if you know Him personally. If the Holy Spirit is dwelling inside of each one of us as believers, we should know and love Him. We should recognize Him and be able to listen to Him with obedience being the result.

Most Christians learn how to feel His conviction. When you are about to sin, you get that gut feeling that what you are about to do is wrong and disobedient. You are given a choice inside. We also know the instant feeling of increased conviction when we choose disobedience. That is just a beginning in learning to respond to the Holy Spirit, and learning to listen to Him.

Many Christians know when the Spirit is prompting them into times of ministry. One afternoon, while sitting in my office, I knew that the Spirit was telling me to go share the Gospel with a young man I had spent a little time with in previous months. But I got busy and didn't go. The next morning, while driving to the church facility, I felt the same prompting of the Spirit. So I drove to the man's home. As I began to talk with him, he told me that he hated people who quoted Scripture at him in hope of evangelizing him. This was definitely a difficult evangelism case. So I told him that I wouldn't quote the Bible to him, but I wanted to talk about Jesus.

After quite a while he did accept Jesus as his Lord and Savior. The Holy Spirit was doing all the work. All I can say is that because I finally responded to the prompting of the

119

Spirit, He included me in bringing this man to Jesus. I know for sure that the times I haven't responded to the Spirit outnumber this example by 100 to 1. As we respond to the Spirit, we begin the process of learning how to listen to Him.

A great example of listening to the Spirit if found in Acts 16:6-10. It says,

"Paul and his companions traveled throughout the region of Phrygia and Galatia, having been kept by the Holy Spirit from preaching the word in the province of Asia. When they came to the border of Mysia, they tried to enter Bithynia, but the Spirit of Jesus would not allow them to. So they passed by Mysia and went down to Troas. During the night Paul had a vision of a man of Macedonia standing and begging him, 'Come over to Macedonia and help us.' After Paul had seen the vision, we got ready at once to leave for Macedonia, concluding that God had called us to preach the gospel to them."

I believe that Paul and his group were intimate with the Spirit, and as they traveled they remained in fellowship with Him. Due to this fellowship they were able to listen to Him when He would not allow them to enter Mysia. Now the Holy Spirit could have kept them from entering Asia and Mysia through circumstances. This is possible, but the passage doesn't say that. The passage doesn't say how the Spirit kept them from preaching in Asia. I think that Paul and the others were intimate with the Spirit and knew when He would say "No."

They were close enough in fellowship with the Holy Spirit to realize that the vision of the man of Macedonia was from Him. He gave it to them in order to direct them in ministry and they obeyed the Spirit.

A classic example of fellowshipping with the Holy Spirit from Reformed History is seen in John Welch, John Knox's son-in-law. John Howie wrote,

> "One night he rose and went into the next room, where he stayed so long at secret prayer, that his wife, fearing he might catch cold, was constrained to rise and follow him, and, as she hearkened, she heard him speak as by interrupted sentences, 'Lord, wilt Thou not grant me Scotland?' and, after a pause, 'Enough, Lord, enough.' She asked him afterwards what he meant by saying, 'Enough, Lord, enough?' He showed her himself dissatisfied with her curiosity, but told her that he had been wrestling with the Lord for Scotland, and found there was a sad time at hand, but that the Lord would be gracious to a remnant." [7]

John Howie also wrote about someone else observing John Welch's fellowship with the Spirit with the following,

> "An honest minister, who was a parishioner of his for many a day, said that one night as Welch watched in his garden very late, and some friends were waiting upon him in his house, and wearying because of his long stay, one of them chanced to open a window toward the place where he walked, and saw clearly a strange light surround him, and heard him speak strange words about his spiritual joy." [8]

John Welch had wonderful times of fellowshipping with the Spirit. He listened to the Spirit and conversed with Him. The "strange light" seen around Welch seems to have been a manifestation of the Holy Spirit while they were spending time together in the garden. We should grow in our spiritual lives so that we go and "watch" before God, letting all else wait as we enjoy His presence. Like Welch, the Holy Spirit wants to draw us into an intimate fellowship with Himself. His dwelling within us is a reality and it is a picture of how close He wants us to be with Him. As we commune with Him we will also learn how He wants to empower us.

R.A. Torrey wrote a great summary of what communing with the Holy Spirit should mean to us as followers of Jesus Christ. The following is from an article in that monumental work called *The Fundamentals*.

> "Do we know the 'communion of the Holy Ghost?'(2 Cor.13:14.) Communion means fellowship, partnership, comradeship. Do we know this personal fellowship, this partnership, this comradeship, this intimate friendship of the Holy Spirit? Herein lies the secret of a real Christian life, a life of liberty and joy and power and fullness. To have as one's ever-present Friend, and to be conscious that one has as his ever-present Friend, the Holy Spirit, and to surrender one's life in all its departments entirely to His control, this is true Christian living." [9]

So, this is part of the Christian life. Listening and talking with the Holy Spirit are the heart of fellowshipping with Him. He leads us and gives us commands as to our specific assignments. As we are following Him in daily life, we receive His love and return our love and admiration to Him.

I can honestly admit that I do not have the kind of fellowship with the Holy Spirit that I would like to have and that I believe I should have. An angel of God once told a man named Paul Cain that, "The people are as close to the Lord as they choose to be." [10] It is my desire to be closer to the Holy Spirit, now I just need to give our relationship some better effort.

## Knowing the Holy Spirit

As we fellowship with the Holy Spirit we grow in our desire to know Him. The Bible teaches us quite a bit about who He is. We begin by knowing His names as given in the Scriptures. He is called the Spirit, Holy Spirit, Spirit of God, Spirit of Christ, and Counselor. This is a basic list, since there are other titles given to Him throughout the Bible. What is important is that these names teach us who He is and what His position is within the Trinity.

His names teach us that He is Spirit. Many Christians know John 4:24 where Jesus said, "God is spirit, and his worshipers must worship in spirit and in truth." God is a spirit being. With this as a foundation, what does it mean when we refer to the Spirit of God?

In Hebrew the word for Spirit is *Ruach*, which means wind, breath or divine power. [11] Alasdair Heron expounded on this definition when he wrote, "Ruach as 'wind' commonly refers to the strong wind of the desert storm, the raging blast from the desert, like the one that divided the Red Sea at the Exodus (Exod. 14:21)." [12]

The Holy Spirit is the wind of God. [13] But don't let a term such as 'wind' take away from the personality of His being. It is a term that describes His movement and fluidity. Think about Jesus' statement to Nicodemus in John 3:5-8, "I tell you the truth, unless a man is born of water and the Spirit, he cannot enter the kingdom of God. Flesh gives birth to flesh, but the Spirit gives birth to spirit. You should not be surprised at my saying 'You must be born again.' The wind blows wherever it pleases. You hear its sound, but you cannot tell where it comes from or where it is going. So it is with everyone born of the Spirit."

The Holy Spirit moves as a wind. He gives birth to us in Christ, but who can tell which way He will blow? Where is He moving? As of this writing, there is revival in Argentina, South Korea, parts of Africa and Florida. But where will He blow revival tomorrow?

While attending an Urbana Conference put on by Intervarsity Christian Fellowship, I was able to watch a seminar that was taking place on the floor of the main arena. During the seminar, the speaker invited the Holy Spirit to come and minister to the students (a few hundred were in attendance). Sitting up in the second floor of this gymnasium I watched as students began to cry. What was interesting is that the crying moved through the crowd. I could see it sweep through the students like a wind through a wheat field. It moved in directions, first moving diagonally then towards the front. This crying was followed by laughter and sounds of joy, following the same movements as if a wind were blowing across the floor. The Holy Spirit is truly amazing!

Jesus also acted as if the Spirit was His breath. In John 20:21-22 it says, "Again, Jesus said, 'Peace be with you! As the Father has sent me, I am sending you.' And with that he breathed on them and said, 'Receive the Holy Spirit.'" In this situation, Jesus was giving them the Holy Spirit. I find it interesting that Jesus didn't just tell them that the Spirit was coming. Instead, He breathed on them. This was a prophetic demonstration that the Ruach (Spirit) of God was coming. But it also showed them the divine nature of the Spirit.

124

Observe how the Spirit arrives in Acts 2:2-4 on the day of Pentecost. The passage reads, "Suddenly a sound like the blowing of a violent wind came from heaven and filled the whole house where they were sitting. They saw what seemed to be tongues of fire that separated and came to rest on each of them. All of them were filled with the Holy Spirit and began to speak in other tongues as the Spirit enabled them." This was a dramatic experience used by God to teach the Church about the nature of the Spirit. He is the "Ruach of God."

His name teaches us that He is holy. We derive the word holy from the Greek word *agios,* which means "holy, morally pure, upright." [14] The Spirit is holy because He is God. The Spirit is pure and does not sin, nor does He lead us into sin. It is not just that He is holy; what He does is holy also. In Reformed theology we acknowledge that we are being sanctified. The Holy Spirit is making us holy. He is purifying us from our sinful lives as He causes us to make war on the desires of our fleshly nature.

Humans are innate sinners. Left to ourselves, we choose to rebel against God and break His commandments. But when the Spirit brought us to faith in Jesus, He sanctified us and started the work of sanctification in our lives. When you interact with the Spirit of God, you will become holy, or you will be convicted of your sinfulness, and sometimes both happen together by Him. So, don't be surprised if you become increasingly holy as you fellowship with the Spirit.

When someone comes to accept Jesus as their Savior, I tell them they are about to change. I don't hand them a list of God's commandments and tell them to do their best to keep them. Instead, I share with them that the Holy Spirit dwells in them making them holy like God and that after their first year of following Jesus they will look back and see that they have changed. The Spirit is the Holy God.

His names teach us that He is of one essence with both the Father and the Son. The names Spirit of God and Spirit of Christ show us just how close the Spirit is with the other persons of the Trinity. He is of one essence with both the Father and the Son.

The Scriptures give us verses that demonstrate the intimacy of the Father and the Spirit. In 1 Corinthians 2:10b-11 it states, "The Spirit searches all things, even the deep things of God. For who among men knows the thoughts of a man except the man's spirit within him? In the same way no one knows the thoughts of God except the Spirit of God." The Holy Spirit searches the "deep things" of the Father and the Son. He knows the Father and the Son in a deep and intimate way.

Yet, in Romans 8:27 the Scriptures also tell us, "And he who searches our hearts knows the mind of the Spirit, because the Spirit intercedes for the saints in accordance with God's will." The Father knows the mind of the Spirit. You could say that the Father knows what is on the Spirit's mind. From these two passages we witness a depth within the Trinity.

To know the Holy Spirit is to know the Father's heart and to know Jesus' heart. To fellowship with the Spirit is to converse with the One who knows the Father and the Son and leads us into that depth of relationship. We begin to know the love of the Father for the Son. And that intimate love begins to fill us and move us in worship and in the service of our great and awesome God. As Jesus prayed in John 17:26, "I have made you known to them, and will continue to make you known in order that the love you have for me may be in them and that I myself may be in them." The Spirit of God puts the love that the Father has for Jesus into our hearts and this is a love that will drive us to be passionate in our relationship with Jesus.

Personally, I have moments when I feel this passionate love in my heart. I can feel the love that the Father has for Jesus, but then I know that His love for Jesus is vast and infinite. I was attending a conference and heard Dr. Jack Deere say that he prays that the Father will fill him with the power to love Jesus the way He does. That is one of the best things I now know to pray, and I believe that if we really pray for this, the Holy Spirit will be faithful to fill us with this love. This isn't something that I can learn by reading about it; this love is something the Holy Spirit gives you. So, ask Him for it!

His names teach us that He has come to fill us and be with us. He is the Paraclete, which means that He is our comforter or counselor. Jesus said in John 14:16-17, "And I will ask the Father, and he will give you another Counselor to be with you forever – the Spirit of truth." The Spirit is another Counselor as Jesus was. As the Spirit of truth, He comes to lead us into all truth (John 16:13). He leads us into the truth of who God is, what God says, what God commands, and what God promises. He leads us into a truthful relationship based on love.

When the Spirit enters into people and begins to regenerate their hearts, He opens their minds to the truth of the Gospel. He also begins the long process of dwelling in us for the rest of our lives. As He lives in us He is faithful to guide us. We can trust that the Spirit will lead us into all truth if we will follow Him.

Besides these names, John Calvin listed the following titles: "spirit of adoption," "the guarantee and seal," "water," "oil," "anointing," "fire," and "spring." [15] These titles speak of His work. As Calvin pointed out, the Holy Spirit is the living water that Jesus offered for those who are thirsty, because it is the Spirit who gives us life in Jesus. Just as He is "water" so He is all of these titles listed by Calvin. Each one shows us what the Spirit does or how He is used by the Father. As we learn who He is, we also learn what He does.

Ask Him to teach you who He is. Yes, you can read about Him in the Scriptures and learn about Him, but there is a difference between knowing about Him and knowing Him. Ask Him to read the Scriptures to you. Ask Him to come and do all that He wants to do with you and to give you all that He wants to give to you.

## The Empowering of the Spirit

There is a time when you first come in contact with the Spirit, or should we say the Holy Spirit comes in contact with you. This is when you begin to come alive in Jesus. Reformed theology calls this process of receiving new life "Regeneration."

The procedure goes something like this: While you are still lost and without Jesus as your Savior and Lord, the Holy Spirit enters your life. He begins to open your heart to the love of God and your mind to the truth of the Gospel. He does this because we humans cannot understand the Scriptures on our own without His empowering us to do so. That is why many people read the Bible and it doesn't make any sense to them, the Spirit hasn't opened their minds to receive the truth.

John Calvin fittingly wrote, "For as God alone is a fit witness of himself in his Word, so also the Word will not find acceptance in men's hearts before it is sealed by the inward testimony of the Spirit. The same Spirit, therefore, who has spoken through the mouths of the prophets must penetrate into our hearts to persuade us that they faithfully proclaimed what had been divinely commanded." [16]

A good example of this is found in Luke 24:44-45. In this passage Jesus is with His disciples immediately following His resurrection from the dead. The verses read, "He said to them, 'This is what I told you while I was still with you: Everything must be fulfilled that is written about me in the Law of Moses, the Prophets and the Psalms.' *Then he opened their minds so they could understand the Scriptures.*" (Emphasis mine.) Jesus wanted them to understand what the Scriptures were saying about Him, so He opened their minds to understand them. The Holy Spirit does the same thing with us as He prepares us to accept Jesus.

Then the Holy Spirit puts saving faith in our hearts and leads us to accept Jesus as Lord and Savior. It is by His work, not ours. It is by His power, not by anything in us. This is the process of regeneration.

So, in the Reformed faith we believe that all those who have come to saving faith in Jesus have the Holy Spirit dwelling in them. We couldn't be true believers unless the Holy Spirit was working in us and putting faith in us. As Titus 3:5 states, "he saved us, not because of righteous things we had done, but because of his mercy. He saved us through the washing of rebirth and renewal by the Holy Spirit." Or as Jesus answered in John 3:5-6, "I tell you the truth, unless a man is born of water and the Spirit, he cannot enter the kingdom of God. Flesh gives birth to flesh, but the Spirit gives birth to spirit." You cannot be saved unless the Holy Spirit renews you and births you into the Kingdom. As I just stated, true believers in Jesus have the Holy Spirit dwelling in them.

For many Christians, it is common to believe that this is the only filling of the Spirit they will ever have or need. It is true that from the time that you believe you can know for sure that the Holy Spirit dwells within you. But the Scriptures show us example after example of subsequent fillings of the Spirit upon the life of a believer.

One of the best examples comes from the book of Acts. Chapter Two tells us about the day of Pentecost, when the Holy Spirit filled the Church. It was a great day accompanied with great blessings from God and the activity of the gifts. Now look at chapter four. Verses 23-30 inform us that Peter and John, after their release from the Sanhedrin, returned to be with the Church. They reported what had happened to them and then led those present in prayer. According to verse 31, "After they prayed, the place where they were meeting was shaken. And they were all filled with the Holy Spirit and spoke the word of God boldly."

These believers who were filled with the Spirit on the day of Pentecost were once again filled with the Holy Spirit. We can see that though you are birthed into the Kingdom by the Holy Spirit and He dwells in you as a Christian, there is still a need to be filled with the Spirit as He plans to use you powerfully in ministry. As Rev. Harold J. Okenga once wrote, "Every Christian has the Holy Spirit (Rom. 8:9). But it is one thing to receive the Holy Spirit and it is another thing to be filled with the Spirit and thus equipped for service." [17]

This filling with the Spirit is a time when the Holy Spirit is poured out on you or anoints you. It is a welling up of the Spirit within you so that His kingdom power and His gifts begin to pour out of you. There may be an initial time when the Spirit is poured out on you, but as was shown in Acts, being filled with the Spirit can happen more than once.

When it takes place is up to the Holy Spirit and you. I believe that some are anointed with the Holy Spirit at the moment they become believers. A classic example is Cornelius and his family in Acts 10:44-46. The passage reads, "While Peter was still speaking these words (sharing the

Gospel with them), the Holy Spirit came on all who heard the message. The circumcised believers who had come to Peter were astonished that the gift of the Holy Spirit had been poured out even on the Gentiles. For they heard them speaking in tongues and praising God." While they were listening to Peter, the Spirit filled them.

So that we don't get too systematic about the timing when the Holy Spirit fills a person, the Bible relates to us the story of John the Baptist's anointing by the Spirit. Luke 1:15b tells us that, "and he (John the Baptist) will be filled with the Holy Spirit even from birth." Now I am not trying to use this example as the norm for how our preconceived ideas of how the Spirit works. John was anointed with the Holy Spirit at birth, before he could ask for it.

So we can see from the Scriptures that one purpose of the Holy Spirit on earth is to anoint us for ministry. By this anointing or filling we are empowered by the Holy Spirit to use the charismatic gifts.

Many want to know if there should be certain gifts accompanying this "filling" of the Holy Spirit. This depends on whom you talk to. Some, such as traditional Pentecostals, will tell you that you will speak in tongues when you are baptized in the Spirit. They have found this to be true in their experience and in their understanding of the Bible. For them, the "baptism" is a separate experience from being saved.

I am not Pentecostal. I fall under a category called the "Third Wave." This term comes from identifying the moves of the Holy Spirit in recent Church history. The first wave of the Spirit in restoring power to the Church was the establishing of the Pentecostal churches. God has done and is still doing great work through this first wave.

C. Peter Wagner teaches that the second wave was the emergence of independent "charismatic" churches and "mini-denominations" [18] that believe in the continuation of the power gifts today. When it comes to their understanding of the baptism of the Spirit, they see it as "distinct from conversion" but are not as adamant about speaking in tongues as the initial evidence of being filled with the Holy Spirit. [19] They believed that one could be baptized in the Spirit, yet Wagner writes that there was not a great emphasis on speaking in tongues.

The third wave is a movement of the Holy Spirit to restore His gifts and power within established denominations. Any gift can be the sign of having been baptized in the Spirit, as He empowers you for service. Wagner also wrote, "the baptism of the Holy Spirit is truly enough a once-for-all experience and that it happens when we are born again." [20] With that he also wrote, "I believe that being filled with the Holy Spirit is something that is not limited to a once-for-all experience (as is new birth), but rather it is something Christians should expect to be repeated from time to time throughout their Christian lives." [21]

It is a mistake for Christians to think that they do not need to be filled with the empowering of the Holy Spirit on the basis that they already believe in Jesus. Acts 8:14-17 tells us, "When the apostles in Jerusalem heard that Samaria had accepted the word of God, they sent Peter and John to them. When they arrived, they prayed for them that they might receive the Holy Spirit, because the Holy Spirit had not yet come upon any of them; they had simply been baptized into the name of the Lord Jesus. Then Peter and John placed their hands on them, and they received the Holy Spirit."

I believe that the empowering of the Spirit is usually a separate event from our conversion experience. It is important for us to ask Him to fill us and to live in that empowering.

Jesus told us that the Father will give the Spirit to those who ask Him. (Luke 11:13)

I see myself as part of the third wave. But I don't want to tell the Holy Spirit how to do His work in me or in the Church. I may be wrong about many aspects of how and when He fills us, but I do want all that He will give me. I am even hoping that there will be a fourth wave of His moving in the Church, and more. God is always causing new moves in us and through us and I want to do what He is doing.

The Apostle Paul wrote in Ephesians 5:18, "Do not get drunk on wine, which leads to debauchery. Instead, be filled with the Spirit." As Christians, let us follow this injunction and seek to be filled with the Holy Spirit. Ask the Holy Spirit to fill you. Ask Him to fill you so that you are overflowing with Him and you are using the gifts He has put in you. If He has filled you before, ask Him to fill you again as the Apostles did in Acts 4:23-31.

## Why Don't We See More of the Holy Spirit in Our Lives and Church?

If we really are birthed into the kingdom by the Holy Spirit and He dwells within us as Christians, then it seems that we should see more of His activity in the local church. In an earlier chapter we looked at the necessity of faith as God uses His power in us and through us. If we do not have enough faith, the mountain will not be moved.

As we are used by the Holy Spirit, He definitely works in conjunction with our faith. A lack of faith will hinder what the Spirit wants to do with us in the world. There are also two other problems that will hinder the work of the Holy Spirit in the Church.

The first of these is grieving the Spirit. Ephesians 4:29-31 says,

> "Do not let any unwholesome talk come out of your mouths, but only what is helpful for building others up according to their needs, that it may benefit those who listen. And do not grieve the Holy Spirit of God, with whom you were sealed for the day of redemption. Get rid of all bitterness, rage and anger, brawling and slander, along with every form of malice."

As Christians, we must be careful not to grieve the Holy Spirit. To grieve Him means to cause Him to be in deep, heartfelt sorrow. From the passage above it would seem that our sin causes Him to be grieved. After all, He is the Spirit of holiness. Our sin and rebellion are directly against who He is. The definition of sin is rebellion against God and His law. To rebel against the commands of God is to rebel against the very words the Holy Spirit inspired us to live by.

Though I think that any of our sins grieve the Holy Spirit, this passage is pointing out sins that bring division. Proverbs 6:19 tells us that one of the things God hates is a person "who stirs up dissension among brothers." Look at the list of sins given in this passage: unwholesome talk, bitterness, rage, anger, brawling, slander, and every form of malice. All of these sins tear people down, divide us from each other and kill our hearts.

I believe that it grieves the Holy Spirit when Christians allow themselves to become filled with pride and speak against other Christians and other denominations. This is a sin of which the Church and her many denominations must repent if we are going to see the Holy Spirit move with power. The

Reformed tradition is as guilty of this sin as any other group. We take pride in our theology and our ways, mocking the other denominations and their theological understandings of the Bible.

What is supposed to come out of our mouths is "what is helpful for building others up according to their needs, that it may benefit those who listen." As the Church we must be one. And as "one" we are to build each other up. Not just building up other Reformed believers. We are to build up all believers and encourage them. In this way we will truly have the love of God in our hearts and instead of grieving the Spirit, we will give the Spirit joy.

The second problem that hinders the Holy Spirit is when we quench Him. In 1 Thessalonians 5:19 the Apostle Paul instructs us by writing, "Do not put out the Spirit's fire; do not treat prophecies with contempt."

It is hard for those who think that the gifts ended with the Apostles to see that they are quenching the Spirit. If there were no more prophecies, then the Spirit couldn't be quenched. But as I have shown in the earlier chapters, the Holy Spirit is still giving the gift of prophecy to the Church. So the belief that the gift of prophecy is dead automatically quenches the Holy Spirit. If you believe that God no longer gives prophecies, you will treat His prophecies with contempt.

The verse above is from the New International Version of the Bible, whereas the New American Standard gives the same verse as, "Do not quench the Spirit." The key Greek word is *un sbennute*, which means to quench, stifle or suppress. [22] This word gives us the idea of seeing a fire and putting it out. The problem here is that the fire is good, because it is the work of the Spirit.

Many Christians have noticed a difference between the ministry of Jesus and the Church of the first century and what we experience now. Jesus never quenched or grieved the Spirit. I also believe that the Church that immediately followed Him did not quench or grieve the Spirit as much as we do.

It is important for us to work with the Holy Spirit if we want Him to work freely within our lives and our church. One of the ways that God demands that we work with Him is to receive His prophecies for us.

We are to desire that God would use the gift of prophecy in us and in our church (1 Corinthians 14:1, 39). We are to fan that gift into flame (2 Timothy 1:6). As that flame turns into fire, we are to be careful not to extinguish it. It is human nature to want to contain a fire and keep it from spreading. But we must know that the Holy Spirit is the Sovereign Lord and ministers to us in order to build us up into the Church He has determined us to be.

This requires that we trust Him. I actually think that many Christians do not totally trust the Holy Spirit when it comes to manifesting His gifts in the Church. The problem is usually found in the difference between what we think is decent and orderly and what God has determined to be decent and in order. For many Christians any activity of the Spirit using His gifts is indecent and out of order, because we are not the ones in control.

It is good to study the manifestations of the Spirit and learn from Him what He does and what to expect when He moves. We must welcome the Spirit and the manifestations He will bring to our churches. Otherwise we will stand in contempt of the Spirit.

# Manifestations of the Holy Spirit

We tend to unnaturally divide the manifestations or experiences of the Spirit into the categories of normal and abnormal in our minds. In reality, all of the manifestations of the Spirit are normal in the kingdom of God. The actual determining factor is what makes us feel comfortable and what doesn't. This artificial line is drawn by our experiences and what we think the Bible teaches.

All of us accept conversion and sanctification as normal manifestations of the Holy Spirit. We know that there is nothing in us by which we can, of ourselves, be saved. So, we know that the Holy Spirit must come and birth each of us into the kingdom. When someone accepts Jesus as Lord and Savior, we know that to be a work of the Spirit.

Likewise, as we begin to grow in Christ, our maturity is a work of the Spirit also. The Holy Spirit dwells in our life and begins the process of making us holy. As He dwells in us, part of the change that comes is the growth of His fruit in our life. Galatians 5:22-23 says, "But the fruit of the Spirit is love, joy, peace, patience, kindness, goodness, faithfulness, gentleness and self-control." As we see these things increase in believers' lives, we know that the Spirit is active in them and they are responding to Him.

But conversion and sanctification are not the totality of the Spirit's work in our lives. Some Christians teach that the fruit has taken the place of the gifts. It goes something like this, "The First Century Church needed the gifts to jump start the Church, but now that the Church is going we only need the fruit of the Spirit." The Apostle Paul would disagree. He wrote in 1 Corinthians 14:1, "Follow the way of love and eagerly desire spiritual gifts, especially the gift of prophecy." The Spirit does not replace His gifts with His fruit. He uses both in our lives.  The gifts are to accompany His fruit.  The gifts without the fruit are nothing.  So it is the will of the Holy Spirit to build both into our lives and ministry.

The Scriptures clearly teach us that all of the gifts are manifestations of the Spirit.  In 1 Corinthians 12:7 we read, "Now to each one the manifestation of the Spirit is given for the common good."  The passage then lists nine gifts of the Spirit.  By looking at the passage we know that each of these nine gifts are manifestations of the Holy Spirit's power.

What does manifestation mean?  The Greek word from which we translate manifestation (*phanerosis*) means "'revelation,' or 'appearance.'" [23]  In other words, the Holy Spirit uses the gifts to reveal His ministry and presence.  You could also say that He makes an appearance in the Church by these gifts.  I like the way that Gordon Fee stated it when he wrote, "Thus each 'gift' is a 'manifestation,' a disclosure of the Spirit's activity in their midst." [24]

When you see the gifts in operation in the Church you know what God is up to.  He reveals His will to heal when gifts of healing are in action.  The Spirit reveals His heart and direction for our lives and ministry when the gift of prophecy is in action.  He reveals His desire to edify us when the gift of tongues is in action.  The Holy Spirit literally appears in the Church and ministers to us when these gifts are in action.

Now for some, this kind of manifestation of the Spirit is undesirable.  When the Spirit manifests Himself in the gifts, He may say something we don't want to hear.  He may make sounds through us that don't make sense to us.  He may do something that is out of accord with how we understand our theology.  It can seem messy to us and we don't like it.

This leads to another form of manifestation of the Spirit that makes people uncomfortable called ecstatic experiences.  The Oxford English Dictionary defines ecstatic with such terms as "trance" and "frenzy." [25] I wouldn't bring this topic up if it weren't something that the Spirit has done in the Bible or in Church history. There are a few examples of this in the Scriptures and I believe that the Holy Spirit is still giving such experiences today.

As for trances there are a couple of good cases in the Book of Acts. The Apostle Paul related the following in Acts 22:17-21, "When I returned to Jerusalem and was praying in the temple, I fell into a trance and saw the Lord speaking. 'Quick!' he said to me. 'Leave Jerusalem immediately, because they will not accept your testimony about me.' 'Lord,' I replied, 'these men know that I went from one synagogue to another to imprison and beat those who believe in you. And when the blood of your martyr Stephen was shed, I stood there giving my approval and guarding the clothes of those who were killing him.' Then the Lord said to me, 'Go, I will send you far away to the Gentiles.'"

In this situation, Paul was telling a crowd about a conversation he had with God. The Lord had chosen to communicate with Paul by putting him in a trance. It was the same for the Apostle Peter. In Acts 10:9-19, we are told of Peter going on a rooftop to pray. While on the roof, he fell into a trance. The vision he received during this trance was used by God to prepare Peter for the ministry God wanted him to do next.

Neither of these two examples states that the trances were the work of the Spirit. Due to the means of communication (visions) we can deduce that this was a manifestation of the Holy Spirit. Both visions were prophetic in nature and it is the Spirit of God who works prophetically in the Church.

There is another kind of ecstatic manifestation of the Holy Spirit that we should recognize. Sometimes the Spirit has taken believers into times when He exerts control over them and they respond with physical manifestations.

1 Samuel 19:18-24 relates the situation when King Saul sent men to arrest David, while David was staying with Samuel.

"When David had fled and made his escape, he went to Samuel at Ramah and told him all that Saul had done to him. Then he and Samuel went to Naioth and stayed there. Word came to Saul: 'David is in Naioth at Ramah'; so he sent men to capture him. But when they saw a group of prophets prophesying, with Samuel standing there as their leader, the Spirit of God came upon Saul's men and they also prophesied. Saul was told about it, and he sent more men, and they prophesied too. Saul sent men a third time, and they also prophesied. Finally, he himself left for Ramah and went to the great cistern at Secu. And he asked, 'Where are Samuel and David?' 'Over at Naioth at Ramah,' they said. So Saul went to Naioth at Ramah. But the Spirit of God came even upon him, and he walked along prophesying until he came to Naioth. He stripped off his robes and also prophesied in Samuel's presence. He lay that way all that day and night. This is why people say, 'Is Saul also among the prophets?'"

The Holy Spirit took each group that came to capture David and caused them to prophesy. The New Revised Standard Version adds to our understanding of what took place before Samuel. It says that each group that came to take David went into a "prophetic frenzy." [26] They not only prophesied, but it could have been that they were experiencing bodily agitations. In King Saul's case, he stripped off his robes while in this state of prophetic frenzy.

The Reformed theologian, Alasdair Heron comments on this passage by writing, "Strange indeed though this behavior may seem to us, it well conveys the understanding of 'prophecy' at that period of Israel's history. It was a wild, ecstatic possession which was ascribed to the influence of God's *ruach*: 'prophet' meant much the same as the Islamic 'dervish.'" [27] He continued writing, "This is probably not quite what we normally have in mind when we repeat the words of the Nicene Creed and say of the Holy Spirit that he 'spoke' by the prophets'; but it is the association between *ruach* and prophecy that was apparently uppermost in that age." [28]

This was not the first time that King Saul had the experience of a prophetic frenzy. The first time was after he was anointed king. In 1 Samuel 10:5-13 Samuel told Saul,

"After that you shall come to Gibeath-elohim, at
the place where the Philistine garrison is; there,
as you come to the town, you will meet a band of
prophets coming down from the shrine with harp,
tambourine, flute, and lyre playing in front of
them; they will be in a prophetic frenzy. Then
the spirit of the Lord will possess you, and you
will be in a prophetic frenzy along with them and
be turned into a different person." (NRSV)

And that is what happened in 1 Samuel 10:10, "When they were going from there to Gibeah, a band of prophets met him; and the spirit of God possessed him, and he fell into a prophetic frenzy along with them." (NRSV) Thus, Saul prophesied by the Holy Spirit. And in the process of causing Saul to prophesy, the Spirit changed Saul so that he was different afterwards.

141

To have the Holy Spirit take over in such a powerful way also happened at Pentecost. In Acts 2 the Spirit so filled the Apostles that they spoke in tongues of many different nations. But Peter's explanation is quite extraordinary. He explained the event by saying, "Fellow Jews and all of you who live in Jerusalem, let me explain this to you; listen carefully to what I say. These men are not drunk, as you suppose. It's only nine in the morning! No, this is what was spoken by the prophet Joel..." (Acts 2:14b-16) Peter was trying to explain their behavior, because many thought them to be drunk.

When someone speaks in a foreign language, we don't usually assume they are drunk. I think that they were doing more than just speaking in tongues. Their manners needed explanation, since they were acting drunk. But why would the Holy Spirit have them act in such a way that would make Peter have to give such an answer to the crowd? I believe F.F. Bruce answered this when he wrote, "The ecstatic utterances had achieved a useful purpose in attracting a large crowd around the disciples." [29]

God uses ecstatic experiences as a sign of the work He is doing in us, through us and for us. For King Saul it was a sign of his anointing as king. For those trying to arrest David it was a sign of God's divine protection over the future king. In Acts 2 it was to get the attention of those in the area so they could hear the Gospel.

There are other ecstatic experiences given in the Bible. Here is a short list: Abraham receiving the covenant from God in a dream (Genesis), Daniel falling into a trance and shaking as he received answers from God by an angel (Daniel chapters 8 and 10), the Apostle John received the Revelation while in the Spirit on the Lord's Day (Revelation 1:9, 10; 4:2), and the Apostle Paul had an out-of-body or in-body experience in which he was caught up into paradise and heard inexpressible things (2 Corinthians 12:1-4).

An example of ecstatic experience is found in American Reformed history. Jonathan Edwards gave this description of what the Spirit was doing in many of the people during the meetings of the Great Awakening,

"Extraordinary views of divine things, and the religious affections, were frequently attended with very great effects on the body. Nature often sunk under the weight of divine discoveries, and the strength of the body was taken away. The person was deprived of all ability to stand or speak. Sometimes the hands were clenched, and the flesh cold, but the senses remaining. Animal nature was often in great emotion and agitation, and the soul so overcome with admiration and a kind of omnipotent joy, as to cause the person, unavoidably, to leap with all the might, with joy and mighty exultation." [30]

And, "Since this time there have often been great agitations of body, and an unavoidable leaping for joy; and the soul as it were dwelling, almost without interruption, in a kind of paradise." [31]

So that we can understand what was going on within those who were being affected so powerfully at these meetings by the Spirit of God, let's look at the writings of Jonathan Edwards' wife Sarah. She wrote out some of the experiences she had in the summer of 1740. For example she wrote,

"To my mind there was the clearest evidence, that God was present in the congregation, on the work of redeeming love; and in the clear view of this, I was all at once filled with such intense admiration of the wonderful condescension and grace of God, in returning again to Northampton, as overwhelmed my soul, and immediately took away my bodily strength." (32)

She described another experience by writing,

"After the prayer, Mr. Buell read two other hymns, on the glories of heaven, which moved me so exceedingly, and drew me so strongly heavenward, that it seemed as it were to draw my body upwards, and I felt as if I must necessarily ascend thither. At length my strength failed me, and I sunk down; when they took me up and laid me on the bed, where I lay for a considerable time, faint with joy, while contemplating the glories of the heavenly world." (33)

And I will give you one last example of what she experienced that summer. She wrote, "This conversation only served to give me a still livelier sense of the reality and excellence of divine things, and that to such a degree, as again to take away my strength, and occasion great agitation of body." (34)

Many of the manifestations described in the Bible and in the writings of Jonathan Edwards are taking place today. The Holy Spirit still manifests Himself in ways that seem strange to the rational mind. In recent revivals and renewals, people have experienced shaking, being slain in the spirit or falling, seeming drunk, laughing, receiving visions during trances and other similar manifestations of the Spirit. Many in the Church today are too quick to judge any manifestation as being wrong and unbiblical. If they did their homework, they would find that the Holy Spirit gives ecstatic manifestations. Just because we are uncomfortable with many of these experiences does not invalidate them.

Yet we know that all manifestations are not from God. So, how do we know if a manifestation is from God? John White wrote the best answer to this question in his book *When The Spirit Comes With Power*. He stated,

> "If we doubt the genuineness of the whole thing we should consider several factors. First, we must examine the teaching under which the manifestations occur (not relying only on gossipy reports since in every revival, critics distort the content of the preaching). Then we must observe the results in the lives of the people in whom they occur." [35]

The fruit in a person's life after a manifestation is the best indicator whether it was a work of the Holy Spirit or not. Does the person have an increased love for Jesus? Does the person show more signs of the fruit of the Spirit listed in Galatians 5:22-23 (love, joy, peace, patience, kindness, goodness, gentleness, faithfulness, and self-control)? Does the person have increased boldness and power to share the Gospel of Jesus Christ? These are the questions that should be answered in order to know if it has been from God.

For many people this just constitutes weirdness. But it is important that we do not reject these manifestations of the Spirit. Yes, we do need to use discernment when we see these manifestations appearing. The enemy will cause manifestations also. He will try to counterfeit the work of the Spirit. Some counterfeit manifestations are easy to detect. John White wrote of common demonic manifestations stating,

"Usually when they occur in Christian settings they include such things as blasphemous utterances, voices other than the person's own voice coming from the throat of an individual, animal-like movements and gestures (such as snakelike writhing)." [36]

The only other source of a manifestation is from a person who is faking the real thing. In this case I feel sorry for them and I hope they will stop. The Holy Spirit does not need their help.

The ecstatic manifestations are not the sum of the Spirit's work in our lives. Though it is great when the Holy Spirit ministers to His people in this way, there is so much more to what He wants to give to us and do through us. He wants to pour out His gifts in His Church.

The Holy Spirit is truly exciting in who He is and what He does. As you can see, when the Bible speaks of Him and what He did, it is some of the most exhilarating things we can read. The Holy Spirit is awesome. He is alive and constantly moving in ministry through and for the Church.

# Chapter Seven
## Why the Holy Spirit Gives the Gifts

We should expect that the Holy Spirit will use His gifts in the normal operation of each local church on a day by day, week by week and a month by month basis. Since every believer has been given the manifestation of the Spirit in the form of the gifts and since all of the gifts are still active today, this is our expectation.

There is so much that the Holy Spirit does within each congregation as He uses His gifts and demonstrates His power. There are many reasons why the Spirit actively uses His gifts and power in the local church.

Yet, many Christians do not see a need for power ministry in their local church and even if they think that the Bible says they should have it, they aren't sure why. They get excited about seeing God use His power in ministry, especially when He uses them, but sometimes they are not grounded enough in Scripture to know why God uses His power in them.

I am also amazed at the way some believers dismiss the relevance of God's ministry of power in our lives and our ministry. Again, I think this is because they have not studied the purposes for which God gives the gifts.

An example of not seeing the value of the gifts is found in the spring 1997 issue of the Reformed Quarterly. Dr. Robert Norris (senior pastor of Fourth Presbyterian Church in Washington D.C.) wrote, "And however much we may long for it and however much we may look for a special movement of God, miracles remain within the freedom of God to move behind the veil of nature. As a consequence, ministry cannot be built upon His unique movements, but rather upon the ordinary requirements that He has set to us." [1]

Dr. Norris' article states that we should base the ministry of the Church upon the example of John the Baptist. He wrote, "one simple verse found in John's gospel reminds us of what we are about." [2] That verse is John 10:41, which states, "and many people came to him (Jesus). They said, 'Though John never performed a miraculous sign, all that John said about this man was true.'" According to Dr. Norris, since this group of people told Jesus that John the Baptist "never performed a miraculous sign" therefore the power of God is unimportant for the Church today.

The article concludes by saying, "The Psalmist has said, 'with my whole heart have I sought Thee.' John, emulating this, was able to dispense with the necessity of miracle, knowing that his whole soul was bent upon carrying out the will of God as best it could be discerned." [3] This article demonstrates a lack of understanding of why God gives His gifts and their relevance for today.

In response to this article, we do not base our ministry in the Church solely upon the example of John the Baptist. As the Church, we must follow the examples of Jesus, the Apostles, and the Church of the First Century. A verse which should actually "remind us of what we are about" is John 14:12 as Jesus stated, "I tell you the truth, anyone who has faith in me will do what I have been doing. He will do even greater things than these, because I am going to the Father." As was shown in chapter two, Jesus was speaking about His miraculous works.

As the Holy Spirit empowers us to minister like Jesus and the Church of the First Century, it is important for us to know why the gifts and the use of God's power are given to the Church. We will start by looking at verses that directly state the purposes of the gifts and then we will examine other Scriptures that give us implied reasons for the gifts.

## #1 - Common Good of Believers

In 1 Corinthians 12:7 it states, "Now to each one the manifestation of the Spirit is given for the common good." The gifts are good and they are given for the benefit of the whole Church. When the Holy Spirit manifests His gifts in the local congregation it is for the good of each person in that congregation.

If you had asked any of the Apostles "Why does the Holy Spirit give the gifts?" I believe they would have answered, "For the common good of the Church." This is why B.B. Warfield's quote in Chapter One is wrong. Let me remind you that he wrote, "Had any miracle perchance occurred beyond the Apostolic Age they would be without significance; mere occurrences with no universal meaning." [4] The universal meaning and significance of God's supernatural power and miracles as displayed through His gifts begins with giving good things to His Church.

A fine example of what we mean by the gifts being given for the common good is found in 1 Corinthians 14:3. Here Paul wrote, "But everyone who prophesies speaks to men for their strengthening, encouragement and comfort." When the Holy Spirit uses the gift of prophecy in the Church it strengthens us. It can strengthen your faith and/or it can strengthen your resolve to follow Jesus during hard times.

A couple in a church I pastored was beginning to have difficulties with the husband's employer. As those troubles were starting, a woman in our church had a dream from God that showed that the troubles and persecution at work were going to get drastically worse, but that God would give him

149

another job where he would be valued. God gave another woman in our church a prophetic word that He was going to take this family to another location for that new job.

Sure enough, the work situation got worse. The boss began to spread gossip about this man in the community, withheld his mail at work, took away many of his health benefits and did other acts of persecution against this man (who was a new believer). But his family was able to stand with God in His strength and comfort due to these prophetic words. In the end, God moved them to another part of the state and he is working for a company that gives him value and respect.

All of the gifts are for the common good. Whether it is discernment of spirits, gifts of healing or any of the other gifts, God gives them for our good. I think that you will see that the other reasons I list for why God gives His gifts to us are also for our common good. As Paul wrote to the believers in Rome, "I long to see you so that I may impart to you some spiritual gift to make you strong – that is, that you and I may be mutually encouraged by each other's faith." (Romans 1:11-12)

## #2 – Building up the Church and Spiritual Growth

Ephesians 4:11-13 tells us, "It was he who gave some to be apostles, some to be prophets, some to be evangelists, and some to be pastors and teachers, to prepare God's people for works of service, so that the body of Christ may be built up until we all reach unity in the faith and in the knowledge of the Son of God and become mature, attaining to the whole measure of the fullness of Christ."

Some see these verses as pointing to offices in the Church, not gifting. Whether you see these five as offices or gifts, I believe that you cannot hold these offices unless the Spirit gives you corresponding gifts. For example, to be a prophet you must have the gift of prophecy. I will refer to these offices and their corresponding gifts as offices/gifts.

The great part of this passage is the list of what these offices/gifts give to the Church. First, these offices/gifts "prepare God's people for works of service." As these five offices/gifts work in the Church, we grow in our readiness to serve our Lord.

These offices/gifts build us up. The goal of this growing and building is so that we will be one in Christ. This unity in the faith mirrors what Jesus prayed for us in John 17:20-21a, "My prayer is not for them (the disciples) alone. I pray also for those who will believe in me through their message, that all of them may be one, Father, just as you are in me and I am in you." Could these five offices/gifts be the answer to our Lord's prayer? God desires that all believers be united in the faith.

Anyone who looks at the Church today knows that we have a long way to go before we reach unity. However, though the Church is not fully united, there are signs that God is moving us towards greater unity. The disunity of the Church is probably due to its rejection of some of these offices/gifts by so many of its denominations. As God continues to restore all of these offices/gifts to the Church, I believe that we will see increased unity in the Church amongst true believers, the kind of unity Jesus prayed that we would have. One day we will present ourselves to the world as one Church, not many churches.

Besides the two reasons for the offices/gifts just listed, the Scriptures give us a few more reasons for the gifts which are implied in different texts in the New Testament. I think that the following reasons are clearly demonstrated in the texts

151

themselves. You will also notice that these following points tend to overlap each other in their significance.

### #3 – To Reveal Jesus

One of the most wonderful things that happens when the Church exercises the gifts of God is that everyone involved has the name and power of Jesus Christ revealed to him or her. The gifts preach and proclaim Jesus. A classic example of this is found in Acts 3:1-26. As Peter and John are on their way to pray they come across a man who was unable to walk since birth. The man asks them for money, but Peter gives him something more. In verse 6 Peter states, "Silver and gold I do not have, but what I have I give you. In the name of Jesus Christ of Nazareth, walk." With this Peter helps the man to his feet and his legs are healed.

That man who was unable to walk had Jesus revealed to him that day. When I read that story I see Jesus displayed as the living God. He is the one who rose from the dead and rules as King. Not only is Jesus revealed in that very act of healing, that moment of power opened up an occasion for Peter and John to witness about Jesus to a crowd of people in verses 17-26.

Jesus Himself used healing, casting out demons and other acts of power to testify to who He is. In the ninth chapter of John, Jesus restored the sight of a man who was born blind. The Pharisees first interrogate the man and then throw him out of the synagogue for acknowledging what Jesus had done for him. I love the following verses of the passage which say, "Jesus heard that they had thrown him out, and when he found him, he said, 'Do you believe in the Son of Man?' 'Who is he, sir?' the man asked. 'Tell me so that I may believe in him.' Jesus said, 'You have now seen him; in fact, he is the one speaking with you.' Then the man said, 'Lord, I believe,' and he worshiped him.' (John 9:35-38) The man believed in Jesus and worshiped Him. That day Jesus was revealed to the healed man as God.

It is clear in the words of Jesus that ministry in power testifies to who He is. In John 14:10-11 Jesus told His disciples, "Don't you believe that I am in the Father, and that the Father is in me? The words I say to you are not just my own. Rather, it is the Father, living in me, who is doing his work. Believe me when I say that I am in the Father and the Father is in me; or at least believe on the evidence of the miracles themselves." The Father did His work through Jesus to show us evidence that Jesus was in the Father and the Father was in Jesus. This is a testimony to the deity of Jesus. His unity with the Father is one way that we see His deity in the Bible.

This passage is like an earlier one in chapter 10 of John. Here Jesus is having a discussion with the Jews. It tells us, "Again the Jews picked up stones to stone him, but Jesus said to them, 'I have shown you many great miracles from the Father, for which of these do you stone me?' 'We are not stoning you for any of these,' replied the Jews, 'but for blasphemy, because you, a mere man, claim to be God.'" (John 10:31-33) Part of Jesus' response to this is found in John 10:37-39 in which He states, "Do not believe me unless I do what my Father does. But if I do it, even though you do not believe me, believe the miracles, that you may learn and understand that the Father is in me, and I in the Father.' Again they tried to seize him, but he escaped their grasp."

Jesus states that the miracles from the Father reveal that He is in the Father and the Father is in Him. The Jews want to stone Him because this is a claim to unity with the Father and His own deity.

The Father worked miracles through Jesus to show the world and us that Jesus is who He claimed to be. As Dr. Jack Deere wrote,

"One clear purpose of miracles was to authenticate the character of Jesus and his relationship with his heavenly Father. In this regard, miracles demonstrate the following: God is with Jesus (John 3:2); Jesus is from God (John 3:2, 9:32-33); God has sent Jesus (John 5:36); Jesus has authority on earth to forgive sins (Mark 2:10-11; Matt. 9:6-7; Luke 5:24-25); Jesus is approved by God (Acts 2:22); the Father is in Jesus and Jesus is in the Father (John 10:37-38; 14:11); in Jesus the kingdom of God has come (Matt. 12:28; Luke 11:20); and Jesus is the Messiah (Matt. 11:1-6; Luke 7:18-23) and the Son of God (Matt. 14:25-33)." [5]

I believe that the Father still does His works in the Church for the same purpose: to show that Jesus is God. There are many testimonies that I hear coming from all over the world of people who see the power of God in works of healing and come to faith in Jesus. This leads us to the next purpose of the gifts and the power of God in the Church.

### #4 – To Bring About Evangelism

One thing I have noticed is that evangelism is much easier when someone has experienced the power of God. This is why John Wimber (Vineyard Christian Fellowship) wrote the book *Power Evangelism*. Wimber explains, "By power evangelism I mean a presentation of the gospel that is rational but that also transcends the rational. The explanation of the gospel comes with a demonstration of God's power through signs and wonders… Power evangelism is evangelism that is preceded and undergirded by supernatural demonstrations of God's presence." [6] I think that he is right and that "power evangelism" is an extremely useful and biblical way of reaching the lost.

We can see the biblical validity of this type of evangelism throughout the New Testament. Though I could list story after story of "power evangelism" from the Gospels and the book of Acts, I would prefer to show it in the writings of the Apostle Paul.

In the book of Romans Paul wrote, "I will not venture to speak of anything except what Christ has accomplished through me in leading the Gentiles to obey God by what I have said and done – by the power of signs and miracles, through the power of the Spirit." (Romans 15:18-19) Gordon Fee comments on these verses by writing, "Paul begins by indicating the two means by which Christ has been effectively at work through him: by 'word' and 'deed.' 'Word' surely refers to his proclamation of the gospel; but 'deed' calls for some explanation, so he immediately adds, 'by the power of signs and miracles.'" [7] Paul did ministry in a two-pronged fashion. He fully preached the Gospel, but he didn't just preach the Gospel by using words. He told them about the good news and he ministered the Gospel by demonstrating its power.

Considering that Paul's letter to the Romans is held by many theologians to be an overview of Paul's theology, is it possible that we are also receiving the same of Paul's philosophy of ministry? If that were the case, we would have to see Paul express the same duality of "word" and "power/deed" in other epistles also. I will show you two other epistles that demonstrate this mixture in addition to the book of Romans.

In 1 Corinthians 2:1-5 Paul states, "When I came to you, brothers, I did not come with eloquence or superior wisdom as I proclaimed to you the testimony about God. For I resolved to know nothing while I was with you except Jesus Christ and him crucified. I came to you in weakness and fear, and with much trembling. My message and my preaching were not with wise and persuasive words, but with a demonstration of the Spirit's power, so that your faith might not rest on men's wisdom, but on God's power."

It is clear in this passage that Paul used a mix of preaching and demonstrating the power of the Spirit to convince the Corinthians to follow Jesus. I believe he did the same thing in Thessalonica.

In 1 Thessalonians 1:4-5 Paul wrote, "For we know, brothers loved by God, that he has chosen you, because our gospel came to you not simply with words, but also with power, with the Holy Spirit and with deep conviction. You know how we lived among you for your sake." Paul brought the Gospel to the Thessalonians "not simply with words, but also with power." Though this passage does not distinctly say that Paul used the gifts, Fee comments, "the Spirit is the key; and there was an evidential expression to the work of the Spirit, that Paul refers to as power, to which he can appeal so as to make his point stick." [8]

So we can see that the use of the gifts and other manifestations of the Spirit can be key to bringing people into a personal relationship with Jesus. God has used deliverance and revelatory experiences to open peoples' eyes to the truth of who He is and what He wants for their lives. The gifts themselves do not save people, but they create an environment of openness in people to hear what a believer has to say.

While I was teaching Bible classes in a Christian High School, I got to know a student named Chris. Once a week we would have a Bible study during lunch. It was during one of those studies that Chris told me of a dream he had the night before. In the dream he died and went to Heaven. Once there, he stood before a table and a man sitting at that table opened a book. After looking through the book the man said that Chris' name wasn't there. Chris then began to fall and landed in darkness.

After telling me the dream he asked me what it meant. I told him that God speaks in dreams and that this dream was pretty clear. But before telling him the meaning of the dream I asked him the classic question. "Chris, if you were to die today why would God let you into Heaven?" He thought for a moment and told me that he had been an altar boy at church a few times. At that point I decided to tell him the meaning of the dream.

I said, "Chris, God has shown you what will happen if you were to die right now. You will not stay in Heaven, but go into the darkness, which is Hell." He immediately decided he didn't want to go to Hell again and asked how to get into Heaven. I led him in the believer's prayer. It was the easiest evangelism I have ever done. I was just glad that God let me be involved in what He was doing with Chris. The Holy Spirit manifested a dream in Chris that would open his ears to hear and accept the Gospel.

Why does God work miracles, speak prophetically, give visions and dreams, cast out demons, and heal people in conjunction with evangelism? He does it to tell us that the Gospel message about His salvation for us in Jesus is genuine. Dr. Jack Deere states,

"A second purpose of miracles was to authenticate the message about Jesus. This was the major function of the miracles as far as the ministry of the apostles was concerned.

Mark says that the Lord 'confirmed his word (that the apostles preached) by the signs that accompanied it' (Mark 16:20). When Luke was describing the ministry of Paul and Barnabas at Iconium, he said that the Lord 'confirmed the message of his grace by enabling them to do miraculous signs and wonders' (Acts 14:3). Notice that in both of these texts the Lord does not confirm the apostles themselves but rather 'his word' or 'the message' that the apostles were preaching." [9]

The only messenger that God authenticated was Jesus Himself. As for the rest of us, including the apostles, God authenticates the message He has given us by using His grace in salvation and works of power. As I have said, there is nothing more exciting than when God is ministering to people in power as we are doing evangelism. It makes it much easier to tell someone about Jesus.

### #5 – To Bring About Repentance

God uses the gifts to bring about repentance both in the process of evangelism and in the life of believers. A good example of the gifts being used by the Spirit to cause someone to repent of their sins is found in 1 Corinthians 14:24-25 in which Paul wrote,

"But if an unbeliever or someone who does not understand comes in while everybody is prophesying, he will be convinced by all that he is a sinner and will be judged by all, and the secrets of his heart will be laid bare. So he will fall down and worship God, exclaiming, 'God is really among you!'"

Here the revelatory gifts are used to expose the hidden sin in a person's life. In the churches I have pastored, the Holy Spirit has used prophecy, words of knowledge and discernment of spirits to bring people to repentance. Sometimes an individual will get a word from the Spirit about a person's sin. One person may have a dream about the situation, another person will get a Scripture, while a third person may know of the presence of a specific demonic spirit that may be feeding off the sin. As a pastor, I have seen a number of people who, once confronted with the information supplied by the Spirit, have repented and sought God's forgiveness.

But miracles and the use of the gifts don't always bring repentance. And if there is not repentance God will speak judgment instead. An example of this is found in Matthew 11:20-23.

"Then Jesus began to denounce the cities in which most of his miracles had been performed, because they did not repent. 'Woe to you, Korazin! Woe to you, Bethsaida! If the miracles that were performed in you had been performed in Tyre and Sidon, they would have repented long ago in sackcloth and ashes. But I tell you, it will be more bearable for Tyre and Sidon on the day of judgment than for you. And you, Capernaum, will you be lifted up to the skies? No, you will go down to the depths. If the miracles that were performed in you had been performed in Sodom, it would have remained to this day. But I tell you that it will be more bearable for Sodom on the day of judgment than for you.'"

Jesus indicates that the cities of Tyre, Sidon, and Sodom would all have repented of their sin if they had witnessed the miracles that Jesus did in Korazin, Bethsaida and Capernaum.

But why didn't the ministry of power and healing bring about repentance in these three cities? Their hearts were hardened to God. An act of God's power is not a guarantee that people will turn to Jesus, but it does make a significant difference in many places where the Holy Spirit has softened minds and hearts to receive His work and word. He can also use His power to do the work of opening people to the Gospel.

I remember hearing stories in seminary of missionaries and church planters who would enter third world villages and offer to heal people in the name of Jesus. Once the village witnessed the power of God, they wanted to hear the Gospel.

### #6 – To Show God's Compassion

This is one of my favorite reasons for believing God uses His power in touching people's lives. He allows our hurts and pains to move His heart. God has sympathy for us. Many times we don't view God in this way. Many Christians see God as an unemotional being who loves us in a theological manner, rather than from the heart. This is a grave mistake. For God loves us both in truth and in heart-felt emotion.

How do I know that God moves in compassion? How do I know that our physical, emotional and spiritual hurts touch God's heart and move Him to reach into our lives and heal us? We can see it in the ministry of Jesus Himself. Jesus healed some simply because He was moved with compassion for them. Let me give you three such cases from the Gospels.

Matthew 14:14 states, "When Jesus landed and saw a large crowd, he had compassion on them and healed their sick." These people had traveled to find Jesus and when they did, He was moved by their need for Him and His powerful ministry. A similar thing happened when two blind men cried out to Jesus for help. Matthew 20:34 tells us that, "Jesus had compassion on them and touched their eyes. Immediately they received their sight and followed him." Jesus had sympathy for these two men who couldn't see. He was moved by their cries for help.

In the third case, Luke relates the situation of a widow whose only son had died. According to custom she was in desperate straits. A widow without a son has no means of supporting herself. She will live by the mercy of others. Jesus meets her and others as they are taking her dead son out of the gates of the town.

"When the Lord saw her, his heart went out to her and he said, 'Don't cry.' Then he went up and touched the coffin, and those carrying it stood still. He said, 'Young man, I say to you, get up!' The dead man sat up and began to talk, and Jesus gave him back to his mother. They were all filled with awe and praised God." (Luke 7:13-16a)

I really like the results when God moves by compassion. Not only do blind men see and dead men come to life, but also people are "filled with awe" and praise Him. Others begin to follow Him.

## #7 – To Demonstrate the Presence of God's Kingdom

Not only does power ministry (miracles and the gifts of the Spirit) work for the common good of believers, build up the Church, reveal Jesus, bring about evangelism, bring about repentance and show God's compassion, it also demonstrates that God's kingdom is a present reality.

As Jesus said in Matthew 12:28, "But if I drive out demons by the Spirit of God, then the kingdom of God has come upon you." As we heal and cast out demons as commanded by Jesus in Luke 9:1-2 and 10:9 we show those around us that the kingdom of God has come upon them.

This is in keeping with Jesus' own ministry as we see in Matthew 4:23, "Jesus went throughout Galilee, teaching in their synagogues, preaching the good news of the kingdom, and healing every disease and sickness among the people." And Matthew 9:35, "Jesus went through all the towns and villages, teaching in their synagogues, preaching the good news of the kingdom and healing every disease and sickness." The Holy Spirit seemed to think it was important to repeat this in the Gospel of Matthew, so He must want us to get the point.

The kingdom of God did not leave when Jesus ascended into heaven. It is still present and it is still powerful. Every time I see the power of God ministered to someone by a follower of Jesus Christ I am reminded of the presence of God's kingdom in our lives and in the world.

## Final Thoughts

I can think of other reasons that God continues to use all of His gifts in the Church. Since casting out of demons is mentioned, we know that the gifts are also given to help in spiritual warfare. The gifts are used to aid the ministry of intercession. The list could go on.

God will use His gifts in any believer for all of the reasons just listed. I can tell you that He will not use His gifts in you to put on a show, to give you financial gain, to fill you with pride so that you feel more important and more spiritual than other believers. The gifts are for the purpose of ministry. They are given to the body of Christ for the advancement of the Church.

Though I have grown in my walk with God in incredible ways because of the Spirit's use of power in the Church as people have ministered to me, I have also grown because of the Spirit using His gifts in me to minister to other people.

I have learned about the heart of God. God loves us intensely. Jesus meant it when He said, "God so loved the world that he gave his one and only Son..." (John 3:16). God really does love the people on this earth. They are His creation and all humans are made in His image. Jesus also meant it when He said, "the Father himself loves you because you have loved me and have believed that I came from God." (John 16:27). Father God loves us and I know this because of the Scriptures and many of the prophecies I have heard. Many times the prophetic word to the local church is about how much God loves them and wants to bless them.

A long time ago I read a book written by a pastor named Buck. I don't remember the man's full name and I don't even remember the name of the book. But I do remember that the pastor had a vision of being in heaven with God and that God had a message for this pastor's church. God said, "Tell them that I love them." That prophetic word from that vision has been engraved on my heart. I think that message is for all of us. God loves His people and wants to minister in power to them and through them. God also loves the people in this world and wants His Church to bring the loving message of the Gospel to them with power.

I have learned about how God wants to touch the hurts people have. I have seen God use His gifts to put people back together again after they have fallen apart physically, mentally, emotionally and spiritually. My uncle, who is a minister of the Gospel, once passed on to me a statement his uncle had told him. "Remember that everyone has hurts and everyone is a little lonely." This dictum is true and we follow a wonderful God who wants to heal those hurts and be with His people. He does much of this through His gifts. He uses each of His gifts in accomplishing this task.

# Chapter Eight
## Spiritual Gifts and How God Uses Them

One of the most exciting things in life is to experience the power of God. This, of course, leads to one of my passions: studying the Bible to learn more about the gifts. As we study the gifts, we will have a better idea of what to expect as God ministers in the Church. There are quite a few misconceptions about the gifts. As we have seen, one misconception is that the gifts have ceased. But there are many other wrong ideas about the gifts. As we define the gifts, we will eliminate many of the problems and outmoded ideas surrounding this area of our spiritual life.

Let me begin by giving you a definition of the gifts of the Spirit. The gifts are manifestations of the Holy Spirit's power that He uses through Christians for ministry. The gifts are not our natural human abilities or talents. As an example, I have heard other Christians call their ability to play the guitar a spiritual gift. God can surely give us the talent to play an instrument, sing or be skilled as a craftsman, but those things are not part of the charismatic gifts of the Spirit.

We will use this chapter to examine the gifts found in 1 Corinthians 12:7-11: the message of wisdom, the message of knowledge, faith, gifts of healings, miraculous powers, prophecy, distinguishing between spirits, tongues, and interpretation of tongues. I will also write on apostleship, since it is inter-related to the rest of the gifts. Many traditions limit the gifts to the list given in 1 Corinthians 12, but others also include those found in Romans 12:3-8; Ephesians 4:11-13; and 1 Peter 4:10-11.

## Healing

The actual translation for "gift of healing" tells us there is more than one type of healing gift. Gordon Fee comments, "the plural *charismata* probably suggests not a permanent 'gift,' as it were, but that each occurrence is a 'gift' in its own right." [1] This may be the case; no one really knows. The understanding I like the most is that there are different gifts of healing for different illnesses. One person may have a gift from God for healing cancer while another may have a gift for healing heart problems. Yet, I have met people with the gift of healing whom God uses to heal many different sicknesses. If you have a gift of healing, then the Holy Spirit manifests through you to heal people.

I define gifts of healing as a manifestation of the Holy Spirit in which He imparts power for healing. The Greek word used in the passage is *iama* and it is translated as a healing or a means of healing. Now there are two other words in New Testament Greek used for healing: *therapeuo* and *sozo*. *Therapeuo* means to attend to, cure or care for the sick. It is used in Matthew 12:15 when Jesus healed the multitudes that followed Him and in Luke 10 when He sent the seventy-two to go before Him and heal. *Sozo* means to make sound or whole and salvation from acute danger. It is used in Mark 5:22-23 when Jairus asked Jesus to come heal his daughter and in James 5:14-15 in which the sick are instructed to call for the elders and they will pray with faith and anoint with oil for *sozo* healing.

We see more of how the gift of healing is used by the Holy Spirit as we look at how the word *iama* is used in the Gospels. Luke 5:17 says "power was present for healing." Luke 6:19 states that "power came forth from Him and healed them all." Then in Luke 8:43-47, when the woman with the flow of blood was healed, Jesus said He felt power go out from Him.  And in Luke 9:1, Jesus gave the Twelve power to heal.  From these verses we can see that *iama* healing involves power manifesting in us for healing.  So, in light of this I would say that a believer who is gifted by the Holy Spirit with gifts of healing will have times when the Holy Spirit will give them power to heal someone; His power will come through them.

Healing is one of the signs that the Kingdom is present.  I believe that any follower of Jesus can pray for someone's healing, those with gifts of healing will see a higher percentage of people being healed.  Gifting operates in *iama* and the rest of us usually operate in *therapeuo* or *sozo*.  That is not to say that the Holy Spirit cannot manifest *iama* healing through any believer, because He can.  The Holy Spirit can use any gift in any believer at any time.  The majority of believers will be used by the Spirit with gifts of healing most of the time.  I have seen God use me to heal people, but healing is not my primary gifting.

Justin, the two-year-old son of a couple in a church I pastored in Santa Maria, California had his leg crushed in an accident.  The parents came to the worship service and said they needed a miracle.  The doctors said that Justin's leg was severely damaged since the growth plates in his bones had been broken.  The parents were told that it would take several surgeries in the coming years to fix the leg, but even then the leg would not grow properly and he would have trouble running.  On top of all this, the parents did not have medical insurance to pay for the surgeries.

Immediately following the worship service a number of elders and church members laid hands on the boy and prayed healing into the leg in the name and authority of Jesus.  We couldn't see whether the leg was healed or not because he was wearing a cast.

Later that week the parents came to see me. With tears in their eyes, they shared that they had taken their son to the doctor earlier that day to prepare for surgery. Upon removing the cast for the surgery, the doctor declared the leg to be as good as new. The parents still wanted to have an x-ray taken of the leg for confirmation. The x-ray confirmed what the doctor said. The healing could have been instant or it could have taken several days, however, the parents received from God what they had asked for. The leg was miraculously healed.

This is just one of the many examples I have seen in the churches I have pastored. But I believe the news more wonderful than this is that God has deposited His gifts of healing in members of every local church.

How do you know if you personally have gifts of healing? You have to try praying for people who are sick and see if God heals them. If someone is sick then follow Jesus' example in Luke 4:40 which says, "At sunset, the people brought to Jesus all who had various kinds of sickness, and laying hands on each one, he healed them." When someone needs healing, ask him or her if you can lay hands on them, and pray for God to heal them. You can pray for healing, rebuke the sickness, or if the Holy Spirit leads you, speak God's healing over them. You can also follow the directions given to elders in James 5:14-15, "Is anyone among you sick? Let them call the elders of the church to pray over them and anoint them with oil in the name of the Lord. And the prayer offered in faith will make the sick person well; the Lord will raise them up. If they have sinned, they will be forgiven."

This brings us to an interesting question: Is all sickness a result of sin? Consider this conversation between Jesus and

His disciples in John 9:1-3, "As he went along, he saw a man blind from birth. His disciples asked him, 'Rabbi, who sinned, this man or his parents, that he was born blind?' 'Neither this man nor his parents sinned,' said Jesus, 'but this happened so that the work of God might be displayed in his life.'" Jesus dismissed the idea that ALL sickness is a result of personal sin.

But before you make the opposite conclusion that no sickness is the result of personal sin, let me quote from 1 Corinthians 11:29-30, "For anyone who eats and drinks without recognizing the body of the Lord eats and drinks judgment on himself. That is why many among you are weak and sick, and a number of you have fallen asleep." I read this as a warning when I serve communion during worship. It is a forewarning that sickness and death can result from the sin of taking communion for the wrong reasons.

So, how do you know if the sickness is caused by sin or not? Is the sickness simply physical, psychological or even from a demonic spirit of infirmity? All of this takes evaluation. Some healings are just physical healings. A person is sick, you pray for them to be healed, and the person is healed. I have seen this happen many times.

Some healings are not just physical healings. As it is written in Luke 13:11-11-13, "and a woman was there who had been crippled by a spirit for eighteen years. She was bent over and could not straighten up at all. When Jesus saw her, he called her forward and said to her, 'Woman, you are set free from your infirmity.' Then he put his hands on her, and immediately she straightened up and praised God." Jesus delivered her from a spirit of sickness.

Some demons have the function of making people sick. Jesus also rebuked such a demon in Matthew 17:14-18.

"When they came to the crowd, a man approached Jesus and knelt before him. 'Lord, have mercy on my son,' he said. 'He is an epileptic and is suffering greatly. He often falls into the fire or into the water. I brought him to your disciples, but they could not heal him.' 'Oh unbelieving and perverse generation,' Jesus replied, 'how long shall I stay with you? How long shall I put up with you? Bring the boy to me.' Jesus rebuked the demon, and it came out of the boy, and he was healed from that moment."

From this passage we see the boy was healed of epilepsy when Jesus cast the demon out. So some healing comes as the result of spiritual warfare. As believers rebuke demons of infirmity, people are healed. This does not mean that every sickness is caused by a demon or that we should rebuke a demon of sickness every time we pray for a person's healing. It takes discernment from the Spirit.

I experienced such an occasion while taking a group of high school students on a short-term mission trip to Reynosa, Mexico. About halfway through our week in Mexico one of the students, named Todd, came to me during my morning quiet-time. He told me that he was feeling sick to his stomach as if he had the flu. I thought, "Lord, the last thing I want to do is to stay here all day and watch Todd throw up." So, we started to pray for his healing. As we began to pray, I felt the Spirit give me discernment that his sickness was not purely physical, but was a demonic attack of sickness against this young man. So I rebuked the sickness. He was soon ready to go to our work site. Not only was he ready, but within the hour, Todd joined us for a huge breakfast before we left for our work.

Many people ask why someone is not healed of a sickness or disability after they are prayed for. I don't have all the answers to that question, but I do think we need to exercise more discernment from the Holy Spirit as we pray. We have to know what kind of healing the person needs. A sickness may seem purely physical, but the person may also be in need of inner healing, may be under demonic attack, or the sickness may be related to personal sin. There is no real formula for knowing which it is. We must listen to the Holy Spirit.

The best way to know if a sickness is caused by a demonic spirit is to have someone with the gift of discerning of spirits evaluate them. Another clue is if the sickness is not responding to medication. It is also true to say that if the sickness is not responding to medication, it could be that the virus has mutated into another strain or the sickness could also be psychosomatic. The point is that we need to ask God for direction and keep praying for the person.

It is always good to keep praying for healing if the healing hasn't happened or there has only been a little improvement. In Mark 8:22-25, "They came to Bethsaida, and some people brought a blind man and begged Jesus to touch him. He took the blind man by the hand and led him outside the village. When he had spit on the man's eyes and put his hands on him, Jesus asked, 'Do you see anything?' He looked up and said, 'I see people; they look like trees walking around.' Once more Jesus put his hands on the man's eyes. Then his eyes were opened, his sight was restored, and he saw everything clearly."

If Jesus prayed for this man twice, we may have to pray for people a bunch of times. Why did Jesus have to minister healing to this man twice? I don't know, He didn't say. But this example keeps me from coming up with a formula that says healing must happen the first time I pray for someone.

We must also exercise more faith when praying for healing. Whichever kind of healing someone needs, it is important for us to exercise the kind of faith found in James 5:15 which says, "And the prayer offered in faith will make the sick person well; the Lord will raise him up." God has been in the process of raising the faith level in the churches I have pastored. Many are getting to the point where they pray with the expectation that God will answer them and will heal those they pray for.

Over the years, God has shown us an increasing level of His power in answer to our prayers. One Sunday at one of my former churches, a church member named Cheryl asked me to pray during the worship service for her grandfather, Vern, who was in the hospital. The doctors had given him two more days before he would die. He had pneumonia, his white blood cell count was low, and his liver was failing. We prayed during the service for his healing. That afternoon Cheryl called me to say that she had gone to visit her grandfather and the doctors said they were going to send him home in two days. They said that somehow that morning the pneumonia cleared up, the white cell count returned to normal and his liver was fine. God added one more year to her grandfather's life.

In another situation, a woman asked me and one of my church elders to pray for her son who lived in another state. He had been in a coma for many months. We prayed and asked God to lift the coma. That very afternoon we received a call with the news that her son had come out of the coma and was well.

This is all very exciting, but I can remember a time when I was fearful about praying for someone's healing. I had serious doubts. What if they weren't healed? How would that reflect on my spirituality? If they weren't healed, would that be a reason for someone to turn away from God or doubt His existence?

I was afraid to pray for healing, but God taught me to get past my fear. I no longer worry about those things. I am excited about the times I see God heal people and touch them with power and I enjoy each testimony that shows God's reality and His mercy. I was able to get over my fears of praying for healing when I began to realize that it was God's will for me to pray that way.

Look again at James 5:14-15: "Is anyone of you sick? He should call the elders of the church to pray over him and anoint him with oil in the name of the Lord. And the prayer offered in faith will make the sick person well; the Lord will raise him up." This is a clear injunction for elders and other members of the church to seek to be healed and to pray for healing when we are sick. We are to give God a "prayer offered in faith" to see people healed. As a pastor, I remind the elders in the churches I pastor that they are to be ready to pray with faith for the healing of someone who is sick. God's will is that they pray for healing in every case.

I also make anointing oil available to each elder when they pray for the sick. The passage tells us to anoint with oil those who are sick. I believe that the oil represents God's authority for using His power to heal. In the Bible, whether the oil is being applied to a new king or a new priest, it is used to anoint and prepare individuals by a show of His authority.

Not only do we pray and anoint with oil, but we also lay on hands in the process of praying for healing. Jesus set this example. In Matthew 8:1-3 says, "When he came down from the mountainside, large crowds followed him. A man with leprosy came and knelt before him and said, 'Lord, if you are willing, you can make me clean.' Jesus reached out his hand and touched the man, 'I am willing,' he said. 'Be clean!' Immediately he was cured of his leprosy." [2] Among the many things we can learn from observing Jesus' ministry, laying hands on the sick is one of them.

We offer to lay hands and pray for anyone who has any form of infirmity in our church during the worship service. One Sunday, a woman named Elizabeth was visiting our church and asked for prayer. She was suffering from cancer and also used an oxygen tank. She told us that she wanted to receive prayer and have us lay hands on her, so we did. Later, she had to leave the worship service before it ended because her oxygen tank wasn't working right and she couldn't go without this extra oxygen for more than a few minutes.

Upon request, I called Elizabeth during that same week. She told me that she had been off her oxygen for a few hours that day and was praising God for it. A couple of days later God had so healed her lungs of cancer that she no longer needed the oxygen tank at all.

To see people healed and to witness God use gifts of healing is wonderful. I wish all Christians could see what I have seen (and I know that I haven't seen as much as other Christians have!) But I have heard some strange objections to praying for healing or allowing the use of that gift in the Church. These objections were used to try to convince me that the Church should not pursue healing.

One person told me of a man who demanded God heal his daughter who was in a coma. She came out of the coma, but lived in a vegetative state the rest of her life. In his mind this healing was the wrong thing to ask for in light of her diminished life capacity.

A missionary told me of a man who was healed and went to tell the elders of his church. The elders did not believe that God heals anymore, so they instructed the man to rebuke the healing. The man did and his body returned to its former infirmity. The missionary told me that this was proof that "Satan is the only one healing now, not God."

Since these were just stories which were told to me, I cannot verify whether they are actually true or not. No one should allow stories like these to be a reason for denying the clear teaching of Scripture to pray for healing.

I believe that all Christians can pray with authority for another person's healing. Healing is a kingdom activity. I base this on Luke 9:1-2 and Luke 10:9 when Jesus instructed the Twelve and the seventy-two to heal the sick and proclaim the kingdom of God. Any Christian can pray for the healing of an infirmity. This is an exercise of authority and power in the name of Jesus. I also believe that those whom the Holy Spirit uses with gifts of healing will see greater frequency of healings as a result of their ministry in this area. The best way to know if you have this gifting is to start praying for people who are sick. In fact, I encourage all Christians to pray with authority for the healing of the sick. Expect God to do great ministry through you, whether you have this gift or not.

How do you know if the Holy Spirit uses this gift in you? Here are some signs of this gift: 1) When you lay hands on people and pray for their healing, a high percentage are healed, 2) You feel power for healing. Some commonly feel heat or power in their hands, 3) You have a deep compassion for people who are sick – Matthew 14:14, 20:34, and 4) The person being prayed for can feel heat or power in the sick or injured body part when you pray for them.

## Prophecy

Within the Reformed tradition there is a misunderstanding as to what prophecy is today. Many think that modern day prophecy is no more than preaching the

175

Word.  In other words, when a pastor gives the sermon at a worship service he is prophesying.  This view started with John Calvin and can be seen in his writings.  In his commentary on 1 Corinthians 12:28 he wrote, "Let us, then, by *Prophets* in this passage understand, first of all, eminent interpreters of Scripture..." [3]  In Calvin's mind, New Testament prophecy is foremost the act of interpreting or expounding the Bible.  I heartily disagree.

The gift of prophecy is not the ability to preach a good sermon or teach a good lesson.  Graham Cooke points out the difference between preaching/teaching and prophecy in this way:

"Put simply, teaching allows us to gain a full understanding of God's **principles** for life, growth and service, etc.  Prophecy imparts the express **purpose** of God in our current situation.  We can understand it better if we think in terms of mind and heart.  Teaching shows us the mind of God whilst prophecy often reveals his heart." [4]

As we try to understand this gift, it is important that we define it.  Prophecy is the supernatural manifestation of the Holy Spirit by which He forth-tells and foretells truth to us.  The Holy Spirit speaks forth what is going on in a given situation or within us.  Sometimes God will use prophecy to reveal hidden sin in our lives, or to encourage us and strengthen us in a given situation.  The Holy Spirit also uses prophecy to speak of events and possible outcomes that will happen in the future; He may give an indication of how He will bless us or of coming problems.

It is exciting when you pore over the Biblical texts which tell us of the prophetic ministry which God has given to the Church.  The foremost of these passages for me is Acts 2:16-18:

"No, this is what was spoken by the prophet Joel, 'In the last days, God says, I will pour out my Spirit on all people. Your sons and daughters will prophesy, your young men will see visions, your old men will dream dreams. Even on my servants, both men and women, I will pour out my Spirit in those days, and they will prophesy.'"

Peter tells us that this prophecy is being fulfilled in the Church, and this tells us some of what God has given to the Church.  Prophecy is for the Body of Christ.  It is for use by the whole Church.  As Jack Deere wrote, "In the Old Testament there were relatively few prophets and seldom did anyone other than a prophet prophesy.  In the New Testament the coming of the Spirit changed all that." [5]  We now live in a time when the Spirit of God can and will use any believer to give a prophetic word.  It is true that while the Spirit still gives the gift of prophecy only to some, it is possible for Him to speak through any other believer at a given moment.

Mike Bickle, founder of the International House of Prayer, gives the best idea of how this works.  He lists four levels of prophetic ministry in his book *Growing In The Prophetic*.  They are: 1) Simple prophetic, "when any believer speaks something God has brought to mind." [6]  2) Prophetic gifting, "Believers who regularly receive impressions, dreams, visions or other types of revelation." [7]  3) Prophetic ministry, in which, "Believers whose gifting has been recognized, nurtured and commissioned for regular ministry in the local church." [8]  and 4) Prophetic office, "They often minister in signs and wonders and are known to speak 100 percent accurate words from God." [9]  Bickle adds, "Their credibility has been clearly established by their proven track record of accurate prophecies." [10] Bickle goes into much more detail in describing each of these levels, but this gives you a general idea. It is important to remember that just because a believer gives a prophetic word to someone, it doesn't mean that person is a prophet or even gifted with prophecy.

How does God give prophecy? The Bible tells us how God imparts prophecy to a believer. In Numbers 12:6-8, God tells Moses, Aaron, and Miriam:

"He said, 'When a prophet of the Lord is among you, I reveal myself to him in visions, I speak to him in dreams. But this is not true of my servant Moses; he is faithful in all my house. With him I speak face to face, clearly and not in riddles; he sees the form of the Lord. Why then were you not afraid to speak against my servant Moses?"

This passage tells us of three methods by which God gives prophecy. The two most common are visions and dreams. Acts 2:17b also states this, "Your sons and daughters will prophesy, your young men will see visions, your old men will dream dreams." The Bible is full of individuals who received prophecy by this method. The list includes: Abraham, Joseph, Ezekiel, Daniel, Peter, Paul and John.

James Ryle writes the definition of a vision as, "to gaze upon, to perceive with the mind and to contemplate with pleasure."[11] Visions usually take place while the person is awake. God can cause them to fall into a trance or He can just show them the vision. As for dreams, I have heard some people call them visions of the night that take place while sleeping.

As the verses in Numbers inform us, much of prophecy through dreams and visions are riddles. We must then seek the Lord for the understanding of the riddle. Even for those who are gifted in interpretation it is not always easy. About the prophet Daniel the Bible says, "And Daniel could understand visions and dreams of all kinds." (Daniel 1:17b) Yet, Daniel received a revelation that he spent considerable time seeking to understand. In Daniel 10:1-3 it says,

> "In the third year of Cyrus king of Persia, a revelation was given to Daniel (who was called Belteshazzar). Its message was true and it concerned a great war. The understanding of the message came to him in a vision. At that time I, Daniel, mourned for three weeks. I ate no choice food; no meat or wine touched my lips; and I used no lotions at all until the three weeks were over."

It was on the twenty-fourth day that Daniel finally had a vision of an angel, who gave him the interpretation of the puzzling revelation.

Sometimes God uses someone else besides the person receiving the dream or vision to interpret the message. That was the case when Joseph interpreted the dreams of the cupbearer, the baker, and Pharaoh while he was in Egypt.

I once had a dream that I was in a white room sitting at a white table having a discussion with a woman. As the discussion went on, we began to argue. Finally a demonic face came forth from the woman's face and I took authority over the demon and commanded it to leave.

I hadn't the foggiest idea what the dream meant. So I went to another pastor in Santa Maria, named Tina Jones, whom God would use prophetically and in dream interpretation. She told me that the white room represented the church I was pastoring. The white table represents the business of the church. The woman was being used by a controlling, religious spirit (a Jezebel spirit). All summed up, the dream was a warning from God that a religious spirit, which has been in the church, would try to regain control of the church. I was to stand my ground and pastor the church by the authority given to me by Jesus.

In the passage from Numbers God also said that He speaks face to face, with clear messages that don't have to be figured out. According to the book of Numbers, this is not the usual way that God speaks prophetically, but that doesn't mean He doesn't speak that way. It just isn't common. When God says "face to face" He means speaking in an audible voice.

On the first day my wife, Diana, and I met, we were teammates on an intramural flag football team at seminary. During practice she was standing on the sidelines and heard a voice say, "You are going to marry him." She happened to be looking right at me as I was coming off the field to talk to her, but no one was within ten feet of her. I think it is worth noting that she did not tell me about that encounter until after we were married.

I am not trying to put my wife on a par with Moses. I write this example simply to illustrate that sometimes God still speaks in an audible way. James Ryle lists at least three other ways God uses to give us prophetic words. The first is through impressions of Scripture. It is common in the churches I have pastored for believers to have a scripture reference come to mind while praying for someone. Many times these verses give direction or affirmation in a given situation. He also speaks in the natural circumstances. For instance, sometimes God will use the weather to give a prophetic picture of His coming works and moves. At other times He speaks through the supernatural realms such as through angelic visitations.

With all of the ways God prophetically speaks, it is important that we learn how to listen to Him. Jack Deere makes the following observation from his own life, "those of us who for years have believed that the only way God speaks to us is through the Bible or through sermons from the Bible, have the most difficult time learning the language of dreams and impressions. It seems unnatural to us that God would speak in any way except the Bible." [12] It takes a move of the Spirit in our hearts for us to want to listen to Him and receive the prophetic messages He has for us. The Holy Spirit has to move on our hearts because we do not value His words as much as we think we do. If we do not want to hear from Him, then we walk in disobedience of 1 Corinthians 14:1 by not especially desiring the gift of prophecy in the Church.

Many come to desire the gift of prophecy when they realize why God gives this gift in the New Testament. For many Christians, their only real study of prophecy is done in the Old Testament. They tend to come away with a negative view of having someone prophesy (except the prophecies about the coming of Jesus). After all, many prophecies in the Old Testament seem to be about judgment and destruction, which God used to correct a sinful people. This is, of course, a wrong way of viewing the purpose of Old Testament prophecy. But let's face it, this is the impression many people get.

So, what does the New Testament say the purpose of prophecy is? In 1 Corinthians 14:3 Paul tells us, "But everyone who prophesies speaks to (people) for their strengthening, encouragement and comfort." These are the three main reasons why any church should desire to have the Holy Spirit give prophecies. An example of this is found in Acts 15:32 which says, "Judas and Silas, who themselves were prophets, said much to encourage and strengthen the brothers."[13] The Spirit wants to strengthen you, encourage you and comfort you like He did the believers in Antioch through Judas and Silas.

Now, the New Testament does not say to simply let believers prophesy. Earlier, I also stated that it is important to remember that just because a believer gives a prophetic word to someone, it doesn't mean that person is a prophet or even gifted with prophecy. God instructs us to test any prophecies that are given. Paul wrote to the Corinthians, "Two or three prophets should speak, and the others should weigh carefully what is said." (1 Corinthians 14:29) The word for weigh in the Greek is *diakrinetosan,* which means to "judge" or "pass judgment." [14] In other words, after a prophet speaks, we are to pass judgment as to whether the prophecy was from God or not.

Paul, likewise, directed the Thessalonians, "Do not put out the Spirit's fire; do not treat prophecies with contempt. Test everything. Hold on to the good. Avoid every kind of evil." (1 Thessalonians 5:19-22) Graham Cooke gave a good summary when he wrote,

> "The New Testament pattern is that we are open to the prophetic gift; we give respectful attention to prophetic revelation; we submit each prophecy to careful Scriptural scrutiny; and we only accept that which passes the test. Most importantly, we deal with prophecy that does not pass muster."
> [15]

The most important thing to remember when dealing with prophecy is that the Bible is supreme. As Christians we acknowledge the Bible to be the final authority for life and ministry. This applies to prophecy as well. All prophecies must be judged by the Scriptures.  Yet some prophecies are hard to judge by the Bible.  So, many who are experienced with prophecy have come up with good lists by which to test prophecies.  Cooke, a man gifted with prophecy, gives a list of five questions by which we should test prophecies. [16]  They are:

1) Does it edify, exhort and comfort?
2) What spirit is behind the prophecy?
3) Does the prophecy conform to Scripture?
4) Does the prophecy glorify the Lord Jesus?
5) Is it manipulative or controlling?

Dr. Jack Deere gives his own list, which includes:
1) Are they honoring Christ and bringing glory to him, or are they bringing attention to themselves?
2) Are they walking in humility, and does their ministry produce humility?
3) Does their ministry produce the fruit of the Spirit?
4) Are their words accurate and do their predictions come true?
5) Does their teaching fall in line with the Scripture? [17]

As you can see, Deere's questions apply more to the ministry of a person or group who have the gift of prophecy.  But, both lists of questions are excellent for weighing and testing prophets and prophecies.

It bothers some Christians that they would have to test prophecy.  It doesn't seem right that they would be in a position to test something that God would give them.  But others don't like the thought that some prophecy would be false and that it would take place in the Church.  I once heard a believer say that they wouldn't want prophecy in their church, because they wouldn't want Satan to be able to give false prophecies to their church.

The Bible doesn't say that if you avoid prophecy you will avoid Satan's schemes. It actually says the opposite. Jesus promised that false prophets would come to the Church. In Matthew 7:15-16 Jesus said, "Watch out for false prophets. They come to you in sheep's clothing, but inwardly they are ferocious wolves. By their fruit you will recognize them." Our Lord warned us that false prophets would come. He also told us what to do. He didn't tell us not to allow prophecy and that all future prophets are false. He told us to test them by looking at the fruit of their ministry.

Then again, false prophets weren't the only things we were warned about. Peter wrote, "but there were also false prophets among the people, just as there will be false teachers among you." (2 Peter 2:1a) The answer to watching for false teachers is not to ban teaching in the Church. Instead, we compare their teaching to the Bible.

So, it is important to have prophecy in the Church and in our local churches. Prophecy speaks the heart of God and God uses it to release and impart wonderful blessings to us in the Church. In 1 Timothy 4:14 Paul wrote Timothy, "Do not neglect your gift, which was given you through a prophetic message when the body of elders laid their hands on you." Timothy's spiritual gift was bestowed on him through a prophetic word.

It is important that we desire to have the gift of prophecy active in our local churches and throughout the Church around the world. I look forward to a time when prophecy is active to the point that we model the Church of the First Century. During that time there were groups of prophets and teachers in the churches. Acts 11:27-30 states,

"During this time some prophets came down from Jerusalem to Antioch. One of them, named Agabus, stood up and through the Spirit predicted that a severe famine would spread over the entire Roman world. (This happened during the reign of Claudius.)"

Based on this prophecy, the disciples gathered money to help the believers in Judea. What a responsive Church! Then Acts 13:1-2 tells us,

"In the church at Antioch there were prophets and teachers; Barnabas, Simeon called Niger, Lucius of Cyrene, Manaen (who had been brought up with Herod the tetrarch) and Saul. While they were worshiping the Lord and fasting, the Holy Spirit said, 'Set apart for me Barnabas and Saul for the work to which I have called them.'"

Barnabas and Saul were then sent off after having hands laid on them. They were commissioned by a prophetic word and they responded. Let's pray that God will once again have prophets and teachers in the churches throughout the world.

As a final note on prophecy, it must be understood that there is one thing God is no longer doing. He is finished writing the Bible. No prophecy is above the Bible, neither will any prophecy given at this time be held as Scripture. But then, I have never heard any Pentecostal or Charismatic believers claim that their prophecies are equal with the Bible.

## Tongues and Interpretation of Tongues

No gift causes more fear and misunderstanding in the churches I have been in than the gift of tongues. For most of the people I have talked to, the gift doesn't make sense to

them.  It sounds like gibberish or sounds made up by someone.
I have also heard comments such as, "If the people in our
church heard someone speak in tongues they would probably
get up and walk out."

Like any of the other gifts, there is no reason to fear the
gift itself.  The gift of tongues is a manifestation of the Holy
Spirit, which He uses for the common good of the Church, by
speaking through a believer either in a human language or in a
heavenly language.

Most Christians like the passage in Acts 2, which
describes the day of Pentecost, due to the excitement of the
event.  Luke wrote,

> "All of them were filled with the Holy
> Spirit and began to speak in other tongues as the
> Spirit enabled them.  Now there were staying in
> Jerusalem God-fearing Jews from every nation
> under heaven.  When they heard this sound, a
> crowd came together in bewilderment, because
> each one heard them speaking in his own
> language.  Utterly amazed, they asked: 'Are not
> all these men who are speaking Galileans?  Then
> how is it that each of us hears them in his own
> native language?'" (Acts 2:4-8)

On that day, the Spirit used the vocal cords of the
disciples to speak the "wonders of God" to people of at least
fifteen different languages.  God did an amazing job of getting
the attention of those people.

I have heard stories of how God spoke in a similar
fashion to minister to people through others who did not know
their language and I've seen God use other languages to
minister through tongues during a worship service.  This

account is memorable – it was an evening service when a man stood up and spoke in tongues. I called for the interpretation and another man stood and gave the interpretation. Someone then asked if this was actually tongues. To my delight one of the church elders, Jim, clarified the moment. He asked if either of the men involved in the tongue and interpretation could speak Scottish Highland Gaelic. Both of the men said, "No." This elder was from Scotland and he grew up with the language that the tongue was spoken in. It was touching to see that the Spirit desired for all involved to know it was a known tongue given by Him.

Most people have problems with this gift when it is no longer a known language, but a heavenly language. I recently read an article on the Internet, which made this statement, "The Bible clearly teaches that the spiritual gift of speaking in tongues always refers to real, known human languages." [18] His point just isn't true. In 1 Corinthians 13:1 Paul wrote, "If I speak in the tongues of man and of angels…" In 1 Corinthians 14:2 he wrote, "For anyone who speaks in a tongue does not speak to men but to God. Indeed, no one understands him; he utters mysteries with his spirit." And finally Paul wrote in 1 Corinthians 14:23, "So if the whole church comes together and everyone speaks in tongues, and some who do not understand or some unbelievers come in, will they not say that you are out of your mind?" I have never heard of someone hearing others speak in a known human language, that is not their own, say, "They are out of their minds." Obviously, from these verses we can see that there is a heavenly language. God can use a heavenly language or He can use a known human language to convey a message, either to others or in prayer to Himself.

The first time I ever really heard the gift of tongues was during my time in seminary. My friend Zach and I had returned from seeing a movie one night. I was dropping him off at his apartment when we decided to pray for each other. I prayed for God to bless him in his studies and then it was his turn. He began to pray, but he ran out of words. He said, "Lord, I want to pray for Tom, but I... I... I don't...." Suddenly, he began to speak in a very beautiful language. I have no idea what he prayed. (We weren't wise enough to ask God for an interpretation.) While he was speaking in tongues, his eyes were big with surprise. And all we know is that we felt the peace and love of God during that moment.

Since then, I have grown a little wiser. While I was the associate pastor of a Filipino congregation in San Francisco, we used to have a prayer meeting the first Friday of every month. It was during one of those prayer meetings that one of the members stood up and began to speak in tongues for the first time in his life. When he finished, the senior pastor and I called for an interpretation. One of the older men of the church stood up and began to speak of how much God loved that church and of His blessings for that church. But before he was finished he became exhausted and another member of the church stood up and finished the message without missing a beat or losing the continuity of the message. We praised God!

The gift of tongues can definitely be misused. In 1 Corinthians, one of the issues the Apostle Paul addressed was not the problem of tongues, but more importantly, how the Corinthians were using the gift. As Gordon Fee points out about the misuse of tongues in the church at Corinth, "They have a spirituality which has religious trappings (asceticism, knowledge, tongues) but has abandoned genuinely Christian ethics, with its supremacy of love." [19] Tongues and their interpretation are good gifts, but they are not to be used as a sign that you are spiritually right with God when you are allowing gross negligence of God's ethics and love in your life. Anytime someone uses the gift of tongues as an exclusive sign of true spirituality it is being misused.

People can get kooky about this gift. Many years ago, Diana and I had two ladies try to "help" us speak in tongues during a break from a conference. They grabbed our cheeks and told us to begin making sounds. After a couple of seconds, we politely told them we would wait for the Spirit. Their hearts were in the right place, but our faces were not the right place for their hands.

When it comes to this gift, we must remember the questions Paul asks in 1 Corinthians 12:29-31, "Are all apostles? Are all prophets? Are all teachers? Do all work miracles? Do all have gifts of healing? **Do all speak in tongues?** Do all interpret? But eagerly desire the greater gifts." (Bold letters mine) This series of questions have as their answer, "no." So, just as not everyone in the Body of Christ is an apostle, neither do we all speak in tongues.

Some theological backgrounds see a difference between the gift of tongues for use in ministry (as was demonstrated on Pentecost) and a personal prayer language. This prayer language is found in the passages speaking of "praying in the Spirit." Two examples are Ephesians 6:18a, which says, "And pray in the Spirit on all occasions with all kinds of prayers and requests." And also Jude 20, "But you, dear friends, build yourselves up in your most holy faith and pray in the Holy Spirit."

The idea of praying in the Spirit is a foreign concept for many in the Christian faith. So, let's look at how Paul describes it in 1 Corinthians 14:14-15. He wrote, "For if I pray in a tongue, my spirit prays, but my mind is unfruitful. So what shall I do? I will pray with my spirit, but I will also pray with my mind; I will sing with my spirit, but I will also sing with my mind." Though I do think that there is a difference in the use for tongues in ministry and in the use of a personal prayer language, they are interrelated. They stem from the same gift. Yet, due to 1 Corinthians 12:29-31, I would still say that not all believers who are anointed by the Spirit speak in tongues, but too many are not even asking God if He gave them that gift.

Jack Hayford, pastor of Church On The Way, states it well by writing,

"There were (and are) too many people whom I know living power-filled lives under the touch and gifts of the Holy Spirit, though never having spoken with tongues. I determined to cease contending for another definition of their fullness and to refuse to deny their anointed ministry as being other than fully Spirit-filled. But as surely as to deny that would have been dishonest, it would have been equally unwise for me to retreat from what I was discovering of tongues as a provision for all believers – for prayer and praise."

Proven results in my own ministry evidenced people almost always receiving spiritual language when they welcomed the fullness of the Spirit into their lives. I had no reason to cease teaching this expectation, but how was I to merge these two convictions I was reaching?

1. I was convinced I couldn't *demand* tongues as an evidence of Holy-Spirit-fullness; and
2. I was convinced I couldn't *deny* the availability or value of tongues if welcomed by those seeking His fullness." [20]

Not all believers will speak in tongues, but we must not belittle the gift either. Like all of the other gifts, it is to be sought in our lives and in our churches. Not all believers will receive the gift of tongues when they are saved and filled with the Spirit like Cornelius' family in Acts 10:44-48 or the disciples of John in Acts 19:6. The Spirit is free to bestow the gift as He desires. Some speak fluently like my friend Zach did and some only get a few words at a time. Like all of the gifts, it must be fanned into flame (1Timothy 1:6).

There are a couple of rules that govern the use of this gift in the Church. First, in 1 Corinthians 14:27-28 we are told, "If anyone speaks in a tongue, two – or at the most three – should speak, one at a time, and someone must interpret. If there is no interpreter, the speaker should keep quiet in the church and speak to himself and God." As was the case at the church in San Francisco, when someone speaks in tongues in the church I call for an interpretation. If there is no interpretation, we disregard it and go on with worship.

The second rule is found in 1 Corinthians 14:39. Paul instructed us, "Therefore, my brothers, be eager to prophesy, and do not forbid speaking in tongues." Most Reformed churches should be worried about having broken this command of God, rather than the first one.

A good example is found at the Orthodox Presbyterian Church's web site. They have a section called "General Assembly Decisions" and written under that heading is the following: "Tongues Speaking – In 1976 the Assembly upheld a presbytery's discipline of a minister who practiced the private exercise of 'speaking in tongues.'" [21] They were biblically wrong in disciplining that minister. Let's not make the same mistake. We must not only "not forbid speaking in tongues" me must encourage the gift. It is one of the wonderful manifestations that the Spirit will give to a receptive Church. Ask God if He will give you that gift.

## Word of Wisdom

1 Corinthians 12:8 reads, "To one there is given through the Spirit the message of wisdom." This is one of the revelatory gifts and as with all of the revelatory gifts, it can seem to overlap some of the other gifts. Many times the lines between prophecy, a word of knowledge, discernment and a word of wisdom can seem to blur. When this happens it is okay, as we think and evaluate what we are experiencing from a western, linear perspective and like to see clear lines of separation and definition between the gifts.

A good definition for this gift is a manifestation of the Holy Spirit that imparts wisdom into a group or into someone's life for direction, decision, or Godly living.

Let's get into the meaning of wisdom. The Oxford English Dictionary defines it as, "Capacity of judging rightly in matters relating to life and conduct; soundness in judgment in the choice of means and ends." While, you can generally live a wise life by reading and doing what God has told us to do in the Bible, there are times and situations when we don't know how to proceed in wisdom. There are events or decisions in which we need God to impart wisdom to us. This is when the Holy Spirit uses this gift.

I have seen the Holy Spirit impress on one with this gift the right advice for the right time. When people are asking for advice, the person with this gift will suddenly say the right advice. And the person with this gift is usually surprised by the wisdom that comes out of their mouth. As one person with this gift said just after a ministry time when the Holy Spirit used this gift, "That was really wise advice, but that wasn't me, it had to be God." As God speaks His wisdom through this gift it has a wonderful nature to it. James 3:17 states, "But the wisdom that comes from heaven is first of all pure; then peace-loving, considerate, submissive, full of mercy and good fruit, impartial and sincere."

The Holy Spirit will also use this gift when elders or others are meeting, especially when the group comes to an impasse on an issue. Though none can agree on an issue, suddenly a person with this gift will say an idea that all will agree is the right course to take. Or I have seen that one will call for a time of prayer, though they weren't planning on asking the others to pray.

I have seen the Holy Spirit give one with this gift the right words to say at a crucial moment. Jesus said this would happen in Luke 12:11-12, "When you are brought before synagogues, rulers and authorities do not worry about how you will defend yourselves or what you will say, for the Holy Spirit will teach you at that time what you should say." And He continued in this thought in Luke 21:12-15,

> "But before all this, they will seize you and persecute you. They will hand you over to synagogues and put you in prison, and you will be brought before kings and governors, and all on account of my name. And you will bear testimony to me. But make up your mind not to worry beforehand how you will defend yourselves. For I will give you words and wisdom that none of your adversaries will be able to resist or contradict."

Jesus is saying He will use the gift of word of wisdom through the Holy Spirit in us at those times.

I have seen the Holy Spirit give one with this gift understanding of a passage of Scripture. Now I love my personal library and I especially like my collection of commentaries, but I also know that scholars are imperfect. As much as I value their good biblical exegesis, sometimes the Holy Spirit has to open a passage to our understanding during times of ministry. It looks a lot like what Jesus did in Luke 24:45, which reads, "Then he opened their minds so they could understand the Scriptures." While good, biblical scholarship is of value, I have seen the Holy Spirit give deep understanding of a verse or passage through this gift.

I have seen the Holy Spirit give one with this gift the right judgment for a situation. One of the best examples of this from the Bible is 1 Kings 3:16-28, in which King Solomon had to make a judgment between two women on the life of a baby. The Holy Spirit will give wisdom to a person with this gift when the empirical evidence is unclear or confusing.

But there is more to this gift. There is a definition for *sophia* (Greek word for wisdom) that adds another dimension to how the Holy Spirit uses this gift: Dream Interpretation. Walter Bauer's A Greek English Lexicon gives one of its definitions of *sophia* as "The gift of unveiling secrets." And Kittel's Theological Dictionary of The New Testament says, "God endows special people with wisdom in an extraordinary way, e.g., Joseph, Solomon, and Daniel. In this regard one may refer to prophetic inspiration (Jer. 9:11), artistic ability (Ex. 28:3), and nocturnal revelation (Job 4:12)." Or if you go online to BibleStudyTools.com and look up *sophia* in their KJV New Testament Greek Lexicon you will see one of the definitions as "the act of interpreting dreams."

We can see this gifting in Joseph and Daniel:

Genesis 41:12 "Now a young Hebrew was there with us, a servant of the captain of the guard. We told him our dreams, and he interpreted them for us, giving each man the interpretation of his dream."

Daniel 1:17 "To these four young men God gave knowledge and understanding of all kinds of literature and learning. And Daniel could understand visions and dreams of all kinds."

How does this gift work? First, let me say how it doesn't work. I once heard a pastor say about another pastor, "I need to give him a word of wisdom." This gift is not the accumulation of wisdom through study of the Bible and many life experiences. Here are some symptoms of having this gift. You are praying over someone and a word of advice comes to your heart and thoughts. A person with this gift is usually amazed at what came out of their mouth, knowing it was God and not from their own mind and experiences. God gives you an interpretation to a message or dream when you hear them and your interpretations are accurate and come to pass.

## Word of Knowledge

The second half of 1 Corinthians 12:8 reads, "to another the message of knowledge by means of the same Spirit."
Dr. Bobby Clinton gave the best definition of this gift when he wrote, "The gift word of knowledge represents the capacity to receive supernaturally revealed knowledge which otherwise could not or would not be known." [22]
Since this is a spiritual gift and supernatural by God's design, I can tell you that you don't have this gift if you have stored up a lot of knowledge. I was visiting in the home of a retired pastor, and enjoying a good conversation about ministry. At least it was going well until he leaned forward

and said, "Let me give you a word of knowledge."  Right away I knew that he didn't understand what this gift is when he proceeded to share with me his own knowledge.

Words of knowledge commonly come in the form of an impression that you need to pray for someone and God may also tell you what to pray for them.  It can be the impression of a verse or chapter of Scripture while ministering to someone.  The Spirit may give you a picture of an event or a word or a sentence that describes the situation of the person being ministered to.  You will know something about the person you are praying for.  You may have pain in any area of your body or the feeling of sickness that you don't normally have as your own ailment.  You can feel heartbreak when someone in the room or area has a broken heart.  These are all common ways in which the Holy Spirit gives words of knowledge at the churches I have pastored.

Dr. Bobby Clinton wrote of John Wimber saying, "In healing situations he actually feels the pain in the organ of the body in which the like situation is present in a person." [23]  Do not let this list limit how the Holy Spirit may give a word of knowledge.  He is the Lord who gives this manifestation.

Diana and I participated on a ministry team in a Presbyterian Church in San Diego, California.  A man in the church approached us and asked us to pray for him as he had terrible back pain and wanted to be healed.  As we were praying for him, the Holy Spirit gave us the word "forgive." So, I told him that we felt God had given us the word "forgive" for him.  I asked him if he had anyone in his life that he knew he needed to forgive.  He jokingly grabbed me by the shoulders and shook me saying "Yes, but I don't want to forgive him."  We told him that the pain in his back may be tied an unforgiven offense in his heart and that he might want to seek God about this during the week.

The following Sunday, he came to Diana and me and told us with a smile on his face that God had healed his back during the week. We asked if God had called him to forgive anyone. He told us that the person he had to forgive was his dad and when he verbally forgave his dad for some past things that had taken place between them, his back was healed at that moment.

## Miracles

Though all of the gifts could be seen as miraculous because they are supernatural, this gift refers to the manifestations beyond the rest of the gifts. This gift would not include healing, though some healings are miraculous.

So, when the Holy Spirit uses this gift in a believer we can expect such things as raising the dead, taking a little food and multiplying it, making poisonous food or drink edible, and the like. The list I have given you is not exhaustive. It is just a list of some of the miracles that took place in the Bible. But those miracles are definitely within the definition of this gift.

For many Christians it is easy to think of God doing a miracle, whether it is in our lives or in recent history. For example, while I was staying in Hungary with a Reformed pastor named Istvan Bojtor, he told me of the following miracle. In the 1500's as the Reformed movement was growing in Hungary, the Catholic bishop in the city of Debrecen took a dead stick of wood and jammed it down into some mud. He said, "The Reformation is like this stick." The people of Debrecen left that stick there and it eventually grew into a tree. God decided to give life to a dead stick, which was being used to make fun of the Reformation.

As I have just written, many Christians can find encouragement from such a story and even believe that God will do similar acts today. That is, if He is doing it by Himself. But many Christians have a hard time accepting that God will gift believers with that same miraculous power.

God has continued to manifest miraculous power in Christians to this day. In chapter three, I related the story of John Knox's son-in-law, John Welch, being used by God to raise a man from the dead. I believe God is doing the same works today.

While I was on that same trip to Eastern Europe, I had the privilege of getting to know a Christian obstetrician and family doctor who was from Czechoslovakia. She told me of a wonderful thing that happened one day when she was delivering a baby. When the baby came out of the birth canal, the doctor had realized that something was wrong. The baby was a stillbirth. She could find no vital signs, no signs of life at all. She was brokenhearted, because she was a good friend of the couple who were giving birth. She told them the bad news, and then began praying over the baby through her tears as she held the child in her arms. After about ten to fifteen minutes of praying over the baby, she felt warmth come into its little body. The baby opened his eyes and began to cry.

God used this Czechoslovakian doctor to raise this baby from the dead. I have heard other stories of God's miraculous power doing similar things all over the world. And I believe that we will see an increase in the use of the gift in the years to come.


### Faith

Let's be clear from the beginning. This gift of faith is not the basic faith of salvation. Every Christian does not have this gift of faith, though every Christian has faith, which is a gift from God. Gordon Fee put it best when he wrote, "what is in mind here is the special gift of supernatural faith that can 'move mountains,' mentioned again in 13:2.  It probably refers to a supernatural conviction that God will reveal his power or mercy in a special way in a specific instance." **(24)**

As was mentioned earlier in this work, I believe there are a few levels of faith:  The first level being saving faith and the top level being a faith that expects miracles and answers from God.  I think that the "gift of faith" presented in 1 Corinthians 12:9 is this kind of faith that believes the miraculous and knows that God will move in this way in specific situations through His Church.

Now all followers of Jesus know that God is all-powerful.  We accept this theologically and acknowledge God to be omnipotent.  But this gift is not a theological subscription to the attributes of God.

A person with this gift does not struggle with nagging doubts that many other Christians have to deal with.  When confronted with an impossible set of circumstances, the Holy Spirit supernaturally implants faith in them to know that the impossible is possible.  When God calls them to walk on water, they walk.  When God tells them to move a mountain, they start pushing in prayer.  When they read a verse like Philippians 4:3 ("I can do everything through him who gives me strength.") they don't rationalize it away.  You might read this verse as if it said, "I can do everything that is within reason and humanly possible through Him who gives me strength," which is how many Christians read it.  But the person with this gift reads "everything" as literally meaning everything!

## Discerning of Spirits

A gift that is highly overlooked, but quite necessary to the local church is the gift of discerning of spirits. It is also known as distinguishing between spirits. The main thrust of this gift is for the Holy Spirit to tell us when something is of God and when it is not.

I do not want to limit how God uses this gift, but I have seen two central ways in which it functions. First, the Spirit manifests this gift in a believer to help the church know where a prophecy or teaching is coming from. In any given situation in the church there are three possible origins of a prophecy or a teaching. It could be from God, it could be from a demonic source, or it could be merely human.

Now, you might say, "Well, we don't need this gift; we already have the Bible for our teachings." Let's look at what the Bible has to say. In 1Timothy 4:1 it tells us, "The Spirit clearly says that in later times some will abandon the faith and follow deceiving spirits and things taught by demons." The "later times" are any time between Pentecost and Jesus' second coming. In this verse, God is warning us that even though we have the Scriptures we must be careful of things taught by demons entering the Church.

How does this happen? Jesus warned us in Matthew 24:11 saying, "and many false prophets will appear and deceive many people." False prophets have come and they will continue to come until Jesus returns. This does not mean to avoid prophets or the gift of prophecy. God has given us the gift of discernment to know which ones to allow to speak. Those with the supernatural gift of discernment are part of those Paul alluded to in 1 Corinthians 14:29 when he wrote, "Two or three prophets should speak, and the others should weigh carefully what is said." Part of weighing the prophecy is letting those with the gift of discernment hear the Spirit tell them the source of the prophecy. But false prophets are not the only problem.

The Apostle Peter wrote in 2 Peter 2:1, "But there were also false prophets among the people, just as there will be false teachers among you. They will secretly introduce destructive heresies...." Just as we must watch for false prophets, so we must look for false teachers also. We still need this gift even though we have the Bible, commentaries and systematic theologies. Theologians can still buy into a destructive heresy. After all, Church history is full of problems stemming from wrong teachings and wrong interpretations of Scripture. I agree with some recent writers that the theology of Cessationism is a doctrine of demons. That teaching robs believers of much that God has given them (i.e. authority, power ministry and the gifts empowered by the Spirit). Demons must love it when parts of the Church willingly give up some of the tools God has given us to fight with.

The second way that I have seen God use this gift is to supernaturally tell a believer what type of spirits we are dealing with in a time of ministry. A person with this gift knows what kind of demonic spirit is attacking or using a person being ministered to, or is in the vicinity of our ministry. There are different kinds of demons as Jesus pointed out when He said, "this kind can come out only by prayer and fasting" in Mark 9:29. The kinds of demons can differ according to the kinds of sin, addictions, and illnesses that are possible in the sphere of human life. In addition, Paul tells us that there are rulers, authorities, powers of this dark world, and spiritual forces of evil in Ephesians 6:12.

In order to know what kind of demonic spirit we are coming up against and how to best deal with it, we need someone with the gift of discernment to hear from God on the issue. Though we can do spiritual warfare without someone with this gift, it is just easier and more efficient to have this gifting present.

Some people with this gift actually can, at times, see angels and demons. There have been children and adults, in churches I've pastored, who have seen angels during worship services. This reminds me of a Bible study I was leading at a member's home. I was teaching on the topic of obeying God when one woman started welling up with tears. I asked her what was on her mind and she said that she could see an angel in the corner of the room. She began to describe what she was seeing, how bright and wonderful the angel looked. She was amazed!

God also uses this gift to show demons to those doing ministry. I have been with a few people whom God will allow to see the demon or demons we are coming up against and also will tell them what kind of demon it is. I can tell you that those who see the enemy do not like to see the demonic, but they reveal what they're discerning which is very helpful for obvious reasons.

## Final Thoughts

I will not be writing about the gifts of teaching, evangelism, exhortation, or service. Though I do believe any Christian can teach, share their faith, exhort, or serve in a local church, there are some whom God has gifted to do these ministries. Almost everyone in the Church can teach, but there are individuals who touch my heart because God is anointing the teaching by gifting. We can all share our faith and are commanded to do so, but there are some with the gift of evangelism who will see great numbers of people accept Christ because God supernaturally ministers through them to present the Gospel and open their hearts. It is the same with giving, exhorting and serving.

A pastor named George Woods once visited me and said something very interesting. "If you can account for the things that happen in your ministry by human effort, then that is what happened. But if you look back and are amazed at what has taken place and know that it wasn't you, then God has been at work." Sometimes He chooses to bless our efforts and sometimes He moves with power through us. I want Him to increase His gifts in the Church.

# Chapter Nine
## How You and Your Church Can Move Into the Gifts

The first time I ever experienced the gifts of the Holy Spirit was in 1985 when I co-led a short-term mission trip to minister to a church in Mexico. During one night of the trip, we were praying with the church's pastor for a woman from the church. While we were praying I began to smell marijuana. I couldn't believe that someone would smoke that substance in a church so I began to look around to see who it was. No one was smoking it and the windows and the doors were shut, so I knew that it wasn't coming from outside.

At the end of the ministry time I told the pastor with whom I was traveling about the smell. He said that he had smelled the same thing and asked our interpreter if he had smelled it. He said, "No." He had used drugs during his lifetime before following Jesus and would have recognized it. The pastor told me that the Holy Spirit had given us a word of knowledge. He then told the woman's pastor what to look for in the woman's life and suggested that she may need further ministry.

When we returned to the hotel, I spent the rest of the night in tears. It was so wonderful to experience a manifestation of the Holy Spirit. I thanked God and just enjoyed His loving presence. That night launched me in a desire to know more of how the Spirit uses His gifts.

### Getting Into the Gifts

So, how does a Christian become equipped with the Spirit's gifts? The first step is to read the Scriptures and study them. As 2 Timothy 3:16-17 teaches, "All Scripture is God-breathed and is useful for teaching, rebuking, correcting and training in righteousness, so that the man [or woman] of God may be thoroughly equipped for every good work." The Holy Spirit inspired lots of Scripture to teach you and equip you for receiving and ministering in the gifts.

In chapter two I listed many of the passages of Scripture that support the continuance of the gifts. Many of these same passages also instruct us about the nature of the gifts themselves. In my view, much of the Bible gives us insight for how God uses His gifts in us. Study both the Old Testament and the New Testament. See the way God uses His gifts in the lives of the people in the Bible. Pore over the passages that show how God gives prophetic words, how God speaks through dreams, how God used biblical figures to heal, and many other aspects of God's power in the lives of His people.

I believe that almost the entire Bible is applicable for life today. Of course, there are parts that no longer apply to our relationship with God, such as the sacrificial laws that have been completed in the crucifixion of Jesus. Some Christians have a belief system that says that only the epistles of the New Testament are really for our guidance, the rest of the Bible is an historical document. As Paul wrote, "All Scripture is God-breathed and is useful for teaching, rebuking, correcting and training in righteousness,"

Study 1 Corinthians 12-14 and see how the gifts are to function. Pay close attention to how Jesus healed, cast out demons and ministered in power. Spend some time in the book of Acts reading of believers like Agabus, Stephen, and Philip in whom God used power and prophecy.

In addition to studying the Bible, it is important to go where the action is. I wish I could tell you that if you read the

Bible you will have all you need to operate in the gifts, but that is not always the way in which the Spirit fills us with His gifts.

The gifts are caught as well as taught. A classic example of this idea is found in 1 Timothy 4:14 where Paul wrote, "Do not neglect your gift, which was given you through a prophetic message when the body of elders laid their hands on you." When the elders laid hands on Timothy, the Holy Spirit gave a spiritual gift to Timothy. This gift was imparted to him. I think that Timothy was quite knowledgeable in the Scriptures or Paul would not have sent him to Ephesus, but it was not through the Scriptures that Timothy was empowered with his gift. His investment came by the laying on of hands.

Some received gifts by being in the presence of others who are functioning in the gifts. This was the case for King Saul when he was anointed king over Israel. The Prophet Samuel told Saul to be ready for this when he said, "As you approach the town, you will meet a procession of prophets coming down from the high place with lyres, tambourines, flutes and harps being played before them, and they will be prophesying. The Spirit of the Lord will come upon you in power, and you will prophesy with them; and you will be changed into a different person." (1 Samuel 10:5b-6) This took place as Samuel had said.

When Saul came in contact with the prophets, the Holy Spirit caused him to prophesy with them. I am not saying that Saul was a prophet, but this situation in Saul's life demonstrates the principle I am writing about. Sometimes the Holy Spirit chooses to impart gifts to us by bringing us in contact with others through whom He is manifesting His gifts.

This is why it is good to invite people who are used powerfully by the Spirit to come and minister in your church. It is good to invite those with the gift of prophecy and healing to come and minister prophetically and to do healing services.

Many times that will release the gifts of healing and prophecy in your church. If nothing else, those with prophetic gifts will prophesy and impart gifts to people as in the case with Timothy. This is a great way to discover what people's gifts are, even before they begin to exercise them. The Spirit knows what He is going to manifest in His people for ministry.

This leads us to the most important step in this process of learning about the gifts and seeing them used in us; ask God for them. As Jesus said in Luke 11:13, "If you then, though you are evil, know how to give good gifts to your children, how much more will your Father in heaven give the Holy Spirit to those who ask him!" Ask the Father for more of the Holy Spirit in your life. Ask that the waters of the Spirit will well up in you. This goes hand in hand with the command to desire the spiritual gifts in 1 Corinthians 14:1.

As Christians, we are not very good at really asking God for the blessings He wants to pour out on us. As James wrote, "You do not have, because you do not ask God. When you ask, you do not receive, because you ask with wrong motives," (James 4:2b-3a) Many Christians do not see the gifts of the Spirit operating in their lives and in their church, because they have never asked God for them. If you have been taught cessationism, you won't bother to ask God for these gifts because you will think that they are no longer given to the church.

I need to offer a word of caution, however, for those seeking the gifts. Check your heart. There are some who ask to see these things to prove they are false. God knows the motives of the heart. We should know not to test God! Yet, I have heard many testimonies of people who doubt that God still gives His gifts to the Church who are being used by the Spirit against their own theology.

A pastor, named Richard, who mentored Diana and me in the gifts, was just such a person. Before he became active in the gifts of the Spirit, his father asked him to attend a meeting at the Anaheim Vineyard one Sunday evening, just to check it out. He had been hearing about things going on at Anaheim Vineyard that were outside his personal experience and theology. During the ministry time John Wimber had a word of knowledge about a woman who was suffering from scoliosis. The woman happened to be sitting in front of Richard. When it was time to pray for healing, many people began to lay hands on her back and somebody took Richard's hand and put it on her back as well. To his amazement he could feel the bones move under his hand as the back was healed. Richard knew this wasn't a hoax, because the woman was a friend who had travelled with them to the service.

Others may ask for the gifts for their own reasons rather than God's. Some want to be exalted and looked up to. God does make some believers very high in profile, but that is not a reason to want the gifts. They are for ministry, not self-promotion.

This self-promotion can be seen in the book of Acts with Simon the Sorcerer. It says in Acts 8:9, "Now for some time a man named Simon had practiced sorcery in the city and amazed all the people of Samaria. He boasted that he was someone great, and all the people, both the high and low, gave him their attention..." The passage tells us that Phillip came and preached the Gospel so that many, including that Simon, believed and were baptized.

The apostles in Jerusalem got wind of this work and sent Peter and John to check it out. These two began laying hands on these new believers for the infilling of the Holy Spirit. Simon saw this and wanted to be filled with the Spirit also. He was even willing to pay them money for it. But his motive for wanting the Holy Spirit was wrong, so Peter replied, "May your money perish with you, because you thought you could buy the gift of God with money! You have no part or share in his ministry, because your heart is not right before God. Repent of this wickedness and pray to the Lord. Perhaps he will forgive you for having such a thought in your heart. For I see that you are full of bitterness and captive to sin." (Acts 8:20-23)

Again, when seeking the gifts of the Spirit, it is important to check your heart. The Spirit and His gifts are given freely to those who believe and want to minister for the sake of Jesus and His kingdom. Just ask the Holy Spirit to use His gifts in you and let you know which of His gifts He has given to you.

An important component to welcoming the Holy Spirit's movement in the gifts is to pray for each other and the Church. Ask God to use His gifts in your brothers and sisters in Christ. And then go on to pray that the Spirit will bless your whole church with His gifts. On any given Sunday, when I am preaching before my congregation I realize that God has filled that church with all of His gifts. It is my desire, as a pastor, to know who has what gift and pray that God will activate these gifts in each believer. I know that He will and when He does, our church will walk in more love and more power, to do what He commands of us.

Think about what the apostle Paul prayed for the church in Ephesus, "I keep asking that the God of our Lord Jesus Christ, the glorious Father, may give you the Spirit of wisdom and revelation, so that you may know him better." (Ephesians 1:17) In commentary on this passage Gordon Fee wrote, "The upshot of all this, then is that Paul is herewith praying that God will gift them with the Spirit yet once more, and that the

Spirit in turn will supply the wisdom to understand what he also reveals to them about God and his ways." [1]

I believe Paul was asking the Father to send the Holy Spirit in order that wisdom and revelation would be given to that church. The church in Ephesus would increase in wisdom as well as the revelatory gifts of word of wisdom, word of knowledge, prophecy, tongues and interpretation of those tongues.

Some may think that Paul was just asking for God to give them some wise understanding rather than these gifts of the Spirit. But as Fee explains, "Whereas one might be able to understand 'a spirit of wisdom' to mean something like 'a wise disposition' or 'a wise spirit,' to speak this way of 'revelation' is to speak nonsense. What, one wonders, can 'a spirit of revelation' possibly mean in *any* sense in English?" [2] His answer to the question is, "the prayer is not for some further Spirit reception, but for the indwelling Spirit whom they have already received to give them further wisdom and revelation. The emphasis, therefore, is not in receiving the Spirit as such, but on receiving (or perhaps realizing?) the resident Spirit's gifts." [3] So we should pray this for our local church and for the Church around the world. Pray that God would increase all of His gifts.

### What Should I Expect?

There are many ideas of what it should be like to experience the gifts. Most people I talk to think that they will black out or get struck with lightening or some other fantastically supernatural experience. Surely God can do these kinds of things when someone first encounters Him using His power through them. But I have not always found this to be the case. As in my first experience of the gifts, I just smelled something that wasn't physically there.  It actually took me by surprise and was quite subtle.  This seems to be the same for many others.

There are many people who do have dramatic experiences with God as He begins to use His gifts in them.  Pentecost was a dramatic experience and God may give you a "Pentecost."  The gifts can come in like a flood.  Think about what happened at Cornelius' house in Acts 10:44-46, "While Peter was still speaking these words, the Holy Spirit came on all who heard the message.  The circumcised believers who had come with Peter were astonished that the gift of the Holy Spirit had been poured out even on the Gentiles.  For they heard them speaking in tongues and praising God."  So, there are believers who know right away what gifts the Holy Spirit is using in them and walk in them very powerfully.

Some have experienced the Holy Spirit manifesting His gifts in them since childhood.  There are children, like the prophet Samuel, who have known God's voice since they were little and have grown up knowing what God is saying to them.  They receive prophetic words or angelic visitations that have prepared them for serving God as they grow up.  The French Calvinists, called the Huguenots, had children who were gifted with prophecy.  Some children have discernment of spirits, while God may gift others with healing gifts.  Children find it very easy to trust God and have faith in what He will do.

Not all Christians, including myself, have that sort of immediate gifting of the Spirit.  The Apostle Paul instructed Timothy by writing, "For this reason I remind you to fan into flame the gift of God which is in you through the laying on of my hands." (1 Timothy 4:14)  Like Timothy, the Spirit of God has gifted all of us, but it must be fanned.  Paul is giving the picture of a burning ember or spark that must be fanned so that it will turn into a burning fire.

But what does it mean to fan our gifts into flame?  As I wrote in an earlier chapter, the gifts operate in proportion to faith.  And that faith has to grow.  I have found that the more someone operates in their gifting, the more faith they have that God will use them.  If you have a gift of healing, then pray over everyone you can, from the sniffles to cancer.  As you see people being healed you will have more faith that God will heal others that you pray for and lay hands on.  If you have the gift of prophecy, you may start by getting impressions in your thoughts of people's needs for prayer or occasional dreams and visions, but you must ask God to continue to speak to you and be faithful with what He gives you.  It is the same with all of the gifts.  The more you follow the Spirit in your gifting the more you will learn how He uses that gift in you.  Pretty soon the Holy Spirit is using you to minister to others on a regular basis.

This may sound like a leap of faith and that is exactly what it is.  You have to step out in faith.  Timothy knew what his spiritual gift was by prophetic utterance, and then had to fan it into flame.

The bottom line on what to expect is actually very simple, don't have expectations about how God will initiate and use the gifts in your life.  It may be gradual or the Spirit might give you an immediate flood.  The Holy Spirit may have gifted you since childhood, or you may learn your spiritual gifts in your elderly years.  It doesn't matter.  Just be willing to follow the Holy Spirit and walk by His leading.

## Bringing the Gifts into the Local Church

Trying to bring the gifts into a church that is not currently using them or allowing their use by the Holy Spirit is never an easy task.  Whether you are a layperson who has come to believe that the Scriptures do teach their use today or if you are a pastor who wants to introduce them to the congregation, it can seem like an uphill road.

James Ryle, pastor of a church in Boulder, Colorado, once received a dream from God on this subject. During the fall of 1989, Ryle dreamed he was looking at a beautiful "English garden" in his backyard from inside his home. The sights and fragrances of the garden were wonderful. Then he saw the following,

"A sudden movement to the right of the garden caught my eye, and I turned to see a man enter it uninvited. I was somewhat affronted by his presumptuous intrusion, but when I saw what followed after him I became flabbergasted! Trailing behind the man like a domestic pet was a huge hippopotamus! The man was leading it along with reins he held firmly in his hand. I collected myself from the shock of the outrageous sight of the hippo in my garden and called to the man, 'What is that? What are you doing there?' At that precise moment I woke up. The oddity of the dream jarred me from my sleep." (4)

As for the meaning of the dream Ryle continues,

"I lay awake in my bed in the early morning hours contemplating the curious and unsettling sight. I asked, 'Lord, what was the meaning of that?' I was surprised by His answer. 'I am about to do a strange thing in My church,' He said, 'It will be like a man bringing a hippopotamus into his garden. Think about that.' 'What is the strange thing You will do?' I asked. He answered, 'I will surely pour out a vast prophetic anointing upon My church and release My people as a prophetic voice into the earth. It will seem so strange and

213

out of place – like a hippo in a garden – but this is what I will do.'" [5]

James Ryle dreamt about a prophetic movement God is bringing into the Church, but I think his dream is also applicable to God pouring His gifts out in any local church. It is seen as out of place and strange to many Christians because they are not used to it. Yet, there are definitely believers who welcome these moves of God and are very excited by anything God does. I think that every church has people in it who just wish that they would see God move in them with power in the same way He moved through others in the Bible.

I have heard people who belong to other churches who have had their pastors say such things as, "I have studied this issue and the gifts don't happen anymore, so we won't have those things in our church." There are others who begin to grow in the Spirit and are activated in the gifts, but then become frustrated in their churches because their pastors try to shut them down and ignore God's manifestation in their lives. These pastors think that any use of power is really from Satan, or they are unlearned in the gifts and don't know how to handle the situation. As Dr. Charles Kraft wrote, "Typically, the traditionalists who think they know how God behaves become the opponents of the new things God wants to do." [6]

So, how does your church get started in the gifts? The most important thing to remember is that only the Holy Spirit can bring this kind of change and renewal. The gifts are His manifestations and He is the One who interacts with the heart. At times, the Holy Spirit has even introduced the gifts into churches that have no real idea what they are or do not want them.

While Diana and I were praying through the dilemma of whether to pastor a church in Santa Maria, California, we called the previous pastor of the church to ask him some questions. During our phone conversation, I told him of my charismatic beliefs and he said something like, "That church will never accept the gifts." Diana and I had to really consider if this was the church for us.

The decision to pastor this church was made by God. One night I woke up at around 3 a.m. and God impressed Ezekiel 36 on my mind. I immediately got up and read the chapter. It was an outline of many of the things God would do in that church while I was their pastor, but one section stood out to us in relation to bringing the gifts to that church. In Ezekiel 36:26-27 it says, "I will give you a new heart and put a new spirit in you; I will remove from you your heart of stone and give you a heart of flesh. And I will put my Spirit in you and move you to follow my decrees and be careful to keep my laws." We knew that God was going to fill this church in a new way with the Holy Spirit. We accepted the call. During our time there, that church began to follow His decrees in relation to the gifts, and it grew stronger in upholding His law. As the gifts were poured out, there was an urgency to obey God.

But how does the Spirit bring about this kind of change? (I can only give you my idea of how He does this.) He changes the way we think, and then He changes the way we do church. Sometimes we will have an experience of the supernatural power of God that will cause us to reconsider the way we see this issue. Or the Spirit may open our eyes to certain passages of Scripture that show the power of God continuing today. Some believers change because of the testimony of God's power in others' lives. These are just a few examples. I am sure there are many other ways the Holy Spirit uses to bring this change.

What we are talking about is a shift of how we view reality and truth. This is commonly called a paradigm shift. [7] When you became a believer, you were taught how to read the Bible and how to relate to God. You experienced a paradigm shift. Many believers have been given the idea that God has ceased to use His power and gifts in people the way He did in the Bible. This idea becomes a stronghold in the mind that must be broken by the Holy Spirit. Though this ideology is not biblical, it is seen as the truth and supported with makeshift theology. Another paradigm shift is needed. The Holy Spirit comes to bring the shift and free us from this training and way of thinking.

James Belasco, in his book on corporate change, gives the following illustration, "Remember the elephant training parable. Trainers shackle young elephants with heavy chains to deeply embedded stakes. In that way the elephant learns to stay in its place. Older elephants never try to leave even though they have the strength to pull the stake and move beyond. Their conditioning limits their movements with only a small metal bracelet around their foot – attached to nothing. Yet when the circus tent catches on fire – and the elephant sees the flames with its own eyes and smells the smoke with its own nostrils – it forgets its old conditioning and changes." [8]

So, what is this smoke and fire the Holy Spirit uses to free the local elephants (I mean churches)? The fire is His love and power. As 1 Thessalonians 5:19-20 tells us, "Do not put out the Spirit's fire; do not treat prophecies with contempt." For many people, fire comes with brimstone and is equated with God's judgment. In thinking this way, they run the risk of missing out on God's burning love for us. When we speak of God's fire, it is a passionate love and refining element, which is demonstrated through His gifts.

Hebrews 12:29 says, "…for our God is a consuming fire." And as for His love, God says to us in Song of Songs 8:6-7a, "Place me like a seal over your heart, like a seal on your arm; for love is as strong as death, its jealousy unyielding as the grave. It burns like blazing fire, like a mighty flame. Many waters cannot quench love." This fire of God came to rest on the believers on the day of Pentecost as seen in Acts 2:1-4,

"When the day of Pentecost came, they were all together in one place. Suddenly a sound like the blowing of a violent wind came from heaven and filled the whole house where they were sitting. They saw what seemed to be tongues of fire that separated and came to rest on each of them. All of them were filled with the Holy Spirit and began to speak in other tongues as the Spirit enabled them."

Sometimes the Holy Spirit shows us His fire through His gifts and we want to see it spread. We see God's passion for us and for the lost and we become excited. We break free from any false chains holding our feet in place and run with the Spirit limited only by the true boundaries of the Bible.

The Holy Spirit moves some of us with His fire by letting us smell the smoke. The smoke makes us wonder what the fire is really like. Dr. Kraft wrote, "One of the felt needs many Evangelicals experience is the sense that there must be more to Christianity than we have witnessed so far. 'Why is our experience of Christianity so different from what we read about in the New Testament?' we ask. 'What is wrong with our brand of Christianity? Is there more?'" [9]

The fire of God once burned red hot in the Scottish Reformation and as a Presbyterian I don't want just to smell the smoke left over from that fire by simply reading the history. I want that fire to burn again and even brighter. As I pointed out in chapter three, the Presbyterian Church was born in the midst of prophecy and miracles. It is time for us to return to our roots. But even more, the New Testament Church was born of the Word and power of God. It is time for the whole Church to seek its roots as well.

The first Reformation of the 1500's brought the Church back to New Testament doctrinal purity based on the Scriptures alone. It was a move of God that made us orthodox in our faith and belief. But I don't think God considers that move to be complete. Many people mention that God is bringing a second reformation to the Church. I agree that we are in this next reformation and I believe that one of the things God is doing is moving us to return to act like the Church in the New Testament. He is making us orthopraxy in our mission, life and power as the Church. Just as there is right doctrine, so there is right practice. And having the Holy Spirit restore His gifts and works of power to the life of the Church is part of the life and ministry of the New Testament that we are missing.

### Knowing the Word and Power of God

As you may suspect from reading this book, I see no discrepancy between holding to the Bible and also holding to God's power and gifts in our present time. As I showed in a previous chapter, the apostle Paul brought people to faith in Jesus by presenting them with the truth of the Gospel and the demonstrations of the Spirit. He wanted their faith to be based on the power of God and upon the truth of His Word. But that wasn't limited to Paul alone.

Many of you are familiar with a discussion between Jesus and the Sadducees in Matthew 22:23-33. This group of religious leaders in Israel came to Jesus with a question about life after death. In response to their question Jesus gave this answer in verse 29, "You are in error because you do not know the Scriptures or the power of God." Though Jesus was dealing with the issue of the resurrection, He did not limit the power of God in His answer. Jesus did not say, "The Scriptures or the power of God for resurrection. He simply stated that they were in error, "because you do not know the Scriptures or the power of God."

The point I am making is that as Christians we must know both the Scriptures and the power of God in our lives. To focus on one of these to the neglect of the other is to leave us open to the consequences of error in our walk with God. I am not saying that a believer who knows both the Scriptures and the power of God is going to live completely void of error in belief. We all have much to learn about God and His ways. But Jesus put a value on knowing both.

As R.T. Kendall stated,

> "Take those of us who represent the Reformed tradition, as I do. We say, 'We must earnestly contend for the faith once delivered unto the saints. We must recover our Reformation heritage. We must return to the God of Jonathan Edwards and Spurgeon. We must be sound in doctrine.' Take those who come from a Pentecostal or charismatic perspective. They say, 'We must recover apostolic power. The need of the day is for a renewal of the gifts of the Spirit. Signs and wonders were seen in the Book of Acts; we too must see them. What is needed is a demonstration of power.' My message to you today is this. The church generally will struggle

on and on in its plea for God to restore the
honour of his Name until it is not one or the
other, but both: the Scriptures and the power of
God." [10]

The gifts and the power of God compliment the
Scriptures, because it was the Holy Spirit who breathed God's
word in written form and backs it up with endowments of
grace. The gifts are not given by the Spirit to upstage and
replace His Scriptures. The Scriptures are supreme and are the
guide and rule for the right use of God's power.

## What a Charismatic Church Looks Like

I once had breakfast with a man who had visited a
church I was pastoring. He had some questions for me on
different biblical topics. During our talk we came around to
the subject of the gifts of the Spirit. He made the statement
that the church I was pastoring didn't seem like a charismatic
church.

He obviously had some preconceived ideas of what a
charismatic church is like. It is interesting to hear what people
think goes on in a charismatic church. Some think that
everyone is speaking in tongues all the time. Others think that
prophecies are spoken constantly, or the people are crazy and
out of control.

I have worshipped in a number of churches that operate
in the gifts. I have been to some wild worship services and I
have been to some rather calm charismatic services. Is there
any stereotype or generalization that I can make about those
services of worship? Yes. They all love God very much and
like to have joyful and expressive worship in an informal
setting. By expressive I mean that they like to sing a lot of

praise to God and allow people freedom to enjoy being in God's presence.

Being a charismatic church does not mean that people are running around and yelling during the worship. But there is a freedom given to the Holy Spirit to do what He wants during the worship service. I have been to worship where there has been much in the way of ecstatic manifestations of the Spirit, yet I have been to many charismatic worship services where there have been no such manifestations. Remember that if you had attended a worship service led by the Reformed theologian Jonathan Edwards during the Great Awakening, some people would have cried out and there would be those with great agitations of their bodies. Also remember that if you had attended a worship service led by the apostle Paul that two or three would have spoken in tongues and or prophesied during the worship.

As a bottom line let me say that the type of worship practiced in a church does not dictate that the church is charismatic in its theology. There are many cessationist churches that also have a contemporary style of worship and also plenty of churches that are theologically charismatic but also have a traditional style of worship. You can have any style of worship as long as you allow for the Spirit to move and speak freely. Most charismatic churches have a contemporary style of worship, because it tends to allow for the most freedom of the Spirit's expression.

A church that is charismatic represents more than just what takes place in the worship service. You have to look at all of its ministries.

Let me use the church I pastored in Santa Maria as an example. First, we were charismatic because of what the Bible teaches and how that informed our theology. We taught the gifts and their use in the life and ministry of the church. That is why I was able to answer the man at breakfast that even though our church did not fit his notion of a charismatic church, we were such a church.

Second, we were charismatic in our worship. We took the answer to the first question of the Shorter Catechism of the Westminster Confession of Faith seriously when it states that, "The chief end of man is to glorify God and enjoy Him forever." We liked to glorify God and enjoy Him in our worship service.

Our worship was made up of three parts. First, we glorified God in praise songs and hymns. While we were singing we encouraged people to worship God freely. They could stand, raise their hands, sit where they were, or kneel before Him. People worshiped as God directed them. The second part of the service was devoted to prayer. We took prayer requests from the congregation and read them in the service. If someone was sick, we asked permission to lay hands on him or her and pray for their healing. This was the portion of the service where prophecy and tongues with interpretation were to be spoken. The third part of the service was devoted to the preaching and exposition of the Scriptures.

If there was a deeper need for ministry, we had a ministry team available after the worship service. This was a time when we did inner healing, deliverance or just prayed for guidance in a given situation in a separate room for confidentiality.

We also encouraged the use of the gifts during our small group home gatherings. They were encouraged because this was a safe place to try praying for others and listening to God.

It is important that the local church not only believe that the gifts are for their use, but also to be used by them. I have heard many pastors and other believers say that they are open to the gifts. This statement usually means that it is acceptable to them if the Holy Spirit uses others in that way, but they have no real intention of seeking the use of the gifts in their own life or in the life of their church.

In the life of any believer there is the need to transition from a paradigm shift to a change in practice. James 1:22 states, "Do not merely listen to the word, and so deceive yourselves. Do what it says." It is like a person who believes in learning the Word of God, but never studies what it says; or a person who believes in evangelism, but never shares their faith with an unbeliever. So it is with a person who believes in the gifts, but never seeks to have the Holy Spirit use them in his or her life or church.

A person must make the change in practice along with a change in belief. Sometimes the change in practice happens as fast as the change in belief, and sometimes it takes a little while. As Dr. Kraft wrote, "I had come through a change of perspective (my paradigm shift) to the point where I now thoroughly believed that God does heal people today. I had even come to the point where I was willing to join with others as they prayed for someone. But it was a frightening thing for me to imagine launching out and taking authority over an illness myself." [11]

## Launching Out in the Gifts

The best way I know of to launch out into the use of the gifts is to lay hands on someone and start praying for them. As I instruct the elders at our church, do what the book of James tells you in 5:14-15, "Is any one of you sick? He should call the elders of the church to pray over him and anoint him with oil in the name of the Lord. And the prayer offered in faith will make the sick person well; the Lord will raise him up. If he has sinned, he will be forgiven." I like to give a small vial of anointing oil to each of the elders in the churches I pastor and tell them to anoint anyone who is asking for healing and pray with faith for their healing.

Pray with faith for someone as you lay on hands. Pray for as many people as you can. I believe you will see God move in ways that will leave you in awe.

# Chapter Ten
## Dealing with Fears Related to the Gifts

As some Christians think about the gifts of the Spirit and functioning in them, one of their initial responses is fear. Yet, the Scriptures tell us not to have fear. 1 Timothy 1:6-7 says, "For this reason I remind you to fan into flame the gift of God, which is in you through the laying on of my hands. For God did not give us a spirit of timidity, but a spirit of power, of love and of self-discipline." Other versions of the Bible translate timidity as fear or cowardice. The Greek word for timidity in this passage is *deileia* of which Gordon Fee wrote, "It is frequently used in contexts of struggle or warfare of those who pull back from the struggle as cowards." [1]

### Fear #1 – Loss of Control

As Diana and I began to teach about the gifts of the Spirit at Santa Maria Community Church, we heard many people express anxiety. There was the fear of the loss of personal control. Members would say, "I don't want to do those kinds of things." I think that in their minds they pictured themselves experiencing some of the more wild manifestations of the Spirit they had heard about or seen.

There was also an anxiety of loss of control during congregational worship. Some would say, "What do you think the congregation would do if someone spoke in tongues or was slain in the Spirit?"

What these brothers and sisters really had to deal with was the fear of the unknown. Have you ever tried to get a child to eat something new? Sometimes the child won't even taste it because they think it is going to taste bad, even though it may taste sweet. My son, Andrew, usually judged whether he was going to try a new food by how it looked. If it looked good or if it looked like something else he liked, then he might try it. Otherwise, he had to be pretty hungry to try a new food.

I think it is the same thing with the gifts. Many Christians don't want to try the gifts because they don't think they look good or they are not part of what they are familiar with in their practice of the faith. They have seen or heard of wild things taking place in churches that use the gifts and they avoid the whole issue. Or they associate the gifts with people in questionable ministries and don't want to be seen as being like them.

What the average Christian needs to know about the gifts is that he or she won't necessarily experience the ecstatic manifestations of the Spirit when used by Him in His gifts. Will some Christians be offended by the activity of the gifts in the church? Yes, I think some will. What happens when the Spirit speaks in tongues in the congregation? Some people don't like it and decide to leave, but those who listen and wait for an interpretation are blessed. If you have a mindset that says God does not use tongues, you will be offended. But if you humble yourself before God, you will be blessed whether there are ecstatic manifestations or not when the Spirit moves in the Church.

I have attended a few prophetic conferences in which there was a common message from God to His Church: Acting strangely for the sake of acting strangely is wrong in the Church. But sometimes God does things that seem strange and out of place to us. This is why God gave us 1 Corinthians 14:39-40 which states, "Therefore, brothers, be eager to prophesy, and do not forbid speaking in tongues. But everything should be done in a fitting and orderly way."

Many Presbyterians have heard that people should worship and act "decently and in order." The image such people have is that there should be two hymns, one read prayer and a sermon in an orderly worship service. This passage is not saying that a worship service where prophecy and tongues are practiced is out of order. It is saying that the gifts are to be used in a fitting and orderly manner. The gifts are fitting and part of the order of the Church. Our concept of "fitting and orderly" can be different from God's.

I believe what happened to the believers on the day of Pentecost was done by the Spirit in a fitting and orderly way. Yet, they were accused of being drunk at an early hour of the morning, showing that others found them out of order. I like worship services where everything is "fitting" as much as anyone else, but I also want all that the Holy Spirit will pour out on us. If that means some things will take place when the Spirit is using His power and that makes us uncomfortable, then I want that too.

I know enough about God to know that His goal is not chaos. God is, by His own revelation, a God of order. By His order, He is building His Church. But the power He uses and the means by which He displays His ministry are not always done in a fashion that is acceptable to many believers.

It is important for those who are being used by the Spirit to respect others around them. While attending a conference a woman approached a pastor I knew and told him that God was calling people to dance like a child. He very nicely told her that she could dance if she wanted in the back of the church, but God wasn't calling him to dance.

### Fear #2 – Problems and Separation in the Church
Some Christians do not want the Holy Spirit to use His gifts in their church because they are afraid that there will be

problems and possible separation in the very fellowship of believers they love.  Many of us are familiar with the common saying, "If it isn't broken don't fix it."  Our local church may seem as if it is doing just fine without the gifts functioning. But, if the Bible says that we are to desire the gifts, then I am willing to say that our churches are malfunctioning without the Holy Spirit's using His supernatural gifts is us and through us.

I have seen too much healing and direction given by the Spirit through His gifts to say that I would want to pastor a church without the gifts.  I have witnessed more freedom and peace in the lives of those who have been ministered to in power than I could give them in pastoral counseling.  I have also seen churches grow in faith and in awe of God by His demonstrations of supernatural ministry.

For some pastors, the gifts are controversial and they would rather avoid them.  We all want peace in our churches, but I don't want peace at the cost of excluding of the Holy Spirit.  This is too high a price to pay for that kind of peace.

The Bible never tells us to avoid the supernatural gifts and power of the Holy Spirit.  It does give us other things we are to avoid within the local church:

1.  Titus 3:9, "But avoid foolish controversies and genealogies and arguments and quarrels about the law, because these are unprofitable and useless."

2.  1 Timothy 6:20, "Turn away from godless chatter and the opposing ideas of what is falsely called knowledge."

3.  2 Timothy 2:16, "Avoid godless chatter, because those who indulge in it will become more and more ungodly. (Just before this Paul warned about quarreling about words.)

4.  2 Timothy 3:5, Paul instructs Timothy to avoid people who have a form of godliness, but who

deny its power. (In this passage, Paul tells Timothy to avoid other types of people besides those who deny the power of God.)

Why are we to avoid these people in the Church? These types of people like dead faith. Their faith consists of chatter, controversies and arguments, which only bring division in the body of Christ. I feel sorry for believers who think that the power of Christianity is found in winning arguments and proving other people wrong. Surely we, as followers of Jesus, stand for the truth. But the truth is to be given to others in love.

I used to love to debate anyone I could find, especially during my college years. I thought that if I could beat the other person by proving how wrong he or she was, I was doing the work of God. It didn't really matter what the point of contention was, I was going to win. A funny thing happened to me during those college years, God took away my ability to debate. I knew in my heart that God was displeased with what was coming out of my mouth. And what comes from your mouth shows what is in your heart. I then realized that I could win a debate, but be a detriment to the kingdom of God. The Spirit showed me that He wanted me to convey the truth with a heart full of love. More people will listen if you speak the truth with love than if you speak the truth with a callous heart and all the right ammunition.

Why does God tell us to avoid those who argue and mull over controversies? Proverbs 6:19b tells us that God detests, "A man who stirs up dissension among brothers." Our job as Christians is to build the Church. We are to build each other up. Arguments and controversies tear believers down and leave them vulnerable to the demonic.

So, if the supernatural gifts are controversial, shouldn't Christians avoid them? No. We are told by God to desire the gifts in the church. We are also told not to put out the Holy Spirit's fire by treating prophesies with contempt. When used properly, the gifts are one of the greatest tools of encouragement the Spirit uses in building His Church.

I am not saying that there aren't problems associated with the use of the gifts; there are. But if there are problems related to the gifts, it is not because of the Spirit Himself. He is Almighty God and does His work perfectly. Any problems associated with the supernatural gifts are first due to human error and sin. Of course, the sinful nature of the flesh is the key ingredient to most if not all of the problems we have in our churches and in the world.

Our sinful human nature causes us to doubt when God calls for faith in praying for healing. Our lack of holiness causes us to foul up a prophetic utterance of the Spirit when we try to intimidate someone with the information or add our own thoughts to it. Our sinful pride allows us to make the gift of tongues a spiritual litmus test.

There are also perceived problems with the supernatural gifts when they are used in the presence of a rigid and legalistic governmental structure in the Church. As I quoted Heron earlier, "As the Church consolidates into an ordered institution, there increases the danger of treating the Spirit as the possession of the church, which grows hardened and is no longer open to the Spirit's free energies. The resultant tensions between Spirit and structure have surfaced repeatedly through Christian history." [2] The Holy Spirit will challenge elders for the control of the local church as well as whole denominations. But if the elders reject the Spirit's control, the Spirit will lessen His involvement in that church. Those elders have put out the Spirit's fire.

This is why some have noticed that there were times in Church history when it seemed that the gifts had ceased. As Heron noted, "Up to about the middle of the second century, there appears to have been a general decline both in charismatic manifestations and in the vital sense of the living presence of the Spirit." [3] This would correspond to growth in the institutionalized Church.

The problem is that the institutionalized Church can confuse the actual leading of the Holy Spirit with the Church's own governmental acts. While attending a denominational meeting, I heard an official of the Evangelical Presbyterian Church make an extremely near-sighted statement. Following a vote on a controversial issue, he said, "When the Assembly has voted the Holy Spirit has spoken." I couldn't believe he let that out of his mouth. But it is an example of the way the institutionalized Church will try to replace the "living presence of the Spirit." Though the Holy Spirit can use individuals to speak in such meetings and can influence the vote of a court of the Church, a vote by members of the Church is not to be taken as prophecy or the expressed will of the Spirit.

Once the Church has established its rules for operating, it may not like the changes God may bring. The Spirit is expected to be a gentleman who will observe the Church's rules. Jesus had to address this amongst the Jews in Mark 7:1-9 which says,

"The Pharisees and some of the teachers of the law who had come from Jerusalem gathered around Jesus and saw some of his disciples eating food with hands that were 'unclean,' that is, unwashed. (The Pharisees and all the Jews do not eat unless they give their hands a ceremonial washing, holding to the tradition of the elders. When they come from the marketplace they do not eat unless they wash. And they observe many other traditions, such as the washing of cups, pitchers and kettles.) "So the Pharisees and teachers of the law asked Jesus, 'Why don't your disciples live according to the tradition of the elders instead of eating their food with 'unclean' hands?'" "He replied, 'Isaiah was right when he prophesied about you hypocrites; as it is written: "These people honor me with their lips, but their hearts are far from me. The worship me in vain; their teachings are but rules taught by men. You have let go of the commands of God and are holding on to the traditions of men. And he said to them: 'You have a fine way of setting aside the commands of God in order to observe your own traditions!'"

Though I function as a pastor under a Book of Order, which lists the rules and procedures for governing the local church and the other courts of the denomination, I know that it is really the traditions of the elders of the Presbyterian Church. I think that it is a good book, but I am sure that it could also get in the way of following the Spirit.

Our theologies can also be the "traditions of the elders" mentioned by Jesus. As was stated in the beginning of this book, many of the Reformed churches have allowed for a tradition that says that the supernatural gifts ceased when the Apostles died. This fallacy has become institutionalized within much of the Reformed faith. They have set aside the clear teaching of Scripture for the use of the gifts by the Spirit in the Church, and instead observe their tradition of cessation. The spirit of the Pharisees is still active in the Church. It can take hold of us all at different times and over different issues. This is just one example.

Pentecostals and Charismatics can do the same thing. They can see the Spirit move in some wonderful way and assume this is how He will always move. Though we can identify some systematic ways in which the Holy Spirit manifests Himself in the Church, we must recognize that He does new things as well.

Since the supernatural gifts are rejected by many and misused by others, there will be growing pains in the Church that may lead to discipline, or worse, separation in some churches. But this is not a reason to avoid this ministry of the Holy Spirit. Some Christians will still value the safety of a church that is quiet and does not have to deal with these issues. For those who feel this way, let me quote Admiral Grace Hopper who once said, "Ships are safe at port, but that is not what ships are made for."

## Fear #3 – Demons and Demonic Influence

I remember hearing a person tell Diana and me that she wouldn't want the gifts in her church, because she wouldn't want any demonic activity to take place. The underlying belief is that the gifts have ceased, so any supernatural activity is really from the demonic. As has been shown in this book, the gifts have not ceased, so you shouldn't attribute all supernatural uses of power to the enemy.

Some don't want the gifts, though they know God still uses them, because they also know that the demonic will try to counterfeit what God is doing. John Calvin had some good insight when he wrote, "And we may also fitly remember that Satan has his miracles, which, though they are deceitful tricks rather than true powers, are of such sort as to mislead the simple-minded and untutored." [4] God heals, so the enemy will use power to heal. God gives prophecy, so the enemy will give divination of the future. (This comes in the form of false prophecies, horoscopes, psychic powers, palm reading, etc.) Just because the enemy can counterfeit the work of God it doesn't mean we should avoid what God is doing. We uphold teaching in the Church even though we know that the enemy can twist the Scriptures and introduce wrong theology. We teach and encourage learning in the Church, because we know to test the teaching in light of the Scriptures and trust that the Holy Spirit is supremely powerful to instruct us as we grow in Christ.

Others just want to live a peaceful life without having to deal with the demonic at all. They don't want to test any works to see if they are counterfeit. They don't want anything to do with spiritual warfare at all. But that is not the reality of being a Christian. We were not called to run from the enemy. Instead, we have been given the armor of God and told that the gates of Hell will not prevail against the Church. Yet, some want peace at all costs, even the cost of not having all that God wants for us.

General H. Norman Schwarzkopf, the commanding general of Desert Storm, wrote of this mentality, which he encountered while commanding a battalion in Vietnam. He states, "On a couple of occasions, troops on ambush patrol simply let the Vietcong walk by. The men had figured out that if they didn't shoot at the VC, the VC wouldn't know they were there and so wouldn't shoot either." [5]

Not having the gifts or operating in the supernatural power of God does not mean that the demonic will not attack you or your church. The gifts of the Spirit are some of the most powerful weapons God has given to us for combating the enemy. I am afraid that some Christians would rather sit quietly and let the enemy move freely.

But you might think, "If I don't allow the gifts, then the demonic cannot infiltrate my life or the life of my church with false power and false words." Counterfeit gifts are only one way in which the demonic will try to infiltrate your life and the life of your church, but there are other schemes of the enemy beside false gifts. Some Christians and churches have religious spirits operating in them and through them.

Rick Joyner, a pastor who is gifted with prophecy, defines this type of spirit by writing, "A religious spirit is a demon which seeks to substitute religious activity for the power of the Holy Spirit in our lives." [6] This is a demonic spirit particularly dangerous to the life of a congregation, because the members of that church can act and feel very religious without the presence of the Holy Spirit.

Joyner points out that one of the ways in which this type of demonic spirit works is from a foundation of pride. He wrote, "When a religious spirit is founded upon pride, it is evidenced by *perfectionism*. The perfectionist sees everything as black and white." [7] He further states, "One with a religious spirit can usually point to problems with great accuracy, but seldom has solutions, except to tear down what has already been built." [8]

This kind of perfectionism comes from and leads to an increased amount of pride in a believer. The religious spirit will then convince a believer that it really knows what is best for their church and everyone else is basically wrong and lacking in true knowledge. Ultimately this unclean spirit will drive the believer to seek to gain control in their church, so that the church will be "right." Such a person will become rigid in his or her viewpoints and will oppose any change to the "correct" way of conducting the church, including opposition to changes brought by the Holy Spirit Himself.

The worst form of this demonic spirit has been labeled a Jezebel spirit, after King Ahab's wife Queen Jezebel in 1 and 2 Kings and also from Revelation 2:20. Joyner wrote, "The Jezebel spirit usually gains its dominion by making political alliances, and often it uses a deceptively humble and submissive demeanor in order to manipulate. However, once this spirit gains authority, it will usually manifest a strong control spirit and shameless presumption." [9]

Just as Queen Jezebel opposed the prophet Elijah, so the Jezebel spirit opposes God's prophetic ministry in the Church today. [10] Joyner pointed out the problem when he wrote, "The Jezebel spirit especially attacks the prophetic ministry, because that ministry has an important place in preparing the way for the Lord." [11] And prophecy is, "the primary vehicle through which the Lord gives timely, strategic direction to His people." [12]

I think that the Jezebel spirit was freely using the Roman Catholic Church to shut down the Scottish Reformation and kill the reformers, such as George Wishart and John Knox, because of the powerful prophetic ministry God was manifesting in that movement. Likewise, today these types of demonic spirits move quickly to shut down the prophetic ministries God is raising up. These spirits do not want the Church to live in the power of the Holy Spirit and will do what is necessary to keep the Church in a "form of godliness, but denying its power." (2 Timothy 3:5)

Surely the demonic can use counterfeit power to try to fool the Church, but God has given us spiritual gifts to detect this. One of the things I like about charismatic churches is their knowledge and experience in deliverance ministry. Many of these churches have come to recognize the activity of the enemy as God activates the gift of discernment in those fellowships. The Holy Spirit will warn members with this gift by telling them when the demonic is at work as what kind or type of demonic spirit it is.

I am not trying to say that churches that have the supernatural gifts in operation are impervious to the schemes of the enemy. The enemy will try to infiltrate and control any Christian and any church.

## Fear #4 – Unity With Other Christians

One of the best things the Spirit gives us is the unity He builds amongst Christians.  But that can cause many to be uncomfortable.  Some fear that they will have to work with other Christians who do not share their understandings of the Bible and theology.  I have met people who want nothing to do with a Calvinist and I have known Calvinists who would rather avoid anyone who isn't a Calvinist.  For that matter, I have met Calvinists who don't want to associate with other Calvinists because of some minor theological differences.

Some Christians separate over versions of the Bible.  Some people are King James Version only and others know that God can use other versions just as well and just as accurately.  Some separate over worship styles.  Within some Reformed churches there is an adherence to what is called the regulative principle of worship.  If the Bible doesn't give you permission to do something then you can't do it.  I believe that if the Bible doesn't forbid something then it is permissible.  These are only a couple of examples of the things that divide believers.

I think that there is an inbred pride within the Reformed tradition that keeps it separated from other movements and theological backgrounds.  I remember a moderator from a Presbyterian General Assembly who exhibited an amazing amount of "Reformed" pride when he addressed the Presbytery of which I was a member.  He basically said that "true" theology was the gift that the Reformed faith had to give to the rest of the world, and that any other denomination that held to another theological understanding of the Bible was wrong.  He made fun of how they did ministry.

As I sat there and listened to him, I was really upset by what he said.  I knew that God couldn't be pleased with his arrogance.  In Proverbs 6:16-19, God states the seven things that are detestable to Him.  Read how it starts, "There are six things the Lord hates, seven that are detestable to Him: haughty eyes…" The first thing on the list of things God hates is haughty eyes.  In other words, God hates it when someone is arrogant.

As the Holy Spirit calls for unity in the Church, that "Reformed" pride will be an opposing factor.  I am not saying that the Reformed churches are the only ones who allow their pride to alienate them from what God is doing.  That kind of haughty arrogance runs through many traditions and movements in the Church.  This attitude is the kind of garbage that religious spirits feed on and encourage in the Church. And that arrogance allows different theological traditions to feel as if they are called by God to be the sole defenders of all that is sacred and true.  They forget that the call of God is to preach the Gospel, not guard it against other Christians.

The reality is that many in the Reformed tradition have no problem being separated from other Christians.  But I think they do this to their detriment.

In the April 1992 edition of National Geographic magazine, there is an article on lions living in the Ngorongoro Crater in Africa.  The crater is isolated from the Serengeti Plain and so the researchers did a study to determine the amount of inbreeding that has taken place in the crater.  They found that most, if not all, of the lions were the descendents of four lionesses.  There had been a devastating increase of biting flies in the early 1960's, which attacked the seventy or so lions in the crater and left only a handful to repopulate.  After much research they found, "a striking lack of genetic variability in the crater lion's immune defense systems.  This loss of genetic variability could render a population especially susceptible to an epidemic." [13]  The researchers actually believe that the lions were susceptible to the biting flies because of many generations of inbreeding in the crater. This resulted in a weakness in their immune defense system.

I think that it is much the same for the Church. As different theological traditions become isolated from each other, they begin to show signs of hereditary defects. Bad strains of theology are allowed to stay, rather than rooted out. Cessationism is a good example. But I have read other such problems in other denominations, such as the belief that Christians cannot be demonized. It is based on the thought that demons cannot be where God is and since a Christian is filled with the Holy Spirit, he or she cannot be possessed by demons. Yet, I know of too many Christians involved in deliverance ministry who have freed fellow believers from demonic control in sinful areas of their lives. As long as those who believe Christians cannot be demonized remain isolated in their belief, they remain an open target for the enemy. They need to be united with those who know better.

The good news is that the Spirit does unite Christians with His supernatural power, and for a reason. I make a point of regularly meeting with groups of pastors from different church backgrounds in the different cities where I have pastored. Ordinarily I would have had little in common with them, since we are from different denominations. What we have in common is our love for Jesus, an evangelical theological perspective and the use of the gift of the Spirit.

We take seriously what the apostle Paul wrote,

"As a prisoner for the Lord, then, I urge you to live a life worthy of the calling you have received. Be completely humble and gentle; be patient, bearing with one another in love. Make every effort to keep the unity of the Spirit through the bond of peace. There is one body and one Spirit – just as you were called to one hope when you were called – one Lord, one faith, one baptism; one God and Father of all, who is over all and through all and in all. But to each one of us grace has been given as Christ apportioned it."

We are from different denominations and diverse theological backgrounds, but we are one in the Spirit. The reason that the Spirit brings Christians together is that no one denomination or movement has all that God has to give. There are wonderful things that I have to learn from Pentecostals. I have benefited as I have learned from them.

Being united with them in the Spirit doesn't mean that I totally agree with them in theology. I know our differences, and some of those differences may never be resolved until Jesus returns. I am willing to live with that. But the Holy Spirit has used each of us to minister to each other in power and with the gifts. We listen closely to the Spirit to know how to pray for our city, state and nation. What it has changed inside of me is that it is more important for me to be known as a child in the kingdom of God, than as a Presbyterian.

There is a greater goal that the Spirit has in mind beyond the imparting of theology and experience to each other. In John 17:20-23 Jesus said,

"My prayer is not for them alone. I pray also for those who will believe in me through their message, that all of them may be one, Father, just as you are in me and I am in you. May they also be in us so that the world may believe that you have sent me. I have given them the glory that you gave to me, that they may be one as we are one: I in them and you in me. May they be brought to complete unity to let the world know that you sent me and have loved them even as you have loved me."

Our unity was so extremely important to Jesus that He put it in His prayer in John 17, which is commonly known as the "High Priestly Prayer." God desires that Christians live in unity. He did not say that we have to embrace heretics. But when Christians are able to hold to the central truths of the Gospel, we are one. When we can dwell as one, it is one more confirmation to the world that the Father sent the Son as the Messiah.

It is the Holy Spirit who builds this unity among Christians. He is the One who is building a spiritual house as a dwelling for the Most High. So, it doesn't surprise me that those who are used by the Spirit with supernatural gifts are drawn to each other. God pours His grace for salvation and power on all denominations and movements. What is surprising is when people who claim to have the Holy Spirit dwelling in them can easily separate from other Christians and isolate themselves. Some Christians justify it by declaring that they hold to true theology, and the other groups don't.

What I have learned and found to be true is that God is no respecter of theology. I have seen Him use His gifts of power in Calvinists and Arminians. Of course, God does not use those who deny the basic tenets of the faith. I do not believe that God uses His grace in Mormons, Jehovah's Witnesses, United Pentecostals or any other cult or any other religion.

I know that some Christians fear that they will have to accept other Christians as brothers and sisters if they get involved in the gifts. Some Christians have radically different styles of worship, which we may not like. Some experience manifestations that we question. And some may have differing opinions on some Scriptures that are very important to us. But those things are okay. Just because someone is not "truly" Reformed in his or her view of Scripture doesn't mean

241

that we can have nothing to do with them. As long as we share the essentials of the faith, we should extend friendship.

Don't let your traditions and theological pride keep you from joining in what the Holy Spirit is doing and from what He wants to do in you. As the apostle Peter wrote, "All of you, clothe yourselves with humility toward one another, because, 'God opposes the proud but gives grace to the humble.'" (1 Peter 5:5b) Being humble is the true prerequisite for God to use His kingdom power of grace in doing supernatural work through you. That humility also means accepting those whom He accepts and being used with those whom He uses.

### Fear #5 – Not Being Used With Power

What if I pray and nothing happens? That was one of my greatest fears when I would think about praying for someone's healing. There is a part of us that hates the idea of failing and falling down.

I remember when my sister, Lynn, was teaching me how to snow ski. We were on a ski trip at Lake Tahoe and she had left me to practice on an easy run. When she returned, she noticed that I was skiing carefully so that I wouldn't fall down. She told me that I would never learn how to ski well if I didn't take more risks. In other words, wiping out in the snow means that you are learning.

As you launch out into the gifts, you are going to wipe out now and then. You may pray for someone's healing and that person won't be healed. You will have what you think is a word for him or her, and you will be wrong. It is all a process of fanning your gift into flame and learning to hear God's voice.

There are two words of advice that I have heard and found helpful. First, be a fool for God. If you think God is leading you to minister to someone, then do what you think God is telling you to do. It may seem foolish to you, but God may be doing something really powerful.

I have heard several testimonies by people who risked doing something they thought God was telling them to do, and as a result saw God do awesome, supernatural work. Everything from sharing the Gospel with someone they didn't know at all to praying for someone's healing then seeing results.

The second word of advice is this: pray for as many people as you can. Minister to people. There is a good chance you won't see the gifts if you don't minister to others. That is why God gives them. Even if you pray for the healing of one hundred people and only one is healed. That one person was healed by the power of God! So, pray for two hundred people and see if two more are healed by God's gracious power.

### What We Should Really Fear

As you can see, I don't think we really need to fear these five things listed above. If the Spirit is leading us, we should be bold in following Him. What we should really be anxious about is quenching the Holy Spirit's fire. I am afraid of not seeing the life of the Spirit in my church. I want all that the Holy Spirit wants to give to the church that I worship in. I want them to hear His voice, see His power and grow closer to Jesus.

I am also afraid that much of the Church will ignore many of the moves that the Holy Spirit is doing today. Because of ignorance of how the Holy Spirit moves, many parts of the Church may miss seeing what God is doing and how He is ministering to a hurting world. As Heron wrote, "It is…that non-charismatic Christianity may be insufficiently open to the movement of the Spirit on experiential levels other than those that have been safely institutionalized, sacramentalized, intellectualized, or otherwise comfortably domesticated in the household of faith." [14] The Church cannot be so presumptuous as to dictate rules to the Holy Spirit.

# Conclusion
## Keep in Step With the Spirit


In Galatians 5:25 the apostle Paul wrote, "Since we live by the Spirit, let us keep in step with the Spirit." The Holy Spirit is working in our lives, our churches and throughout the world. It is imperative for us to follow the Spirit's leading in our lives and in ministry. As John Calvin wrote, "Every day we need the Holy Spirit that we may not mistake our way." [1] When we stop listening to the Spirit and giving Him the freedom to move in our churches, we are at serious risk of mistaking our way.

The Father, Son and Holy Spirit want to pour so many blessings out upon us it is almost unimaginable. The apostle Paul listed some of these blessings when he wrote, "I pray also that the eyes of your heart may be enlightened in order that you may know the hope to which he has called you, the riches of his glorious inheritance in the saints, and his incomparably great power for us who believe." (Ephesians 1:18-19a) As saints we have an inheritance that God is giving us. It is an inheritance of being called a child of God, which comes with authority to heal the sick and broken-hearted and cast out demons. God has also given us great power, the kind of power that demonstrates His supernatural ministry to a Church and a world in need of His compassionate touch.

All of this is based on a loving relationship with Him. He loves us so much. His heart is passionate in caring for us and giving us the wonders of His kingdom. Allow God to supernaturally call you to be close to Him. As James wrote, "Come near to God and he will come near to you." (James 4:8)

Seek God with all of your heart. Keep the first commandment and love God with all of who you are.

What is of true value in the Faith? It is following the living God. It is knowing Him and being made known by Him. He cleared the way for us to receive all that He has for us through the atonement of Jesus on the cross. God has removed our sin. He has regenerated us by the Spirit and called us into a passionately loving relationship with Him.

Worship Him in Spirit and in truth. Know the Word and the power of God. The Holy Spirit will show us His wonders and cause us to be in awe of the Father. He will lead us so that, like King David, we will say, "One thing I ask of the Lord, this is what I seek: that I may dwell in the house of the Lord all the days of my life, to gaze upon the beauty of the Lord and to seek him in his temple."

Come Holy Spirit and put this desire deep inside of us. Empower us and use us for the name of Jesus Christ and to the glory of the Father. Let this passion well up inside of us, so that the world can see and thirst for the living water.


I hope by reading this book you see that the Holy Spirit has never stopped using His power and gifts in the Church. We can embrace the ministry of the Spirit from a Reformed (or Calvinistic) perspective and welcome His work in our local church.

# Bibliography

Ahlstrom, Sydney E. *A Religious History Of The American People*. New Haven: Yale University Press, 1972

Augustine, *Confessions*, Book III, XI, as translated by R.S. Pine-Coffin. New York: Pengine Books, 1961

Bauer, Walter, William F. Arndt, F. Wilbur Gingrich, and Frederick W. Danker. *A Greek-English Lexicon Of The New Testament and Other Early Christian Literature*. Chicago: The University of Chicago Press, 1979

Belasco, James A. *Teaching the elephant to dance: the manager's guide to empowering change*. New York: Penguin Group, 1990

Berkhof, Louis. *Systematic Theology*. Grand Rapids: Wm. B. Eerdmans Publishing Co., 1941

Bickle, Mike. *Growing In The Prophetic*. Orlando: Creation House, 1996

Boettner, Loraine. *The Reformed Doctrine Of Predestination*. Phillipsburg: Presbyterian and Reformed Publishing Company, 1932

Bromiley, Geoffrey W. *Theological Dictionary Of The New Testament, Abridged In One Volume*. Gerhard Kittel and Gerhard Friedrich, eds. Grand Rapids: William B. Eerdmans Publishing Company, 1985

Bruce, F.F. *The Book Of Acts, The New International Commentary On The New Testament.* Grand Rapids: William B. Eerdmans Publishing Company, 1988

Bruce, F.F. *The New Century Bible Commentary, I & II Corinthians.* Grand Rapids: Wm. B. Eerdmans Publ. Co., and London: Morgan & Scott Publ. Ltd., 1971

Bruner, Fredrick Dale. *A Theology of the Holy Spirit.* Grand Rapids: Wm. B. Eerdmans Publishing Company, 1970

Burgess, Stanley M., Gary B. McGee and Patrick H. Alexander, eds. *Dictionary of Pentecostal And Charismatic Movements.* Grand Rapids: Zondervan Publishing House, 1998

Cain, Paul and R.T. Kendall. *The Word and the Spirit.* Eastbourne: Kingsway Publications, 1996

Calvin, John. *Commentary on a harmony of the Evangelists, Vol. 3.* Trans. Rev. William Pringle. Grand Rapids: Wm. B. Eerdmans Publishing Company, 1949

Calvin, John. *Commentary on the First Epistle To The Corinthians.* Trans. Rev. William Pringle. Grand Rapids: Wm. B. Eerdmans Publishing Company, 1949

Calvin, John. *Institutes of the Christian Religion.* John T. McNeill ed., Philadelphia: The Westminster Press, 1960
Clinton, Bobby. *Spiritual Gifts.* Beaverlodge: Horizon House Publishers. 1985

Cooke, Graham. *Developing Your Prophetic Gifting*. Kent: Sovereign World Ltd., 1994

Deere, Jack. *Surprised by the Power of the Spirit*. Grand Rapids: Zondervan Publishing House, 1993

Deere, Jack. *Surprised By The Voice Of God: How God Speaks Today Through Prophecies, Dreams, and Visions*. Grand Rapids: Zondervan Publishing House, 1996

Edwards, Jonathan. *Thoughts On The Revival Of Religion In New England, "Nature of the work in a particular instance," from The Works of Jonathan Edwards, Volume 1*. Carlisle: The Banner of Truth Trust, 1987

Elwell, Walter A., ed. *Evangelical Dictionary of Theology*. Grand Rapids: Baker Book House, 1984

Fee, Gordon D. *God's Empowering Presence, The Holy Spirit in the Letters of Paul*. Peabody: Hendrickson Publishers, Inc., 1994

Gardner, Rex. *Healing Miracles*. London: Darton, Longman and Todd, 1986

Hawthorne, Gerald F. *The Presence & The Power, The significance of the Holy Spirit in the life and ministry of Jesus*. Dallas: Word Publishing, 1991

Hayford, Jack. *The Beauty Of Spiritual Language: Unveiling the Mystery of Speaking in Tongues*. Nashville: Thomas Nelson Publishers, 1996

Heron, Alasdair I. C. *The Holy Spirit*. Philadelphia: The Westminster Press, 1983

Hodge, Charles. *Systematic Theology, Vol. 2*. Grand Rapids: Wm. B. Eerdmans Publishing Co., 1997

Howie, John. *Scots Worthies*. Revised by Rev. W. H. Carslaw. Edinburgh: Johnstone, Hunter, and Company, 1870

Joyner, Rick. *Overcoming the Religious Spirit*. Charlotte: MorningStar Publications, 1996

Knox, John. *The History Of The Reformation Of Religion Within The Realm Of Scotland*. Edited by C.J. Guthrie, Q.C., London: Adam and Charles Black, 1898

Kraft, Charles H. *Christianity With Power*. Ann Arbor: Servant Publications, 1989

Kraft, Charles H. *Defeating Dark Angels, Breaking Demonic Oppression in the Believer's Life*. Ann Arbor: Vine Books, 1992

Kuyper, Abraham. *The Holy Spirit*. New York: Funk & Wagnalls Company, 1900

Kydd, Ronald A. N. *Charismatic Gifts in the Early Church*. Peabody: Hendrickson Publishers, 1984

Ladd, George Eldon. *A Theology of the New Testament.* Grand Rapids: William B. Eerdmans Publishing Company, 1974

MacNutt, Francis. *Healing.* Notre Dame: Ave Maria Press, 1974

*New Bible Dictionary.* Wheaton: Tyndale House Publishers, Inc., 1982

Newman, Barclay M., Jr. *A Concise Greek-English Dictionary of the New Testament.* Stuttgart: Biblia-Druck, 1971

Nienkirchen, Charles W. *A. B. Simpson And The Pentecostal Movement.* Peabody: Hendrickson Publishers, 1992

Olson, Bessie G. *John Knox, A Great Intercessor.* Des Moines: The Boone Publishing Co.

Ridley, Jasper. *John Knox.* Oxford: Clarendon Press, 1968

Ryle, James. *Hippo In The Garden: A Non Religious Approach To Having A Conversation With God.* Orlando: Creation House, 1993

Smellie, Alexander. *Men of the Covenant, The Story of the Scottish Church in the Years of the Persecution.* London: Andrew Melrose, 1903

Schwartz, Hillel. *The French Prophets, The History of a Millenarian Group in Eighteenth-Century England.* Berkeley: University of California Press, 1980

Schwarzkopf, General H. Norman. *The Autobiography, It Doesn't Take A Hero.* New York: Linda Grey Bantam Books, 1992

*The Book of Confessions, Presbyterian Church (U.S.A.).* New York: Published By The Office Of The General Assembly, 1983

*The Compact Edition Of The Oxford English Dictionary, Vol. 1, A-O.* New York: Oxford University Press, 1971

Torrey, R. A. *"The Personality and Deity of the Holy Spirit." The Fundamentals.* Los Angeles: The Bible Institute Of Los Angeles, 1917

Warfield, Benjamin B. *Counterfeit Miracles.* Edinburgh: The Banner of Truth Trust

Wagner, C. Peter. *How To Have A Healing Ministry In Any Church.* Ventura: Regal Books, 1988

Wagner, C. Peter. *Signs & Wonders Today.* Altamonte Springs: Creation House, 1987

Wagner, C. Peter. *Spreading the Fire.* Ventura: Regal Books, 1994

Wells, David F., ed. *Reformed Theology In America, A History Of Its Modern Development*. Grand Rapids: Baker Books, 1997

*The Westminster Confession of Faith, An Authentic Modern Version*. Signal Mountain: Summertown Texts, 1992

White, John. *When The Spirit Comes With Power*. Downer Grove: InterVarsity Press, 1988

Williams, Don. *Signs, Wonders, and the Kingdom of God*. Ann Arbor: Vine Books, 1989

Wimber, John. *Power Evangelism*. San Francisco: Harper & Row Publishers, 1986

# Endnotes

## Preface

1        From a document of the Evangelical Presbyterian Church, called The Essentials.
2        The Westminster Confession of Faith, Revised EPC Edition, 1992, page 5.
3        1 Corinthians 2:5b, NIV

## Introduction

1        The five points of Calvinism are the result of rulings given by the Synod of Dort from 1618 to 1619. The Synod gave the five points of Calvinism in response to five points developed by followers of James Arminius. The five points of Calvinism are well known by the acronym TULIP (Total depravity, Unconditional Election, Limited Atonement, Irresistible grace, and Perseverance of the saints). You need not hold to all five of these points to be truly Reformed. These points are a great outline of Reformed thought and a wonderful starting place for anyone who would like to learn and grow in Calvinist theology.
2        de Witt, John Richard, What Is The Reformed Faith? (Edinburgh: The Banner of Truth Trust, 1981), p.4
3        de Witt, John Richard., p.4
4        The more well known Pentecostal denominations being the Assemblies of God, the Four-Square Gospel, and the Pentecostal Holiness. These have all shown themselves to be great denominations, which share in the basic essentials of Orthodox theology. There has been at least one heretical branch known as the United Pentecostal Church. A major theme of its theology is the denial of the Trinity, otherwise known as "Oneness Theology."

## Chapter One

1        Michael Horton, Power Religion (Chicago: Moody Press, 1990) p.332
2        James Montgomery Boice, The Subject of Contemporary Relevance (Chicago: Moody Press, 1990) p.134
3        B.B. Warfield, Counterfeit Miracles (Edinburgh: The Banner of Truth Trust) p.27-8

4      Alasdair I. C. Heron, The Holy Spirit (Philadelphia: The Westminster Press, 1983) p.102

5      John Calvin, Institutes of the Christian Religion, John T. McNeill ed. (Philadelphia: The Westminster Press, 1960) p.1454 4-19-6

6      John Calvin, p.17 From the Prefatory Address To King Francis

7      John Calvin, p.57 1-5-5

8      John Calvin, p.185 1-15-2

9      B.B. Warfield, Counterfeit Miracles (Edinburgh: Banner of Truth Trust, 19??) p,9

10     B.B. Warfield, p.23

11     B.B. Warfield, p.22

12     B.B. Warfield, p.6

13     B.B. Warfield, p.6

14     Luder G. Whitlock, Jr. "James Henley Thornwell" in Reformed Theology in America, A History Of Its Modern Development, David F. Wells, ed., (Grand Rapids: Baker Books, 1997) p.242

15     D.F. Kelly on "Scottish Realism" in Evangelical Dictionary of Theology, Walter A. Elwell, ed., (Grand Rapids: Baker Book House, 1984) p.990

16     Sydney E. Ahlstrom, A Religious History Of The American People (New Haven: Yale University Press, 1972) p.355

17     Sydney E. Ahlstrom, p.355

18     Mark A. Noll, "The Princeton Theology" in Reformed Theology In America, A History Of Its Modern Development, David F. Wells, ed. (Grand Rapids: Baker Books, 1997) p.242

19     Charles H. Kraft, Christianity With Power (Ann Arbor: Vine Books, 1989) p.41

20     Charles H. Kraft, p.41

21     Abraham Kuyper, The Holy Spirit (New York: Funk & Wagnalls Company, 1900) p.189

22     Jack Deere, Surprised by the Power of the Spirit (Grand Rapids: Zondervan Publishing House, 1993) p.19

23     Jack Deere, p.101

24     Jack Deere, p.104

25     Rudolf Bultmann, New Testament & Mythology And Other Basic Writings (Philadelphia: Fortress Press, 1984) p.1

26     Rudolf Bultmann, p.3

27     Rudolf Bultmann, p.4

28     Rudolf Bultmann, p.4

29     Rudolf Bultmann, p.5-6

# Chapter Two

1    Rev. Jack Lash, The Biblical Observer, Vol.3, No.1, The Gifts of the Spirit: Have They Ceased?, p.2

2    Walter Bauer, William F. Arndt, F. Wilbur Gingrich, Frederick W. Danker, A Greek-English Lexicon of the New Testament and Other Early Christian Literature (Chicago: The University of Chicago Press, 1979), p.308

3    Don Williams, Signs, Wonders, and the Kingdom of God (Ann Arbor: Vine Books, 1989) p.131

4    The Jesus Seminar is a group of theologians and others who meet annually. They give one of four ratings to each saying of Jesus in the New Testament. These ratings decide if Jesus said a given statement, might have said a given statement, might not have said a given statement, or Jesus didn't say a given statement. I believe they do the same thing with each of the events in Jesus' life and ministry. Their thinking is definitely wrong in their approach to the Bible.

5    John Calvin, Commentary on a harmony of the Evangelists, p.388

6    Calvin, of course, only saw this power continuing into the Early Church.

7    John Calvin, Commentary on a harmony of the Evangelists, p.388

8    C. Peter Wagner, Spreading the Fire (Ventura: Regal Books, 1994) p.68

9    Bauer, Arndt, Gingrich and Danker, p.849

10   Gordon D. Fee, God's Empowering Presence, The Holy Spirit in the Letters of Paul (Peabody: Hendrickson Publishers, Inc., 1994) p.88 n.24

11   Gordon D. Fee, p.85

12   F.F. Bruce, The New Century Bible Commentary, I & II Corinthians (Grand Rapids: Wm. B. Eerdmans Publ. Co., and London: Marshall, Morgan & Scott Publ. Ltd., 1971) p.128

13   Luder G. Whitlock, Jr., "James Henley Thornwell" in Reformed Theology in America, David F. Wells, ed. (Grand Rapids: Baker Books, 1997) p.245

# Chapter Three

1    Ronald A. N. Kydd, Charismatic Gifts in the Early Church (Peabody: Hendrickson Publishers, 1984) p.15

| 2 | Ronald A. N. Kydd, p.16 quoting from Ignatius, "to the Philadelphians," 7:1 and 2, ed. Camelot, Ignace d'Antioch: letters, ed. P. Th. Camelot (Sources chretiennes, 10) (4th ed. Paris: Cerf, 1969) p.126 |
|---|---|
| 3 | Ronald A. N. Kydd, p.15 quoting from Ignatius, "Polycarp," 2:2, Ignace d'Antioch: Lettres, ed. P. Th. Camelot (Sources chretiennes, 10) (4th ed., Paris: Cerf, 1969), p.148 |
| 4 | John Wimber, Power Evangelism (San Francisco: Harper & Row, Publishers, 1986) p.157. John Wimber is quoting from Justin Martyr's Dialogue with Trypho (Coxe 1:240) |
| 5 | John Wimber, p.158. This quote is also from Justin Martyr's Dialogue with Trypho (Coxe 1:243). |
| 6 | Ronald A. N. Kydd, p.29 |
| 7 | Ronald A. N. Kydd, p.44 |
| 8 | Ronald A. N. Kydd, p.45, his footnote reads, Irenaeus as quoted by Eusebius in Ecclesiastical History, 5, 7:6, Kirsopp Lake, (Loeb Classical Library), 1:451 & 455 |
| 9 | Ronald A. N. Kydd, p.71, his footnote reads, Epistulae Cypriani (Letters of Cyprian), 78, 2, ed. G. Hartel, (Corpus Scriptorum Ecclesiasticorum Latinorum, 3, 2) (Vindobon: C. Geroli, 1871), p.837 |
| 10 | Ronald A. N. Kydd, p.72, his footnote reads, Cyprian, Epistulae, 66, 10, (Corpus Scriptorum, 3, 2), p.734 |
| 11 | Ronald A. N. Kydd, p.73-74, his footnote reads, Cyprian, Epistulae, 16, 4, (Corpus Scriptorum, 3, 2) p.520 |
| 12 | Ronald A. N. Kydd, p.74 |
| 13 | Ronald A. N. Kydd, p.74 |
| 14 | Ronald A. N. Kydd, p.78, his footnote reads, Origen, Against Celsus, 1, 46, Chadwick, p.42 |
| 15 | Ronald A. N. Kydd, p.78, his footnote reads, Origen, Against Celsus, 2, 8, Chadwick, p.72 |
| 16 | Ronald A. N. Kydd, p.82-83, his footnote reads, Dionysius in Eusebius' Ecclesiastical History, 7, 7:3; Oulton, 2:143 and 145. |
| 17 | St. Augustine, Confessions, Book III, XI, as translated by R.S. Pine-Coffin (New York: Penguin Books, 1961) p.68 |
| 18 | St. Augustine, Confessions, Book VIII, XII, p.177 |
| 19 | St. Augustine, Confessions, Book VIII, XII, p.178 |
| 20 | St. Augustine, Confessions, Chapter 8 |
| 21 | St. Augustine, Confessions, Chapter 8 |
| 22 | St. Augustine, Confessions, Chapter 8 |
| 23 | St. Augustine, Confessions, Chapter 8 |

24      John Knox, The History Of The Reformation Of Religion Within The Realm Of Scotland, edited by C.J. Guthrie, Q,C. (London: Adam and Charles Black, 1898) p.52

25      John Knox, p.57

26      John Knox, p.58

27      John Knox, p.58

28      John Knox, p.58

29      John Knox, p.59

30      John Howie, The Scots Worthies, revised by Rev. W.H. Carslaw (Edinburgh: Johnstone, Hunter, and Company, 1870) p. 30

31      John Howie, p.31

32      Jasper Ridley, John Knox (Oxford: Clarendon Press, 1968) p.504

33      John Howie, p.63

34      Jasper Ridley, p.526

35      Bessie G. Olson, John Knox, A Great Intercessor (Des Moines: The Boone Publishing Co.) p.20

36      John Howie, p.61

37      John Howie, p.61

38      John Howie, p.60

39      Jasper Ridley, p.519

40      Samuel Rutherford, A Survey Of The Spiritual Antichrist. Opening The Secrets of Familisme and Antinomianisme in the Antichristian Doctrine of John Saltmarsh, and Will. Del, the present Preachers of the Army now in England, and of Robert Town, Joh. Crisy, H. Denne, Eaton, and others. (London: Printed by J.D. and R.I. for Andrew Cooke, 1648) p.42

41      John Howie, p.117

42      John Howie, p.120

43      John Howie, p.124

44      John Howie, p.124

45      John Howie, p.121

46      John Howie, p.127

47      John Howie, p.123

48      John Howie, p.129

49      John Howie, p.130

50      John Howie, p.131

51      John Howie, p.124-125

52      John Howie, p.134

53      John Howie, p.133

54      John Howie, p.148

| 55 | John Howie, p.149 |
| 56 | John Howie, p.148 |
| 57 | John Howie, p.148 |
| 58 | Alexander Smellie, Men of the Covenant, The Story of the Scottish Church in the Years of the Persecution (London: Andrew Melrose, 1903) p.374 |
| 59 | Alexander Smellie, p.331 |
| 60 | Alexander Smellie, p.335 |
| 61 | Alexander Smellie, p.335 |
| 62 | Alexander Smellie, p.379 |
| 63 | Alexander Smellie, p.379 |
| 64 | Alexander Smellie, p.381 |
| 65 | Alexander Smellie, p.381 |
| 66 | Hillel Schwartz, The French Prophets, The History of a Millenarian Group in Eighteenth-Century England, (Berkeley: University of California Press, 1980) p.17 |
| 67 | Hillel Schwartz, p.17 |
| 68 | Hillel Schwartz, p.18 Here he quotes a few sources such as Pierre Jurieu, Reflections. |
| 69 | Hillel Schwartz, p.18 |
| 70 | John Wimber, p.172 |
| 71 | Hillel Schwartz, p.69 |
| 72 | Rex Gardner, Healing Miracles (London: Darton, Longman and Todd, 1986) p.88 |
| 73 | Rex Gardner, p.88 |
| 74 | Rex Gardner, p.88 |
| 75 | Charles W. Nienkerchen, A.B. Simpson And The Pentecostal Movement (Peabody: Hendrickson Publishers, 1992) p.1 |
| 76 | Charles W. Nienkerchen, p.13 |
| 77 | Charles W. Nienkerchen, p.66 and note 61 |
| 78 | Jasper Ridley, p.504. Here he quoted from Melville's Diary |

# Chapter Four

| 1 | Loraine Boettner, The Reformed Doctrine of Predestination, (Phillipsburg: Presbyterian and Reformed Publishing Company, 1932) p.375 He quotes Schaff from his book The Swiss Reformation, II., p.818 |
| 2 | George Eldon Ladd, A Theology of the New Testament (Grand Rapids: William B. Eerdmans Publishing Company, 1974) p.70 |

3        John Calvin, The Institutes of the Christian Religion, 4-20-2, p.1487

4        Charles Hodge, Systematic Theology (Grand Rapids: Wm. B. Eerdmans Publishing Co., 1997) Vol. 2 p.599

5        Louis Berkhof, Systematic Theology (Grand Rapids: Wm. B. Eerdmans Publishing Co., 1941) p.409

6        Don Williams, Signs, Wonders and the Kingdom of God, A Biblical guide for the Reluctant Skeptic (Ann Arbor: Vine Books, 1989) p.107

7        C. Peter Wagner, Signs & Wonders Today (Altamonte Springs: Creation House, 1987) p.53  Wagner does not give a reference for Ridderbos' quote.

8        The Westminster Confession of Faith, An Authentic Modern Version (Signal Mountain: Summertown Texts, 1992) p.7.  This is a revised Evangelical Presbyterian Church edition.

9        The Westminster Confession of Faith, p.17

10      Gordon Fee, God's Empowering Presence, The Holy Spirit In The Letters Of Paul (Peabody: Hendrickson Publishers, Inc., 1994) p.14

11      Gordon Fee, p.33

12      Both the word grace (charis) and the word gift (charisma) come from the base root word (chairo) meaning rejoice.  In case you were wondering why we feel so much joy when we come in contact with grace and the gifts of the Spirit.  I believe these are a demonstration of God's joy.

13      Gordon Fee, p.33

14      This is a quote from Proverbs 3:34 and is also found in James 4:6.

15      Louis Berkhof, p.494

16      In verse 21, Jesus added, "But this kind does not go out except by prayer and fasting."  He was referring to a type of demon and the spiritual disciplines it takes to cast it out.

17      Louis Berkhof, p.502

18      Louis Berkhof, p.502

19      C. Peter Wagner, Spiritual Power and Church Growth (Altamonte Springs: Strang Communications Company, 1986) pp.32-34

20      C. Peter Wagner, How To Have A Healing Ministry In Any Church (Ventura: Regal Books, 1988) p.266

21      I normally wouldn't want people to base things on a movie, except that this movie was a close telling of the book of Luke.  Watching this movie is like reading the actual gospel.

# Chapter Five

1     James Montgomery Boice, The Subject of Contemporary Relevance (Chicago: Moody Press, 1990). P.134

2     Gerald F. Hawthorne, The Presence & The Power, The significance of the Holy Spirit in the life and ministry of Jesus (Dallas: Word Publishing, 1991) p.148 Note: Gerald Hawthorne is professor of Greek and New Testament Exegesis at Wheaton College.

3     The Westminster Confession of Faith: An Authentic Modern Version (Signal Mountain: Summertown Texts, 1985) p.15

4     The Westminster Confession of Faith, p.15

5     The Westminster Confession of Faith, p.15

6     The Westminster Confession of Faith, p.15

7     The meaning of this verse is based on the Greek word Kenosis, which translates into "empty, divest" in English. We find the same definition in the BAGD Greek-English Lexicon as, "Of Christ, who gave up the appearance of his divinity and took the form of a slave, eauton ekenosen he emptied himself, divested himself of his privileges Phil. 2:7."

8     The New American Standard Bible

9     Louis Berkhof, Systematic Theology (Grand Rapids: Wm. B. Eerdman's Publishing Co., 1941) p.332

10    Gerald F. Hawthorne, The Presence & The Power, p.208

11    Monophysitism was also known as Eutychianism after one of its teachers, Eutyches (d.454). The main idea of this heresy is that Jesus has only one nature, His divinity. It was a denial of Jesus' two natures, divine and human. This information is from the article on Monophysitism by D.A. Hubbard in the Evangelical Dictionary of Theology, Walter A. Elwell, ed. (Grand Rapids: Baker Book House, 1984) p.730

12    Concerning Jesus' kenosis John Calvin believed that Jesus had just hid His deity under His flesh and decided not to show the wonders of His majesty (Institutes 2-14-3). He teaches as if Jesus' human body was a thin covering over the reality of being God. According to Calvin, Jesus did all of His miracles by His own power (Institutes 1-13-13) and this use of His power shows His divinity.

13    There were more than 5,000 at the first feeding and 4,000 at the second feeding. The passages say these numbers and say this was the count of men "besides women and children."

# Chapter Six

1      R.A. Torrey, "The Personality and Deity of the Holy Spirit," from The Fundamentals (Los Angeles: The Bible Institute Of Los Angeles, 1917) p.323  Torrey was the president of B.I.O.L.A. and Reformed in his theology.

2      The Book of Confessions, Presbyterian Church (U.S.A.) (New York: Published By The Office Of The General Assembly, 1983) Reference 1.3 of the Nicene Creed

3      The Book of Confessions, Presbyterian Church (U.S.A.) (New York: Published By The Office Of The General Assembly, 1983) Reference 5.016 of the Second Helvetic Confession

4      The Westminster Confession of Faith (Signal Mountain: Summertown Texts, 1985) p.34.  This is an Evangelical Presbyterian Church modern version, but this quote is a traditional statement of the Westminster Confession of Faith.

5      Gordon Fee, God's Empowering Presence, The Holy Spirit In The Letters Of Paul (Peabody: Hendrickson Publishers, Inc. 1994)  p.363 n.232

6      Gordon Fee, p.363

7      John Howie, The Scots Worthies, revised by Rev. W.H. Carslaw (Edinburgh: Johnstone, Hunter, and Company, 1870) p.124

8      John Howie, p.124

9      R.A. Torrey, p.337

10      Mike Bickle, "The School of Intercessory Prayer," from The Morning Star Journal (Charlotte: MorningStar Publication, 1992)

11      J.G.D. Dunn, "Spirit, Holy Spirit," New Bible Dictionary (Wheaton: Tyndale House Publishers, Inc., 1982) p.136

12      Alasdair I.C. Heron, The Holy Spirit (Philadelphia: The Westminster Press, 1983) p.4

13      Charles Hodge wrote, "Originally the words (Ruach) and (pneuma) meant the moving air, especially the breath, as in the phrase (pneuma biou); then any invisible power; then the human soul.  In saying, therefore, that God is Spirit, our Lord authorizes us to believe that whatever is essential to the idea of spirit, as learned from our own consciousness, is to be referred to God as determining his nature." From Systematic Theology (Grand Rapids: Wm. B. Eerdmans Publishing Company, 1997) vol.1 p.377

14      A Concise Greek-English Dictionary of the New Testament, prepared by Barclay M. Newman, Jr. (Stuttgart: Biblia-Druck, 1971) p.2

15    John Calvin, Institutes of the Christian Religion, John T. McNeill ed. (Philadelphia: The Westminster Press) pp.540-541 Book 3, Chapter 1, Number 3

16    John Calvin, p.79 Book 1, Chapter 7, Number 4

17    Frederick Dale Bruner, A Theology of the Holy Spirit (Grand Rapids: Wm. B. Eerdmans Publishing Company, 1970) p.116. This is a quote of Harold J. Okenga taken from his publication Power through Pentecost (New York: Fleming H. Revell Co., 1947) p.57

18    C. Peter Wagner, How To Have A Healing Ministry In Any Church (Ventura: Regal Books, 1982) p.21

19    C. Peter Wagner, p.21

20    C. Peter Wagner, p.26

21    C. Peter Wagner, p.25,26

22    Walter Bauer, William F. Arndt, F. Wilbur Gingrich, and Frederick W. Danker, A Greek-English Lexicon Of The New Testament and Other Early Christian Literature (Chicago: The University of Chicago Press, 1979) p.745

23    Geoffrey W. Bromiley, Theological Dictionary Of The New Testament, Abridged In One Volume, Gerhard Kittel and Gerhard Friedrich, eds. (Grand Rapids: William B. Eerdmans Publishing Company, 1985) p.1245

24    Gordon D. Fee, p.164

25    The Compact Edition Of The Oxford English Dictionary, Vol. 1, A-O (New York: Oxford University Press, 1971) p.832

26    Many other versions of the Bible translate this as simply "prophesied." But Ralph Klein writes of this in his commentary, "The spirit of God came on the messengers of Saul, and they exhibited characteristic prophetic behavior... We have designated this behavior as prophetic ecstasy in our translation." (1 Samuel, Word Biblical Commentary (Waco, Word Books, Publisher, 1983) p.198) I think that some theologians see this as frenzy or ecstasy due to the arresting nature of the experience. Some even believe that King Saul lay before Samuel in a state of trance. There isn't much said in the passage except that they were taken over or possessed by the Spirit of God.

27    Alasdair I. C. Heron, p.13

28    Alasdair I. C. Heron, p.13, 14

29    F.F. Bruce, The Book Of Acts, The New International Commentary On The New Testament (Grand Rapids: William B. Eerdmans Publishing Company, 1988) p.60

30      Jonathan Edwards, Thoughts On The Revival Of Religion In New England, "Nature of the work in a particular instance," from The Works of Jonathan Edwards, Volume 1 (Carlisle: The Banner of Truth Trust, 1987) p.376
31      Jonathan Edwards, p.376
32      Sarah Edwards, "Mrs. Edwards. Her Solemn Self-dedications. Her Uncommon Discoveries Of The Divine Perfections And Glory; And Of The Excellency Of Christ. Remarks Concerning Them" from Jonathan Edwards, Memoirs Of Jonathan Edwards (Carlisle: The Banner of Truth Trust, 1987) p.lxiv
33      Sarah Edwards, p.lxiv
34      Sarah Edwards, p.lxv
35      John White, When The Spirit Comes With Power (Downer Grove: InterVarsity Press, 1988) p.77
36      John White, p.77

# Chapter Seven

1       Robert Norris, "Leading A Ministry Without Miracles," from Reformed Quarterly, Spring 1997, p.13
2       Robert Norris, p.12
3       Robert Norris, p.13
4       B.B. Warfield, Counterfeit Miracles (Edinburgh: The Banner of Truth Trust) p.27-28
5       Jack Deere, Surprised by the Power of the Spirit (Grand Rapids: Zondervan Publishing House, 1993) p.103
6       John Wimber, Power Evangelism (San Francisco: Harper & Row, Publishers, 1986) p.35
7       Gordon Fee, God's Empowering Presence, The Holy Spirit In The Letters Of Paul (Peabody: Hendrickson Publishers, 1994) p.629
8       Gordon Fee, p.45
9       Jack Deere, p.105

# Chapter Eight

1       Gordon Fee, God's Empowering Presence, The Holy Spirit In The Letters Of Paul (Peabody: Hendrickson Publishers, Inc., 1994) p.169

2    Other examples of Jesus touching people can be found in Matthew 8:15; 9:29; and 20:34.

3    John Calvin, Commentary on the First Epistle To The Corinthians, trans. Rev. William Pringle (Grand Rapids: Wm. B. Eerdmans Publishing Company, 1949) p.415

4    Graham Cooke, Developing Your Prophetic Gifting (Kent: Sovereign World Ltd., 1994) p.18

5    Jack Deere, Surprised By The Voice Of God: How God Speaks Today Through Prophesies, Dreams, and Visions (Grand Rapids: Zondervan Publishing House, 1996) p.179

6    Mike Bickle, Growing In The Prophetic (Orlando: Creation House, 1996) p.120

7    Mike Bickle, p.120

8    Mike Bickle, p.120

9    Mike Bickle, p.120

10    Mike Bickle, p.120

11    James Ryle, Hippo In The Garden: A Non Religious Approach To Having A Conversation With God (Orlando: Creation House, 1993) p.118

12    Jack Deere, p.169

13    This is the same Silas whom Paul took with him on his journeys after the split with Barnabas in Acts 15:36-41. Paul seemed to want to have a prophet traveling with him and ministering with him.

14    Walter Bauer, William F. Arndt, F. Wilbur Gingrich, and Frederick W. Danker, A Greek-English Lexicon Of The New Testament and Other Early Christian Literature (Chicago: The University of Chicago Press, 1979) p.185

15    Graham Cooke, p.144

16    Graham Cooke, p.146-148

17    Jack Deere, p.181

18    Brian Schwertly, The Charismatic Movement: A Biblical Critique (http://members.tripod.com/-michael_bremmer/sola.htm.)

19    Gordon Fee, God's Empowering Presence: The Holy Spirit in The Letters Of Paul (Peabody: Hendrickson Publishers, Inc., 1994) p.198

20    Jack Hayford, The Beauty Of Spiritual Language: Unveiling the Mystery of Speaking in Tongues (Nashville: Thomas Nelson Publishers, 1996) p.97

21    Orthodox Presbyterian Church, www.opc.org

22    Bobby Clinton, Spiritual Gifts (Beaverlodge: Horizon House Publishers, 1985) p.61

23    Bobby Clinton, p.61

24      Gordon Fee, p.168

# Chapter Nine

1       Gordon Fee, God's Empowering Presence, The Holy Spirit in the Letters of
        Paul (Peabody: Hendrickson Publishers, Inc., 1994) p.676
2       Gordon Fee, p.676
3       Gordon Fee, p.676, note 55
4       James Ryle, Hippo In The Garden, A Non-religious Approach To Having A
        Conversation With God (Orlando: Creation House, 1993) p.258-9
5       James Ryle, p.259
6       Charles Kraft, Christianity With Power (Ann Arbor: Servant Publications,
        1989) p.65
7       Dr. Kraft defines a paradigm as, "a perspective on a sizeable segment of
        reality.  Each worldview is an organization of thousands of such semi-
        independent 'picturings' or renderings of reality."  Charles Kraft, p.82
8       James A. Belasco, Teaching the elephant to dance: the manager's guide to
        empowering change (New York: Penguin Group, 1990) p.17-18
9       Charles Kraft, p.35
10      Paul Cain and R.T. Kendall, The Word and the Spirit (Eastbourne:
        Kingsway Publications, 1996) p.23-24
11      Charles Kraft, p.77

# Chapter Ten

1       Gordon Fee, God's Empowering Presence, The Holy Spirit in the Letters of
        Paul (Peabody: Hendrickson Publishers, Inc., 1994)  p.788, note 141
2       Alasdair I. C. Heron, The Holy Spirit (Philadelphia: The Westminster Press,
        1983) p. 59
3       Heron, p.63
4       John Calvin, Institutes of the Christian Religion, John T. McNeill ed.
        (Philadelphia: The Westminster Press, 1960) p.17 From the Prefatory
        Address To King Francis
5       General H. Norman Schwarzkopf, The Autobiography, It Doesn't Take A
        Hero (New York: Linda Grey Bantam Books, 1992) p.167
6       Rick Joyner, Overcoming the Religious Spirit (Charlotte: MorningStar
        Publications, 1996) p.8

7       Rick Joyner, p.18
8       Rick Joyner, p.18
9       Rick Joyner, p.31
10      Rick Joyner, p.32
11      Rick Joyner, p.32
12      Rick Joyner, p.32
13      Craig Packer, "Captives in the Wild," National Geographic, Vol. 181, No. 4, April 1992, p.130
14      Heron, p.135-136

# Conclusion

1       John Calvin, Institutes of the Christian Religion, John T. McNeill ed. (Philadelphia: The Westminster Press, 1960) Book 2, Chapter 2, 25, p.284

Made in the USA
Middletown, DE
07 September 2023

38096355R00156